Wim Wenders

Making Films that Matter

Edited by
Olivier Delers and Martin Sulzer-Reichel

BLOOMSBURY ACADEMIC
NEW YORK • LONDON • OXFORD • NEW DELHI • SYDNEY

BLOOMSBURY ACADEMIC
Bloomsbury Publishing Inc
1385 Broadway, New York, NY 10018, USA
50 Bedford Square, London, WC1B 3DP, UK
29 Earlsfort Terrace, Dublin 2, Ireland

BLOOMSBURY, BLOOMSBURY ACADEMIC and the Diana logo are trademarks of
Bloomsbury Publishing Plc

First published in the United States of America 2020

This paperback edition published in 2021

Volume Editor's Part of the Work © Olivier Delers and Martin Sulzer-Reichel
Each chapter © of Contributors

For legal purposes the Acknowledgments on p. 193 constitute an extension
of this copyright page.

Cover design: Eleanor Rose
Cover image: Wim Wenders, Los Angeles, 1999 © Donata Wenders

All rights reserved. No part of this publication may be reproduced or transmitted
in any form or by any means, electronic or mechanical, including photocopying,
recording, or any information storage or retrieval system, without prior permission
in writing from the publishers.

Bloomsbury Publishing Inc does not have any control over, or responsibility for, any
third-party websites referred to or in this book. All internet addresses given in this
book were correct at the time of going to press. The author and publisher regret any
inconvenience caused if addresses have changed or sites have ceased to exist, but
can accept no responsibility for any such changes.

Library of Congress Cataloging-in-Publication Data
Names: Delers, Olivier, 1977- editor. | Sulzer-Reichel, Martin, 1962- editor.
Title: Wim Wenders: making films that matter / edited by Olivier Delers and
Martin Sulzer-Reichel.
Description: New York: Bloomsbury Academic, 2019. | Includes bibliographical
references, filmography, and index. | Summary:
"Wim Wenders: Making Films That Matter is the first book in fifteen years to take a
comprehensive look at Wim Wenders's extensive filmography. In addition to offering new
insights into his cult masterpieces, the ten essays in this volume highlight the thematic and
aesthetic continuities between his early films and his latest productions. Wenders's films
have much to contribute to current conversations on intermediality, whether it be through
his adaptations of important literary works or his filmic reinventions of famous paintings
by Edward Hopper or Andrew Wyeth. Wenders has also positioned himself as a decidedly
transnational and translingual filmmaker taking on the challenge of representing peripheral
spaces without falling into the trap of a neo-colonial gaze. Making Films That Matter argues
that Wenders remains a true innovator in both his experiments in 3D filmmaking and his
attempts to define a visual poetics of peace"– Provided by publisher.
Identifiers: LCCN 2019026402 (print) | LCCN 2019026403 (ebook) |
ISBN 9781501356339 (hardback) | ISBN 9781501356322 (epub) | ISBN 9781501356315 (pdf)
Subjects: LCSH: Wenders, Wim–Criticism and interpretation.
Classification: LCC PN1998.3.W46 W58 2019 (print) | LCC PN1998.3.W46 (ebook) |
DDC 791.4302/33092–dc23
LC record available at https://lccn.loc.gov/2019026402
LC ebook record available at https://lccn.loc.gov/2019026403

ISBN: HB: 978-1-5013-5633-9
PB: 978-1-5013-8408-0
ePDF: 978-1-5013-5631-5
eBook: 978-1-5013-5632-2

Typeset by Deanta Global Publishing Services, Chennai, India

To find out more about our authors and books visit www.bloomsbury.com
and sign up for our newsletters.

Contents

1 Introduction: New Perspectives on Wim Wenders as Filmmaker and Visual Artist *Olivier Delers and Martin Sulzer-Reichel* — 1

Part I Watching the Road Trilogy in the Twenty-First Century

2 Search for the Sublime: The Road Trilogy, or Wenders's *Roam-man-ticism* *Oliver C. Speck* — 29

3 Writing in the Blood of the Past: *Wrong Move* and the Search for a Contemporary German Identity *Kristin Eichhorn* — 48

4 The Window-View and the Romantic Vision of the World: Notes on a Visual Leitmotif in the Films of Wim Wenders *Philipp Scheid* — 63

Part II Reimagining Cinema and Photography with Wenders

5 As If It Were for the Last Time: Wim Wenders—Film and Photography *George Kouvaros* — 77

6 Wenders–Salgado: Space, Time, and Transformation in *Salt of the Earth* *Darrell Varga* — 92

7 Wim Wenders's *Pina*: A Cinematic Homage to Pina Bausch *Peter Beicken* — 105

Part III Transnational Wenders

8 Multitrack and Transcultural Narratives in Wim Wenders's Works *Simone Malaguti* — 119

9 "I Can Imagine Anything": The European Project in Wim Wenders's *Wings of Desire* *Mine Eren* — 134

10 Blandness and "Just Seeing" in the Films of Wim Wenders *William Baker* — 154

11 The Heart of Things: Wim Wenders and the Evocations of Peace *Mary Zournazi* — 168

Bibliography	179
Filmography	191
Acknowledgments	193
List of Contributors	194
Index	195

1

Introduction: New Perspectives on Wim Wenders as Filmmaker and Visual Artist

Olivier Delers and Martin Sulzer-Reichel

In a career that spans more than forty-five years, Wim Wenders is still busy adding to his extensive body of work: in the past two years alone, he has released two full-length feature films, exhibited his large-scale landscape photography at the Museum Kunstpalast in Düsseldorf, and announced a new documentary project featuring conversations with Pope Francis. And yet, despite being considered one of the leading figures of New German Cinema and a "cult" filmmaker thanks to films like *Alice in the Cities* (1974), *Paris, Texas* (1984), and *Wings of Desire* (1987), Wenders in recent years has played a relatively minor role in the field of film studies.[1] The last monograph on his films, Alexander Graf's *The Cinema of Wim Wenders: The Celluloid Highway*, was published in 2002,[2] and, if we exclude the sudden proliferation of studies devoted to his collaborations with Peter Handke, research on Wenders has been stagnant and somewhat directionless, in particular for films released in the twenty-first century. No one, for instance, has written about Wenders's ongoing visual and narrative exploration of Los Angeles and the American West in a second trilogy of sorts—*Million Dollar Hotel* (2000), *Land of Plenty* (2004), *Don't Come Knocking* (2005)—and very little has been said about his acclaimed documentaries *Pina* (2011) and *Salt of the Earth* (co-directed with Juliano Salgado; 2014).

Wenders has certainly not been silent or resting on his laurels. On the contrary, over the past fifteen years, he has taken on new challenges, not only by exploring new motifs and using new technology in his substantial filmic and photographic output but also by acting as a champion of European cinema and reflecting upon the power of images in the digital age. Of particular interest to film studies scholars is a recent publication *Inventing Peace: A Dialogue on Perception*, published in 2013. Conceived as a series of dialogues between Wenders and his coauthor

Mary Zournazi, the book addresses Wenders's attempt to be more socially and politically engaged in his later films. It also theorizes what Wenders calls a "peaceful" gaze, a technical and spiritual way of looking at the world, inspired in large part by the films of Yasujiro Ozu, that has the potential to inspire images and films that participate in a new visual language of peace.[3]

Inventing Peace belongs to a larger body of self-reflective and critical writings that Wenders has produced over the years, most notably *The Logic of Images* (1992), *On Film* (2001), and *A Sense of Place* (2004). Along with the fascinating director's commentaries he has recorded for new releases of his films on DVD, these essays and interviews reveal the importance for Wenders of thinking critically, as both a practitioner and a public intellectual, about what images do. They also offer a unique vantage point from which to examine his creative process and to understand what might motivate him to keep making new films. Perhaps the following statement best explains how Wenders sees the role of cinema in the twenty-first century:

> Entertainment today constantly emphasizes the message that things are wonderful the way they are. But there is another kind of cinema, which says that change is possible and necessary and it's up to you. Any film that supports the idea that things can be changed is a great film in my eyes. It doesn't have to be overtly political. On the contrary a film can promote the idea of change without any political message whatsoever but in its form and language can tell people that they can change their lives and contribute to progressive changes in the world. Any movie that has that spirit and says things can be changed is worth making.[4]

For Wenders, the "idea of change" need not be exclusively political but should be apprehended in relation to the idea that cinema has a role to play in helping us, as human beings, move forward and see things from multiple perspectives. What he sees as the power of "another kind of cinema" also sounds like a personal manifesto and a key to reading his films. In other words, following a recipe for success that one has mastered is not enough—Wenders once responded to critics by saying that he no longer knew how to make a film like *Wings of Desire*, for instance.[5] One has to make films that matter *now* and that imbue the auteur perspective with a keen sense of the ethical responsibilities of filmmaking.

Do Wenders's films still matter? And, if so, how do they matter? We attempt in the collection of chapters here to answer these questions by taking stock of research published in the past fifteen years or so and arguing that Wenders studies deal with some of the most pressing questions posed in film studies and, more broadly, cultural studies. Three major themes emerge in the scholarship published on Wenders in the past fifteen years or so: first, the intermedial strategies used by Wenders to adapt texts written by Peter Handke and to make them come alive on the screen; second, the problematic representation of the non-European other and of subaltern spaces in several Wenders films; and, third, the transnational and translingual dimension of his *oeuvre*. We also pay particular attention to Wenders's newer films and show how they direct us toward new ways of questioning film as a medium. Wenders's unique painterly gaze channels the style, mood, and perspective of realist painters like Edward Hopper or Andrew Wyeth. In this respect, several of his films are decidedly transmedial, moving seamlessly between an original written text, its visual translation into film, and references to painterly images that inform the meaning of particular scenes. Wenders is also a pioneer in 3-D auteur filmmaking and has used the technology to capture the movements and energy of Pina Bausch's *Tanztheater* in *Pina*, to establish closer emotional identification between characters and viewers in *Every Thing Will Be Fine* (2015), and to explore the proximity of stage and filmic storytelling in *The Beautiful Days of Aranjuez* (2016). Finally, we focus on the theoretical underpinnings of Wenders's visual aesthetic of peace and analyze its implementation in his films, arguing that the concept, even though it stems from Wenders's own faith and personal vision, can be useful for thinking about making films that matter in the twenty-first century.

* * *

Adaptation and intermediality, the first overarching theme that stands out in the recent scholarship on Wenders, both harkens back to the beginning of his career (*The Goalkeeper's Fear of the Penalty* in 1972, a film adaptation of a novel with the same title by Peter Handke) and is directly relevant to one of his latest films (*The Last Days of Aranjuez*, also drawn from Handke's repertoire). No less than four books on the collaboration between the two men were published between 2004 and 2011: David Coury's *The Return of Storytelling in Contemporary German Literature and Film: Peter Handke and Wim Wenders* (2004), Carlo Avventi's *Mit den Augen des richtigen Wortes: Wahrnehmung und Kommunikation im Werk Wim Wenders und Peter Handkes* (also in 2004), Simone Malaguti's *Wim Wenders' Filme und ihre intermediale Beziehung zur Literatur Peter Handkes* (2011), and Martin Brady and Joanne Leal's *Wim Wenders and Peter Handke: Collaboration,*

Adaptation, Recomposition (2011). This outpouring is not particularly surprising since, as Brady and Leal have noted, the Wenders/Handke relationship is "perhaps the most important collaboration between a writer and filmmaker in the history of European cinema."[6] Of course, Wenders has adapted works or coauthored scripts with other major literary figures: Patricia Highsmith for *The American Friend* (1977), Sam Shepard for *Paris, Texas* and *Don't Come Knocking*, and Peter Carey for *Until the End of the World* (1991), to name only the most important ones. But the Wenders-Handke partnership offers a particularly interesting case study because it reflects a range of adaptational strategies and challenges the assumption that an adaptation is a mere "copy" that should be as faithful as possible to the original. Their collaboration exemplifies some recent advances in the field of adaptation studies: adaptation is about "the mutation of forms across media" and should be understood as "metamorphosis," "transvocalization," "performance," or "actualization."[7] Handke, in a joint television interview with Wenders, added another, more loaded, term to characterize their work together: "betrayal." Whereas Handke felt that it was unnecessary, for instance, to represent the act of writing the dialogue between the two lovers in *The Last Days of Aranjuez*, Wenders argued that the person standing behind the typewriter had to be represented because it was also him, the film director—both the eyes that frame images and the brain in charge of transposing the story he is adapting.[8] Hence, "betrayal" is not necessarily a negative term. On the contrary, it is a central aspect of the complex relationship between two different media with their own strengths and limitations and between two ways of thinking about authorship and its textual presence.

While adaptation theory can certainly offer new concepts or metaphors for deciphering the multiple dimensions of the Wenders-Handke relationship, the films born out of their collaboration have the potential to complicate our sense of what it means for them to work together and to enter into a creative dialogue through words and images. At one end of the spectrum, adapting means translating a novel into a different medium and bringing to life both Handke's "goalkeeper" and his concerns with the ways in which language frames our perception of reality. At the other end of the spectrum, it means living with Handke's texts and drawing inspiration from them, even if they are not referenced directly in the film itself (as was the case when Wenders was preparing for and shooting *Alice in the Cities*).[9] Sometimes, adaptation involves a ménage à trois of sort. For *Wrong Move* (1975), Handke rewrites one of Goethe's masterpieces for the screen, inspiring Wenders to cast Rüdiger Vogler as an angst-ridden

Wilhelm Meister and Nastassja Kinski as a nymphet Mignon. *Wings of Desire* also functions as a polytextual film, in which Paul Klee's painting *Angelus Novus* and Walter Benjamin's reference to the "Angel of History" cross paths with Handke's poem "Song of Childhood" and Wenders's own vision of angels roaming around a divided Berlin that still bears the scars of the Second World War. These four creative encounters make it possible for Wenders to stretch the limits of what cinema, as a medium, can convey. He can "reflect essayistically," "assimilate images and music," "address the problem of writing through the iconography of German Romantic painting," and "commission poetic dialogue to signify the capacity of film to tell stories that were once the province of the oral tradition." In that sense, the Wenders/Handke films constitute "a tetralogy on the strengths and weaknesses of literary cinema and . . . a protracted experiment in different modes of collaborative productions."[10]

In the 1970s, that experiment addressed openly some of the debates that agitated New German Cinema: the overreliance on literary texts by filmmakers even as they tried to emancipate themselves from traditional narrative modes, but also the more fundamental question of the inherent "literariness" of cinema. In his early films, Wenders wonders whether it is "possible for the camera to film objects without embedding them in language" and whether "one can 'see' the world without 'reading' it."[11] The nature of language is still a central theme in later Wenders films, even as he progressively moves away from "the tradition of anti-narrative cinema" and displays "a newfound advocacy for storytelling."[12] But language is now explored in connection with the waning power of images and the interaction of words and images in a medium that is as obviously visual as it is inescapably entangled in words. Brady and Leal explain that

> [Wenders's] initial faith in the authenticity of images gives way to a growing distrust of their signifying power, not least as his awareness of their co-option and manipulation by the entertainment and advertising industries goes. As he becomes more suspicious of the image, his belief in the auratic power of literary language increases, precisely because it would seem able to resist the co-option for nefarious purposes to which images are so susceptible. A growing commitment to language as integral to cinematic signification is coupled with an increased conviction in the vital function of narrative in the process of structuring and making human experience liveable.[13]

The different layers of this transition are methodically laid out in film essays such as *Tokyo-Ga* (1985) and *Lisbon Story* (1994), but this new outlook on cinema is perhaps best represented in *Wings of Desire*, admittedly the high point of the Wenders-Handke relationship and the film in which the common thread of their collaboration, "melancholy self-reflexivity," is most fully realized.[14] In *Wings of Desire*, self-reflexivity is not meant to draw attention to the construction or sheer materiality of the film, or, in other words, it is not used as a postmodern way of "defamiliarizing" the viewer. Instead, it participates in the articulation of a complex intermedial poetics, refined through a series of drafts that enter into dialogue with one another. Wenders said that he could only imagine *Wings of Desire* because he had made *Tokyo-Ga* a few years earlier; likewise *Lisbon Story* is implicitly about continuing the conversation with the three masters (Truffaut, Tarkovsky, and Ozu) to whom *Wings of Desire* is dedicated. These drafts are also conversations with other texts, literary texts like Handke's poem, palimpsestic historical texts, and of course visual texts, whether they belong to a network of foundational images or are perverted by the omnipresence of commercial signs.

Wings of Desire continues to fascinate film scholars, and some of the most interesting insights about the film concern its complex intermedial dimension and the presence of two full-fledged authorial voices, Wenders's and Handke's. The film explores "issues of authorship, agency, readerly and writerly texts," but it does so by "blurring" different perspectives and foregrounding formal elements: "the intermixing of narrative and non-narrative film styles, the use of color and black-and-white film stock, and characters speaking directly to the camera."[15] Likewise, the successful integration into the film of Peter Handke's "Songs of Childhood" goes beyond its affinity with the main themes and overall mood of the film. It is also part of a quest to make cinema "speak the language of poetry."[16] Thomas Martinec speaks of a "film-poem" and lists a number of cinematic elements that bring to mind the formal features of poetry: "the emphasis on spontaneity in the making of the film . . .; the attempt to film the invisible; the coherence achieved by light and camera treatment rather than a narrative; the concern for audible words; and the musical use of languages."[17] In a 2017 essay, Pablo Gonçalo argues that understanding the intermedial qualities of *Wings of Desire* requires taking a closer look at the script itself, as "an archival record of the development process" and as "a transitional sort of writing, a text that wants to be another text."[18] In a sense, the film and script enter into a relation of "reverse ekphrasis." Instead of being a text that brings a visual text to life in words, the script is a medium that requires its reader to imagine and dramatize what a written text would look like as a series of images. This reversal is important for Handke, "a writer who has transposed poetic dilemmas of ekphrasis between scripts, radio plays, novels and films."[19] It is perhaps even more important to understand another way in which Wenders has used ekphrasis in his films, as a recreation in moving images of paintings that have influenced his own visual universe.

Critics have commented on Wenders's tendency to linger on a particular situation or landscape and suggested that it lends his films a unique atmospheric and painterly quality. Gonçalo, for instance, compares his camera work to Vermeer's paintbrush, but the relation between Wenders and the painters who have influenced him is not only stylistic.[20] It is a mimetic attempt to make a painting come alive and to have it bear both formally and thematically on the film. Brigitte Peucker has linked Wenders's attempt to stage two paintings by Vermeer in *Until the End of the World* to the tradition of the *tableau vivant*.[21] First theorized by Diderot in the eighteenth century, the *tableau vivant* is by definition transmedial. It relies on the potential of three art forms (painting, drama, and sculpture) to produce a strong emotional reaction in the viewer—and, as a result of that reaction, to highlight the moral implications of the situation depicted. In mixing elements of Vermeer's *Girl with a Pearl Earring* and *Young Woman with a Water Pitcher* in a single scene, Wenders adds other representational layers to his *tableau vivant*. In *Until the End of the World*, the characters' visual experiences can also be processed through a special neuro-camera that captures brain waves at the same time as it records images, so that what is recorded can eventually be "seen" by the hero's mother, who has lost her sight. The result is striking. Seen through that filter, the pixelated images look like "animated watercolors"[22] or like an abstract version of a pointillist painting. As Peucker notes, they possess a strong interpictorial presence, in turn bringing to mind the works of Andy Warhol, Gerhard Richter, or Chuck Close.[23] In this case, the intense mise en abyme serves to advance one of the central themes of *Until the End of the World*: both the yearning for original images and the impossibility of reclaiming them, whether they come from childhood memories or have been collected through a lifetime of observing and drawing inspiration from our visual experiences. For Peucker, the presence of *tableaux vivants* in film makes apparent one of the central characteristics of cinema: it is "a medium where different representational systems collide."[24] In a sense, many of Wenders's films explore this collision, either as adaptation of written narrative material or as an ekphrastic inquiry focused on the continuities and tensions between cinema and painting.

In a 2012 TV interview, Wenders confesses that he has been using Hopper's paintings as models since the 1970s and that he likes them for their intensely kinetic and anticipatory qualities: they always give the viewer "the impression that something violent is going to happen next."[25] Hopper's influence can be felt in several early films, both visually—in the green and red tones that dominate *The American Friend*[26]—and thematically, to the extent that the struggles of Wenders's characters in The Road Trilogy, for instance, echo Hopper's central themes, "the futility of action, the difficulty of meaningful connection, and the solace of being alone."[27] In *The End of Violence* (1997), Wenders recreates Hopper's masterpiece, *Nighthawks*, as a scene in an intradiegetic Hollywood crime film, and this reinforces the neo film noir aesthetics of the film itself. Here again, Wenders's filmic ekphrasis is highly self-reflexive: the viewer can see the camera moving along the diner's windowpane and the director following the shooting on his monitor.

In subsequent films, Hopper is quoted in more subtle ways, but, paradoxically, his paintings seem to be everywhere. For instance, many shots in *Million Dollar Hotel* look into private rooms through a window. They bring to mind iconic paintings by Hopper that portray individuals alone and isolated in their room (such as *Hotel Room* [1931], *Room in New York* [1932], and *Night Windows* [1928]). In *Don't Come Knocking*, the cinematography borrows the color tones and poetic realism that define Hopper's style. The buildings and houses filmed by Wenders in Butte, Montana resemble Hopper's rendition of Brooklyn and of small-town life in the 1930s and 1940s (such as *Williamsburg Bridge* [1928], *House at Dusk* [1935], and *Pennsylvania Coal Town* [1947]). Rather than recreating specific paintings, Wenders explores visual motifs and perspectives that recur in Hopper's *oeuvre*: the voyeuristic observation of private lives, the looking in from an elevated outside position or capturing moments when characters stare at a window in a pensive or melancholic way, the importance of windows as frames that double the frame of the painting or the shot, and, more generally, the omnipresence of glass panes (in private homes, diners, or store fronts) that act as both a physical separation and an invitation to enter the lives of others. Hopper and Wenders both like to sketch out stories even if they are never fully realized—except perhaps as aesthetic experiments. As was the case with Handke, one can speak of "non-hierarchical adaptation" when it comes to Wenders referencing Hopper's paintings in his films.[28] Except in instances when he is purposefully creating a *tableau vivant*, Wenders has internalized a large set of images which resurface as visual echoes or retinal memories that viewers may recognize or not. Visual experiences are palimpsestic by nature, and one should always be mindful of the fact that an image can conceal, recall, cite, or transpose many other past images. In other words, Wenders suggests that every image that he has shot exists in relationship with all the images that he has seen or remembers. Hopper kept a quote from Goethe in his wallet that is strangely applicable to Wenders's own creative process and relationship with the visual world: "The beginning and end of all literary activity is the reproduction of the world that surrounds me by means of the world that is in me, all things being grasped, related, re-created, molded and reconstructed in a personal form and original manner."[29] For Wenders, ekphrasis can take the form of a mimetic search that makes an image come to life and activates the story contained in it. It can also be part of a personal aesthetic journey in which the real activates visual memories and is imagined anew in a filmic form in relation to a specific narrative project.

The intermedial relationship between painting and film is complicated by the influence of other media and technologies on Wenders's adaptational and creative endeavors. For example, the first traces of Wenders's fascination with Andrew Wyeth's work can be seen in a 2000 photograph titled *Wyeth Landscape*. More than the lone farmhouse placed at the center of the photograph, it is the Wyethan color palette that Wenders perfectly captures in his shot, particularly in the brownish-yellow tones of the prairie grass and in the subtle grades of blue of the cloudy sky. In *Inventing Peace*, Wenders reflects on Wyeth's most famous painting, *Christina's World*, and sees in it both photographic and filmic qualities. It exudes "a freshness that you think you know only from photo snapshots," and it is not "static"—in fact it gives the viewer the feeling that the "woman might turn around in the next second."[30] Interestingly, Wenders shot a scene based on *Christina's World* for *Every Thing Will Be Fine* but did not include it in the final cut. Still, Wyeth's influence is vividly reflected in the film. It can be felt in the casting of Charlotte Gainsbourg, who shares the same frail silhouette and bony features as Christina; in the rural isolation of the farmhouse where her character lives; in the formal attention to windows and doors; and in the film credits themselves.[31] Wenders's obsession with Wyeth and his paintings produces a complex transmedial relation between the different texts that are interlaced in his film. In the process of being adapted for the screen, the original screenplay by Bjørn Olaf Johannessen makes referencing and recreating certain images possible, and this, in turn, takes the story, the cinematography, and the casting in unexpected directions. Conversely, Wyeth's visual legacy is also necessarily transformed by the narrative material that it influenced, since it now serves as a visual network of references for stories and places that were not originally present in the painter's imagination.

Wenders's painterly gaze is defined by the obsessive behavior of the fan, the careful and detailed work of the artist who takes on the challenge of transposing a painting into a different medium, and the challenge of aesthetic experimentation. Perhaps the best example of this three-pronged approach is the way in which Wenders takes advantage of 3-D technology in *Every Thing Will Be Fine* to convey the sense of depth that characterizes many of Wyeth's paintings. In a short yet beautiful scene, Wenders shoots a sheer curtain floating in the air in front of an open window. The moment is clearly inspired by Wyeth's *Wind from the Sea*, a painting which Wenders also directly references and discusses in *Inventing Peace*. The 3-D version of the film creates a visual separation between the window in the background and the curtain, which slowly moves in front of the viewers' eyes, in a space that is no longer constrained by the flatness of the cinema screen. By translating a visual impression typically achieved by the masterful application of pigments on a canvas into a different medium, Wenders succeeds in rendering in a 3-D film what he sees as the great quality of Wyeth's paintings:

> Wyeth painted the lace of that curtain for months,
> and the momentary and utterly elusive split second of a gust of wind
> that gently moved it.
> Again, as in *Christina's World*, there is the instant and eternity.
> Wyeth teaches us, or helps us, to see both.
> And maybe that's the greatest lesson
> for our damaged and limited perception in need of guidance
> to learn again to be in the moment and outside of its time.
> He makes us see the wonder of both,
> which is exactly what our daily avalanche of images is hiding.
> The more pictures we see,
> the less we see how extraordinary every slice of life is.[32]

The *Wind from the Sea* scene in *Every Thing Will Be Fine* places us close to the objects of everyday life, and, by doing so, transforms our perception of them. They are no longer "in the background" but live and breathe with us, as if the documentary impulse of the filmmaker/photographer created an ontological complicity between the intradiegetic and extradiegetic worlds.

* * *

The fascination with American landscapes and cityscapes has been a constant in Wenders's films, from the views of the New York skyline shot from the Empire State Building in *Alice in the Cities* to the very conscious references to Andrew Wyeth's paintings in *Everything Will Be Fine*. At the same time, the clear shift in his filmography from transatlantic to transnational cinema is hard to miss. The first part of his career can be summarized by the term "Amereurope," which Silvestra Mariniello coined to characterize "the encounter between (or 'the marriage' of) the American landscape (human, sonar and musical, geographic, etc.) and a European gaze replete with memory."[33] Wenders's early films explore the ambiguous relation between German and American cultures, as it relates to both cultural norms and ways of seeing (in *Kings of the Road*, Robert famously says to Bruno: "The Yankees have colonized our subconscious") and also to the conception of what it means to be an auteur filmmaker, a question discussed in *The State of Things* (1982) through a pointed criticism of Hollywood and the film "industry." After *Tokyo-Ga* (1985), *Until the End of the World* (1991) is the first Wenders film to travel to non-Western spaces. Originally conceived to include stops on every continent, the film "tries hard to be a global film" as it takes the viewer from Venice to the Australian outback.[34] The opening scene of *Lisbon Story* (1994) depicts "the first journey across the newly opened European 'frontier'" before making Lisbon the stage of an elusive love story that doubles as a sustained reflection on cinema and sensory memory.[35] In *Land of Plenty* (2004), Wenders returns to a city that he knows well, Los Angeles, but offers a "transnational contribution to the memory of 9/11" by following characters from different faiths and backgrounds and "merging national and transnational experiences in a new understanding of human suffering."[36]

Of course, Wenders's 1998 documentary *Buena Vista Social Club* stands out as another attempt to tell a compelling transnational story. Even though the film was well-received by critics and loved by audiences around the world, it has also been the target of some particularly virulent criticisms. For instance, Tanya Hernandez argues, in an essay titled "The Buena Vista Social Club: The Racial Politics of Nostalgia," that the film foregrounds "a narrative of an ahistorical nostalgia for a prerevolutionary Cuba that was presumably more appreciative of its Black talent than socialist Cuba, and thereby ends up serving as a justification for the unilateral reentry of U.S. corporate interests into the affairs of Cuba."[37] The attack is, to some extent, ideologically motivated, but, in Hernandez's view, the film glorifies Cuba's "faded mansions and glamorous hotels" and implies that "socialist Cuba does not appreciate the talent of its populace in the way a White

North American like Ry Cooder can."[38] While it is true that Cooder's position as the American "expert" who rediscovers the lost talents of a prerevolutionary past is problematic, it is only one part of a broader, more pervasive nostalgia in Wenders's approach to the places and people he films in Cuba.

In fact, it draws our attention to a larger issue that several critics have raised: his lack of interest in challenging Western-centric and neocolonial views in representations of the non-European "other." For instance, Dimitris Eleftheriotis suggests that Wenders's representation of "foreign" places is problematic in *Until the End of the World*:

> The film represents the world as a set of attractive and exotic locations that provide a commercially appealing and visually stunning background to the action. The engagement with "other" cultures is completely superficial as they are often reduced to orientalist stereotypes. While "depth" is required to re-capture Europe's "soul," "surface" is rendered adequate for the representation of Russia, Siberia, China and Japan as the worn out clichés demonstrate.[39]

Others have taken issues with how Wenders represents Lisbon. The city "appears frozen in time at the beginning of the twentieth century" in *Until the End of the World*,[40] while in *Lisbon Story*, "the issue of colonialism and post-colonialism, and of Lisbon's multiculturalism, is almost completely erased from Wenders's film."[41] More generally, there seems to be a discrepancy between the nature of the Wendersian gaze and the imperatives of a postcolonial and postorientalist consciousness for which the act of looking back nostalgically is seen as a betrayal of political ideals that should be shared by "progressive" artists of all types. For many, Wenders's position as one of the figureheads of European auteur cinema means that he has a responsibility at least to gesture toward an awareness of the colonial weight of the European gaze when it is applied to peripheral spaces.

This discrepancy helps us consider why most of Wenders's films, more or less since *Wings of Desire*, have been received with reservations—or, in some cases, misunderstood—by the specialized press. For the most part, Wenders has not created the kind of films that have been expected of him. Critics continually fault him for his elliptical style of storytelling, for instance, but rarely point out the deep thematic continuities that run through both his fiction films and documentaries. In the past thirty years, Wenders has in fact continued to blaze his own trail as a visual artist and theorist, without giving in to the dictates of what auteur films should look like or of the kinds of stories they should tell. Our point here is that the transnational dimension of his films cannot be properly understood without exploring at the same time the type of visual project that underpins them. Representations of cultural otherness in Wenders's films, as fraught as they may be, cannot be detached from his ongoing reflections on the nature and power of images.

Tokyo-Ga provides a matrix of sorts for resolving the tension between the drive to formal innovation and a tendency toward orientalism. On the one hand, a large portion of the film is devoted to what Westerners would typically consider the peculiarities of Japanese culture. On the other hand, the film is less a documentary concerned with the visual transcription of observed reality than a true "film essay."[42] Counterintuitively perhaps, Tokyo is not the main theme or the center of the film. It is a means to an end for a personal reflection on the act of seeing, one that parallels the filmmaker's journey through Japanese images, from Ozu's postwar films to the saturation of signs brought about by the mass production and consumption of television images in the 1970s and 1980s. *Tokyo-Ga* is not about recording reality but about how the act of recording images is deeply connected to the act of seeing, to the impression of having already seen as representation something that is in fact experienced for the first time, and of remembering through the filter of how a particular place has been filmed by others.

Those who fault Wenders for his nostalgic or orientalist tendencies also acknowledge—albeit sometimes unwittingly or in roundabout ways—that Wenders's visual epistemology can complement in productive ways the cultural dimension of his fiction films and documentaries. In *Until the End of the World*, for instance, Wenders's tendency to rely on clichés in filming places like Lisbon, Tokyo, or San Francisco is intimately linked to a mise en abyme of images that are part of our collective memory and that continue to frame our visual approach to these places. The second part of the film makes it clear that visual memories are both what structure our psyches and what threaten to destroy them. In that sense, the film "can be read not only as an allegorical manifesto on the future of cinema but also as a fiction about the future of technologies of vision and vision itself."[43] It also functions as a warning against defining a monolithic transnational aesthetics and as "a humanist critique of the myth of the 'shrinking world': far from bridging the distance between people, or between individuals, and their dreams and desires, modern technologies of vision appear to be alienatory and destructive."[44] Similarly, *Lisbon Story* is constructed as a palimpsestic film which harkens back to the days of silent cinema and Soviet formalism.[45] As Paulo de Medeiros admits: "Wenders has always searched for identification through alterity; but in the case of Lisbon, even though the city can be seen as central to his memory, it is not so much a representation of Lisbon that one finds but rather a phantom of Wenders's own desire."[46] Wenders suggests that we distance ourselves from the immediacy of "meaning" (of the symbolic value and weight of cultural representations) and invites us instead to look at the images that he shoots as being deeply embedded in a journey of self-discovery and in a visual grammar that both defines and organizes fictional and lived experiences.

As Alberto Medina brilliantly explains in his essay "Jameson, 'Buena Vista Social Club' and Other Exercises in the Restoration of the Real," Wenders is not interested in "documenting" or in selecting images that preserve an idealized past. For Medina, filming places like Tokyo, Lisbon, or Havana is an "exercise in restoration," but in the sense that "the very meaning of cinema is restoration, the recovery of a reality whose truth has somehow been lost."[47] This approach offers a more productive way of thinking about Wenders's transnational ambitions. It does not preclude readings of his films focused on storytelling and the exploration of new spaces, yet, at the same time, it ascertains the primacy of the aesthetic process: a process that is dialogic and intertextual in nature (Tokyo and Ozu's films, Lisbon and Manoel de Oliveira) and centrally concerned with reflecting upon what cinema can and cannot accomplish. To put it differently, Medina recognizes that "Wenders' films exist somewhere between the faithful depiction of reality and its nostalgic re-production."[48] But rather than seeing in this a lack of political consciousness, he connects it to an ethical yearning focused on reclaiming a visual essence that has been lost in the postmodern age and to an attempt to "save the truth of images from extinction."[49]

It is not surprising that cameras—and those who use them—are featured prominently in both Wenders's documentaries and fiction films. They serve as a constant reminder that there is something at stake for the filmmaker beyond telling stories or capturing outside reality. Cameras speak, so to say, and they speak different visual languages. Translingualism in Wenders's body of work is a natural extension of his approach to transnational cinema. It invites a dialogue between the different cinematic languages that a filmmaker can learn and speak and the multiple languages spoken in many of his films. In doing so, it also gestures toward a larger aesthetic and ethical ambition: the desire to outline a new visual language of peace that would influence both what cinema does and how it does it.

Wenders himself resorts to the language metaphor, in particular to justify his interest in 3-D technology. As he explains in interviews and in the book *Pina:*

The Film and the Dancers, the challenge of filming *Pina* in 3-D went beyond the necessity of designing, testing, and ultimately using new types of cameras.[50] It also meant learning a new visual grammar and exposing viewers to a cinematic language that they did not speak fluently or that they had perhaps "mislearned." Indeed, for Wenders, 3-D aesthetics were appropriated and defined too quickly by big studio productions and equated with speed, action, and special effects. As a result, its potential for other film genres was not seriously considered, and his 3-D "trilogy" (*Pina*, *Every Thing Will Be Fine*, and *The Beautiful Days of Aranjuez*) stands out as an attempt to try out different modes made possible by 3-D.

Pina, of course, is about Pina Bausch, but the film also posits that the creation of a new cinematic language was necessary to record the language of dance, and that it is only by listening to the nine different languages spoken by Pina's dancers that one can get to the heart of who she was and what she meant to them. The dancers' monologues tell a number of "translingual migration stories" and, in doing so, help "restage a transnational *Academia polyglotta* that variously tests, agitates and elides presumptive contemporary models of multilingual citizenship."[51] The first monologue, however, already indicates a slippage from a literal to a metaphorical understanding of language. "Meeting Pina was like finding a language, finally," one of her dancers tells us. "Before, I didn't know how to talk, and then she suddenly gave me a way to express myself, a vocabulary."[52] The close-up on the dancer's face, enhanced by the depth provided by 3-D, shows the strong emotional bond that Pina had with members of her ensemble. The fact that the dancer is technically not speaking—we hear her voice but her lips do not move—also gives the sensation that we have direct access to her thoughts. At the same time, Wenders's formal choices—3-D, the paradox of a silent monologue, and the foreignness of the spoken languages—all create a certain distance from the scene and hint at its metatextual dimension. The filmmaker himself is looking for a vocabulary and a way to express an art form that is hard to capture for the screen.

These metatextual moments are regularly repeated in *Pina* and systematically foreground the deep connections between spoken language, the language of dance, and the language of cinema. For instance, the presentation in the film of one of Pina Bausch's most celebrated pieces, "Café Müller," begins with the dancers as the performance gets underway. The wide-angle shot of the stage quickly fades into a shot of a small-scale model of the space, with the same white walls, grey floor, and randomly arranged black chairs. In his Director's Commentary, Wenders explains the reason for this transition: distracting the audience's attention from one of the shortcomings of 3-D. From a distance, the actors can appear "as if they were miniaturized."[53] Two of Pina's dancers walk around the model stage and discuss—in French, their native language—their memories of how Café Müller came to be. We learn about Pina's creative process, from her idea of adding chairs, to her set designer's suggestion of having a male dancer move them around to create a safe path for a female dancer who keeps her eyes closed and thus does not see the obstacles in her way. But the scene does more than document Pina's artistry or her dancers' recollections. It links a shot of a stage in 3-D with a three-dimensional model of that stage on which moving bodies finally appear as the film returns to the performance. In "Translating Pina for *Pina*," Carrie Smith-Prei perfectly summarizes what is at stake here:

> The body is the language transferred between the media of stage and film, or between choreographic process and filmic process. . . . Wenders' choice of 3D film causes the medium of film to display its materiality at every turn; while attempting to simulate the real experience of sitting in the Tanztheater, the film shows clearly that this is a staged reality.[54]

In *Pina*, the intermedial process is more than just a formal exercise: it is embodied through the physical presence of the dancers and the polyphony of their voices.

Wenders's translingual approach to cinema culminates in *Pina*, but it is also clearly visible in a number of other films, so much so that one could wonder: Does the presence of multiple spoken languages drive formal innovation in his films? Or is it perhaps the other way around? Suffice it to say that there is a strong codependency between the two. *Salt of the Earth*, for instance, moves seamlessly between English, Portuguese, and French, as the film provides biographic information on its main subject, the Brazilian photographer Sebastião Salgado, makes his photographs come alive in his commentary, and frames his work and life story into a coherent narrative. But the real challenge facing Wenders and his co-director Juliano Salgado had to do with a different kind of "language" issue: How to get the photographer to talk about his work in such a way that it would come alive for the viewers? A traditional interview format in which Sebastião Salgado would look at photographs on a flat surface failed to produce quality footage. Salgado struggled to be both engaged and engaging. The two directors ended up creating a setting that put the photographer in direct conversations with his photographs by having him sit directly in front of the image and concealing the camera behind it. The visual trick made it possible to show Salgado's face superimposed on his images and to let the ruggedness of his facial features—also shot in black and white—speak for themselves and add to his words.

Wenders's preoccupation with language can be traced back to early films like *Alice in the Cities*. Even though Philip Winter can express himself in both German and English, he struggles with a more profound translation issue: he has difficulties putting into words what he has seen and experienced during his road trip from North Carolina to New York. Even a visual language—the "instant" representation through Polaroid pictures of American scenes—has difficulty capturing the essence of particular moments and places.[55] In *The State of Things*, the three spoken languages (Portuguese, German, and English) are loosely connected to three cinematic languages: that of an experimental science-fiction film at the beginning, of European auteur cinema that self-consciously reflects on its own nature and commercial viability, and of a classic Hollywood crime plot at the end. In *Lisbon Story*, the sepia scenes shot with a hand-cranked camera enter into a dialogue with Friedrich Monroe's attempt to remove subjectivity from his films by carrying a camera on his back facing away from him, in a film that is both polyphonic and defined by the music of Madredeus. Of course, a more extended analysis would be necessary to understand how different languages intersect and produce meaning in these films and others.

Wenders's latest theoretical intervention is also fundamentally about language. *Inventing Peace: A Dialogue on Perception* collects a series of conversations with the philosopher Mary Zournazi and includes several short essays by Wenders written in his signature freeform prose—his "reflexive style of writing."[56] Beyond providing a summary of the films, visual artists, and ideas that have influenced him, the book outlines the singular visual philosophy that he has methodically developed over the years. For instance, Wenders and Zournazi spend time considering what makes Yasujiro Ozu's films so special and how his technical choices create an ethical language that leads us toward more "gentle" ways of seeing. They explain that "Ozu takes all the obstacles away between his language and our reception of it" by systematically using a 50-mm lens, making things appear closer to us, and by positioning his camera at the eye level of someone sitting on the floor.[57] Taken together, these two techniques give his films an aura of hospitality and inclusion, as if they were letting the viewer come home, both physically and symbolically.

Other filmmakers are featured prominently in *Inventing Peace*—Robert Bresson and his 1966 film *Au Hasard Balthazar*, for example—but what is particularly striking is to see that Wenders continues to be preoccupied with the same theoretical concerns that already informed his early films: the power of cinema (and photography) to "rescue the existence of things," to use Béla Balázs's expression. The thought that he might be the only person looking at a particular space at a specific moment gives him a "sudden sense of responsibility" and makes him ask: "How much of the 'world' did the history of photography and film cover? How much of it was 'captured,' so to speak?"[58] For Wenders, seeing and recording through a lens is a necessary response to the fact that we are always in a process of losing traces of lived experience. Photography, especially in the pre-digital era, was a way of both remembering and archiving in a physical object moments with ontological potential: "each and every single picture 'represented,' / yes, in the very sense of the word, actually 'stood for' / a single, unique, unrepeatable instant, / a truthful glimpse from one person's existence / and into his (or her) point of view of the world."[59]

Interestingly, Wenders's continued interest in the responsibility of photography and filmmaking to preserve things is related to the increasingly visible influence of Christian thought on his personal and artistic outlook. In his mind, we are all "God's instruments / the 'projectionist' of his (or her) creation / together sharing an ever-shifting moving image of the world, / a 'feedback.'"[60] Seeing, in that sense, is also (and perhaps foremost) a double act of bearing witness. As we record for God our visual experiences on Earth, we also reflect the presence of the divine in our lives. Here, Wenders's spiritual considerations are deeply embedded in his aesthetic thought. The reverse angle is always there in-waiting in any act of seeing and inexorably "reveal[s] the eye behind the lens."[61] In other words, film and photography go inward at the same time as they go outward, creating a continuity between the self and the real that carries with it the possibility of spiritual transcendence.

It is within this framework that Wenders and Zournazi seek to define a new visual language of peace that has the potential of "reenchanting the world."[62] They wonder why images of war and violence are so pervasive when "peace" itself sounds like such an abstract notion, or a fleeting hope, that rarely finds productive translations in artistic representations. As Homer laments in *Wings of Desire*, "no one has thus far succeeded in singing an epic of peace."[63] Inventing peace begins with redefining how we understand the word itself and with a pragmatic reframing of what a more peaceful world would look like. For Wenders and Zournazi, the idea of peace is not meant to exclude preemptively the existence of all conflicts. On the contrary, conflict must be an integral part of a dialectic of peace that is based on "the love of opposing views."[64] Likewise, peace can no longer appear to be a utopian ideal and instead must be grounded in the great social issues of our time and in the practice of compassion. "There is certainly no THINKING ABOUT PEACE today that can be detached from THINKING ABOUT POVERTY," Wenders emphatically claims in a letter to Zournazi, "And there is no valid thinking, PERIOD, that has not known suffering."[65]

As one would expect, the emphasis in *Inventing Peace* is on learning to see in new ways. The book, however, does not read like a manifesto for the transformative power of images, or, for that matter, of cinema. In fact, Wenders's approach to the question in one of his personal essays is surprisingly dialectic and exploratory. On the one hand, he suggests that our intense visual culture might be responsible for the absence of peace. If peace is defined as presence (with "people," "things," "places"), then images, because they are only re-presentations, always create a certain distance from the world. In that sense, they contain "an inbuilt violence" and produce "void, longing, regret, anger" rather than the kind of "concord" and "harmony" that comes with presence.[66] This leads him to a somewhat pessimistic conclusion: "I have a hunch that in order to appreciate PEACE, / and to be able to perceive it again, / we might have to move away from our culture of images, / and come back to the things themselves."[67] On the other hand, Wenders and Zournazi are committed to "redress[ing] the limits of our vision" and do not give up on finding a path for a new visual culture of peace.[68] At the center of their argument lies the idea of fostering "gentle perceptions" based on "good and soothing encounters and experiences."[69] This loving look is best understood not as an idealistic proposition but as an outgrowth of Martin Buber's philosophy: a true "I–You" relationship is one of dialogue and observation in the service of a greater and fuller awareness of the Other. In visual terms, the relationship is mediated by a tool—the camera—that "reflect[s] a very exact mirror image of the emotion you empower them with."[70] Photography and film do create a distance from things, but it is that distance, that mediation, which creates the possibility to see again, to see "with affection," and to reframe our perceptions.[71]

* * *

In Wenders's films and in his theoretical writings, intermedial practices are often deeply integrated with transnational and translingual concerns. In the past forty years, Wenders has produced a coherent body of work based on a visual and narrative system that operates in and evolves with each new project. It feeds into a philosophy of perception that can be traced back to his early films, but has found new expressions and remained relevant through Wenders's creative collaborations and technological innovations. At a panel at the Cannes Film Festival in 2017, Wenders explained that one "cannot intend to make a film that matters," but that sometimes something miraculous happens and "a film that is dear to somebody's heart, like the filmmaker's, becomes dear to other people's hearts and, all of a sudden, the fact that it matters appears as something that you do together, the audience as well as the filmmaker, and that you feel together."[72] We hope that the ten chapters that follow provide ample evidence that Wim Wenders occupies a unique place in the contemporary landscape of auteur filmmaking, not only because he still makes films that matter—aesthetically, culturally, and technologically—but also because his early works keep bringing people together, in this case in the form of new scholarly interpretations and perspectives.

In that spirit, we open with three chapters on films from the 1970s, a period still seen by many as the most accomplished in Wenders's career. The Road Trilogy (*Alice in the Cities*, *Wrong Move*, and *Kings of the Road*) marks Wenders's engagement with New German Cinema, but it also betrays a desire to reference and subvert the German romantic tradition. Oliver Speck's chapter "Search for the Sublime: The Road Trilogy, or Wenders's *Roam-man-ticism*" defines Wenders's male protagonists as postmodern nomads whose circular quest points to the negotiation of national identity in postwar Germany at the same time as it questions the very notion of representation. In the three films, it is not just the characters who roam and wander but also the camera itself as it sketches a new kind of postmodern sublime. In "Writing in the Blood of the Past: *Wrong Move* and the Search for a Contemporary German Identity," Kristin Eichhorn focuses on the symbolic dimension of the second film of the trilogy, arguing that the main character's outburst of violence should be seen as generational inheritance. *Wrong Move* suggests that the great literary and artistic achievements of the nineteenth century can conceal the crimes of the Nazi period for a time, but the film also functions as a call to address the "German catastrophe" openly. In loosely borrowing from the plot of Goethe's *Wilhelm Meister*, *Wrong Move* suggests a disturbing continuity between romantic ideals and the logic of National Socialism. In his chapter, Philipp Scheid explains that Wenders reflects on the act of seeing by using windows and windshields as a metaphor for the lens of the camera. In doing so, Wenders partakes in a long tradition in art history that permeates the works of the German romantics, from E. T. A. Hoffman to

Caspar David Friedrich. In *Alice in the Cities* and *Wrong Move*, most notably, Wenders references this tradition and builds on it to investigate the relation between inner and outer spaces. Windows function as a symbolic barrier or interface that tell us about the mental state of his protagonists as they seek to break boundaries and find a purpose in life or decipher the incomprehensible language of landscape and media.

The second section is devoted to Wenders's deep intermedial engagement with other art forms, namely photography and dance. In "As If It Were For the Last Time: Wim Wenders—Film and Photography," George Kouvaros argues that Wenders's approach to photographic images is central to understanding two recurring themes in his films: how to live with images and how to be conscious of time, of its finite and singular quality. Following Walker Evans, Nicholas Ray, and Yasujiro Ozu, Wenders explores the paradox of photography through prose poems in several photobooks, suggesting that capturing images is both an act of preserving a moment that would have otherwise been lost forever and a way of realizing that we are surrounded by the ghosts of all the images that have already been taken. Darrell Varga's "Wenders—Salgado: Space, Time, and Transformation in *Salt of the Earth*" considers photography and filmmaking as critical interventions into social and political issues, both in Wim Wenders's film essays of the 1980s and in his engagement with the work of Sebastião Salgado in his documentary *Salt of the Earth*. Salgado's life story is presented as a mythical journey that parallels the history of the second part of the twentieth century. The Brazilian photographer's repeated experiences of devastation away from his homeland are not fundamentally different from Wenders's exploration of existential loss in his fiction films. Both are a search for home amid the "wreckage of human history," to borrow Walter Benjamin's expression. In "Wim Wenders's *Pina*, a Cinematic Homage to Pina Bausch," Peter Beicken outlines the strategies used by Wenders to film Pina's complex kinetic structures and to translate motion on the stage into emotion on the screen. Placing his cameras where Pina would have been seated in the theater, Wenders seeks to adopt both her gaze and her method of collaboration with her dancers, based on a creative process of self-representation and self-narration. Beicken shows how the film is both a fascinating human story and a feat of technology, since Wenders was inventing a new visual language from scratch at the same time as he was celebrating the legacy of his friend Pina.

The last section deals with the rich transnational dimension of Wenders's films. Simone Malaguti's essay argues that ecological and transcultural theories can inform our understanding of Wenders's films, photography, and picture-stories. Drawing on examples from films like *Until the End of the World* and *Salt of the Earth*, photobooks like *Once* and *4 Real & True 2*, and the book *Inventing Peace*, she suggests that Wenders's works reveal how a personal poetics of space can function as a communicative strategy and how intermediality and interculturality can bring together aesthetic and cultural reflections in productive ways. In "'I Can Imagine Anything': The European Project in Wim Wenders's *Wings of Desire*," Mine Eren shows that in his portrayal of German identity and counter-identity under the pressures of the Cold War, Wenders subverts fantasies of cultural homogeneity by creating a collective "we" that challenges traditional concepts of home, belonging, and citizenship. *Wings of Desire* presents more than an aesthetic intervention into German political discourse on memory. By capturing the sights and sounds of a "twilight zone" in which Wenders's guardian angels live and observe West German life, the filmmaker invites the film's audiences to experience Berlin as a transnational space. Bill Baker's "Blandness and 'Just Seeing' in the Films of Wim Wenders" draws a comparison between the cinematographic styles of Yasujiro Ozu and Wenders and a wider philosophy of seeing characterized by what the French essayist François Jullien has defined as "blandness." Both Ozu and Wenders seek to facilitate a more direct access to the immediacy of experience by filming bland, everyday scenes that acknowledge universal qualities of human sight and experience. *Alice in the Cities* and *Paris, Texas* feature characters who view the world without expressing thought or judgment: their lack of determinate expression echoes what Wenders posits as a core tenet of his visual philosophy in *Tokyo-Ga*: "Just to look, without wanting to prove anything." In the last chapter of the book, "The Heart of Things: Wim Wenders and the Evocations of Peace," Mary Zournazi builds upon the philosophical and ethical dialogue that she and Wenders began in *Inventing Peace*. Zournazi discusses Wenders's commitment to indispensable images and shows how three broad themes—listening, seeing, and dreaming—can help us better apprehend Wenders's vision of the world and the sense of presence and responsibility with which he infuses his films.

Notes

1 The relative lack of attention to Wenders by film studies scholars is not a new phenomenon. Over two decades ago, in their introduction to *The Cinema of Wim*

Wenders: Image, Narrative, and the Postmodern Condition (Detroit: Wayne State University, 1997), Roger Cook and Gerd Gemünden were already observing that "although Wenders is arguably the leading European filmmaker of the last two decades, he has not received as much attention from scholars either in the United States or Europe as some of his colleagues who also had their beginning in New German Cinema" (24).

2 Alexander Graf, *The Cinema of Wim Wenders: The Celluloid Highway* (London: Wallflower Press, 2002).

3 Wim Wenders and Mary Zournazi, *Inventing Peace: A Dialogue on Perception* (London: I.B. Tauris, 2013).

4 Wim Wenders, "Wim Wenders Talks with WSWS: 'The Culture of Independent Film Criticism has Gone Down the Drain,'" interview by Richard Phillips, World Socialist Web Site, January 10, 2000, www.wsws.org/en/articles/2000/01/wwen-j10.html

5 See Jason Wood, *Last Words: Considering Contemporary Cinema* (London: Wallflower Press, 2014), 147; and Martin Brady and Joanne Leal, *Wim Wenders and Peter Handke: Collaboration, Adaptation, Recomposition* (Amsterdam: Rodopi, 2011), 288.

6 Brady and Leal, *Wim Wenders and Peter Handke*, 19.

7 Robert Stam, "Introduction: The Theory and Practice of Adaptation," in *Literature and Film: A Guide to the Theory and Practice of Film Adaptation*, ed. Robert Stam and Alessandra Raengo (Oxford: Blackwell Publishing, 2005), 25. For more on adaptation theory, see for instance Linda Hutcheon's *A Theory of Adaptation* (New York: Routledge, 2006).

8 François Busnel, in conversation with Wim Wenders and Peter Handke, "Wim Wenders adapte au cinéma la pièce de Peter Handke 'Les beaux jours d'Aranjuez,'" *La Grande Librairie*, October 28, 2016, www.youtube.com/watch?v=A4sLktgdJ0U

9 Brady and Leal, *Wim Wenders and Peter Handke*, 31.

10 Ibid., 286.

11 Brad Prager, "29 February 1972: With *Die Angst des Tormanns beim Elfmeter* New German Cinema Learns to Read," in *A New History of German Cinema*, ed. Jennifer M. Kapczynski and Michael D. Richardson (Rochester: Camden House, 2012), 438.

12 David Coury, *The Return of Storytelling in Contemporary German Literature and Film: Peter Handke and Wim Wenders* (Lewiston: Edwin Mellen Press, 2004), 115.

13 Brady and Leal, *Wim Wenders and Peter Handke*, 251–52.

14 Ibid., 28.

15 Nathan Wolfson, "PoMo Desire? Authorship and Agency in Wim Wenders' *Wings of Desire*," *Film and Philosophy* 7 (2003): 133.

16 Thomas Martinec, "'Some Kind of Film Poem': The Poetry of Wim Wenders' *Der Himmel über Berlin/Wings of Desire*," *Studies in European Cinema* 6, no. 2–3 (2009): 167.
17 Ibid., 176.
18 Pablo Gonçalo, "Film in Words/Words in Pictures: Ekphrasis Modulations in Peter Handke and Wim Wenders' Cinematic Collaborations," *Journal of Screenwriting* 8, no. 1 (2017): 84 and 88.
19 Ibid., 88.
20 Ibid., 93.
21 Brigitte Peucker, "Filming Tableau Vivant: Vermeer, Intermediality, and the Real," in *Rites of Realism: Essays on Corporeal Cinema*, ed. Ivone Margulies (Durham: Duke University Press, 2003), 295–96.
22 Ibid., 311.
23 Ibid., 310.
24 Ibid., 295.
25 Wim Wenders, "Wim Wenders influencé par Hopper," interview by Jean-Pierre Devillers, *Grand Palais*, 2012, www.youtube.com/watch?v=SakYrQaOLJQ (my translation).
26 See Fabien Gaffez's "Le rouge et le vert: D'Edward Hopper à Robby Müller," *Positif* no. 621 (November 2012), 104–5.
27 Carol Troyen, "Edward Hopper's Stories," *Magazine Antique*, April 2007, 84.
28 Brady and Leal, *Wim Wenders and Peter Handke*, 15.
29 Quoted in Barbara Haskell, "Edward Hopper: Between Realism and Abstraction," in *Modern Life: Edward Hopper and His Time*, ed. Barbara Haskell in collaboration with Ortrud Westheider (Munich: Hirmer Verlag, 2009), 52. The quote is from a letter from Goethe to Friedrich Heinrich Jacobi, August 21, 1774. Hopper mentioned it in "Invitation to Art," an interview with Brian O'Doherty, first broadcast on April 10, 1961.
30 Wenders and Zournazi, *Inventing Peace*, 151.
31 "Wim and Donata Wenders would like to thank . . . The paintings of Andrew Wyeth." Wim Wenders, *Every Thing Will Be Fine* [01:58:22].
32 Wenders and Zournazi, *Inventing Peace*, 154.
33 Silvestra Mariniello, "Experience and Memory in the Films of Wim Wenders," *SubStance* 34, issue 106, no. 1 (2005): 165–66. Timothy Corrigan argues that "Wenders's cinema is dislocated between two cultures, between that of Goethe and Heidegger and that of Ray and Ford" ("Wenders's *Kings of the Road*," in *New German Film: The Displaced Image* [Bloomington: Indiana University Press, 1983], 19).
34 Dimitris Eleftheriotis, "Global Visions and European Perspectives," in *Aliens R Us: The Other in Science Fiction Cinema*, ed. Ziauddin Sardar and Sean Cubitt (London: Pluto Press, 2002), 169.

35 Randall Halle, *The Europeanization of Cinema: Interzones and Imaginative Communities* (Urbana, University of Illinois Press, 2014), 17.
36 Bridget Dawes, "Celluloid Recoveries: Cinematic Transformations of Ground Zero," in *Media and Cultural Memory / Medien und kulturelle Erinnerung: Transnational American Memories*, ed. Udo Hebel (Berlin: de Gruyter, 2009), 302.
37 Tanya Hernandez, "The Buena Vista Social Club: The Racial Politics of Nostalgia," *Latino/a Popular Culture*, ed. Michelle Habell-Pallan and Mary Romero (New York: New York University Press, 2002), 61.
38 Ibid., 66 and 67.
39 Eleftheriotis, "Global Visions and European Perspectives," 176.
40 Paulo de Medeiros, "Representing Lisbon: Wenders, Memory and Desire," *Journal of Romance Studies* 1, no. 2 (Summer 2001): 78.
41 Ewa Mazierska and Laura Rascaroli, *Crossing New Europe: Postmodern Travel and the European Road Movie* (London: Wallflower Press, 2006), 208.
42 Nora Alter explains that "*Tokyo-Ga* appears as a film about films rather than a film about reality (or rather about the rest of reality, since obviously film is part of reality), a filmic practice both defined and confined by cinematographic illusion" ("Global Politics, Cinematographic Space: Wenders's *Tokyo-Ga* and *Notebooks on Cities and Clothes*," in *Projecting History: German Nonfiction Cinema, 1967-2000* [Ann Arbor: University of Michigan Press, 2002], 117).
43 Eleftheriotis, "Global Visions and European Perspectives," 170.
44 Ibid., 171.
45 Mazierska and Rascaroli, *Crossing New Europe*, 205.
46 De Medeiros, "Representing Lisbon," 74.
47 Alberto Medina, "Jameson, 'Buena Vista Social Club' and Other Exercises in the Restoration of the Real," *Iberoamericana (2001-)* 7, no. 25 (March 2007), 16.
48 Ibid., 16.
49 Ibid., 16.
50 See Donata Wenders and Wim Wenders, *Pina: The Film and the Dancers* (Munich: Schirmer/Mosel, 2012).
51 David Gramling, "Seven Types of Multilingualism: Or, Wim Wenders Enfilms Pina Bausch," in *The Multilingual Screen: New Reflections on Cinema and Linguistic Difference*, ed. Tijana Mamula and Lisa Patti (New York: Bloomsbury, 2016), 45.
52 Wim Wenders, *Pina*, 15:05–15:16.
53 Wenders, "Commentaries," *Pina*, dir. Wim Wenders, DVD disc 2 (New York: Criterion Collection, 2013), 19:03–19:18.
54 Carrie Smith-Prei, "Translating Pina for *Pina*," in *Translation and Translating in German Studies: a Festschrift in Honour of Raleigh Whitinger*, ed. John L. Plews and Diana Spokiene (Waterloo: Wilfried Laurier University Press, 2016), 182.

55 For more on polaroid photography as a visual "language" of its own, see Wim Wenders, *Instant Stories* (London: Thames and Hudson, 2017).
56 Wenders and Zournazi, *Inventing Peace*, 8.
57 Ibid., 95.
58 Ibid., 58.
59 Ibid., 59.
60 Ibid., 58.
61 Ibid., 59.
62 Ibid., 12.
63 Wim Wenders, *Wings of Desire* [00:40:20–00:40:27].
64 Wenders and Zournazi, *Inventing Peace*, 38.
65 Ibid., 28 (their capitalization).
66 Ibid., 67–68.
67 Ibid., 68–69.
68 Ibid., 76.
69 Ibid., 56.
70 Ibid., 74.
71 Ibid., 73.
72 "Wim Wenders Talks at the Movies that Matter Panel in Cannes 2017," https://www.youtube.com/watch?v=uTdBxy5lwMU (accessed May 1, 2018).

Part I

Watching the Road Trilogy in the Twenty-First Century

2

Search for the Sublime: The Road Trilogy, or Wenders's *Roam-man*-ticism

Oliver C. Speck

More than forty years later, the three films that established Wim Wenders's international reputation—*Alice in den Städten/Alice in the Cities* (1974), *Falsche Bewegung/Wrong Move* (1975), and *Im Lauf der Zeit/Kings of the Road* (1976)—appear very much rooted in their time. Indeed, for a German of my generation, the films of the so-called Road Trilogy clearly evoke nostalgic feelings. The Germany that we see here is the Germany of our childhood.[1] We "see" this Germany through the eyes of a boy, a gaze that Wenders's protagonists—all of them male—constantly try to recapture.[2] It is a Germany where trains run on time, and where you can still open the windows on a train (and this is quite important: Wenders's windows are not just screens through which you stare with romantic longing; they must be opened, or broken with bricks and even bare hands).[3] It is a Germany where adults can be trusted, where the police are happy to help, and where people go about their business without thinking too much about the Third Reich, and without paying any heed to the terror from the left that certainly dominated the headlines in those years leading to the "German Autumn" of 1977. To quote the first line of Wenders's biggest success, *Der Himmel über Berlin/Wings of Desire* (1987), "Als das Kind Kind war...."

We can also see why Wenders, certainly in the eyes of some critics, will always be the distant third in the triumvirate of German New Cinema directors. Just look at the dozen (!) films that Rainer Werner Fassbinder made in roughly the same period. These are angry films, still politically relevant, about people tragically trapped by their milieu and destroyed by capitalism. And who can forget the great trickster Werner Herzog, three years older than Fassbinder and Wenders, with his possessed dwarfs, flying woodcarvers, and raving conquistadores?[4] At least at first glance, Wenders's films in comparison appear heavy, metaphysical, imbued with a Teutonic charm that appeals to American undergraduate students and—as we learn from a recent *New York Times Magazine* feature—Brooklyn indie-rock bands.[5] But suddenly, I realize that my nostalgia for 1970s Germany becomes tinged with the awareness that the memory of this world of my childhood has always been partly fictive, a projection, a facade of full employment and prosperity, while adults pushed the things they sought to ignore into the shadows: the Nazi past, the student revolt, left-wing terrorism. Instead, then, of elaborating on the glory days of New German Cinema, I want to concentrate in this contribution on what will always be new in Wenders's films. It is important here to remember that—with the exception of the documentary filmmaker Harun Farocki—Wim Wenders is the only New German Cinema director who actually went to film school. The moving image always has priority over story and plot in any Wenders film. My chapter will therefore address the movements in Wenders's Road Trilogy, especially those of his camera, as it films his roaming male protagonists and their romantic search. Following the model of Gilles Deleuze, on which I will elaborate later, I then attempt to distill Wim Wenders's main filmic concept out of these movements, an image that I attempt to capture with the portmanteau word "roam-man-ticism."

While the three abovementioned films were not planned as a trilogy and do not share a common format (16-mm black and white, 35-mm color, and 35-mm black and white), all three are road movies that were shot by cinematographer Robby Müller, and all feature the actor Rüdiger Vogler. There is nothing tragic or possessed about the characters Vogler plays in these three films. Philip Winter,[6] Wilhelm, and Bruno Winter are laid-back loners in search of themselves who have trouble relating to women. The protagonist in each film appears hesitant, milquetoast, "ein typischer Softie," as he would have been called back then. His gestures and soft features give him the appearance of a petulant child. Even his few moments of anger—slamming a TV set to the ground, breaking a window with his fists, starting a fight—appear more as an attempt to try out an emotion, as children or teenagers would do—more an act, quickly regretted, than the outburst of genuine frustration.[7] Wenders's male characters do not act—they act out.

In tandem with these immature gestures, the men of the Road Trilogy have their aimless travel in common. Supposed to write a magazine story about "The American Landscape," Philip in *Alice in den Städten/Alice in the Cities* instead takes hundreds of Polaroids. When he is put in charge of accompanying nine-year-old Alice back to Germany by her mother, a chance acquaintance, he agrees, probably because he has a crush on the mother. After Alice's mother doesn't show up at the meeting point, Philip is forced to take responsibility and sets out to locate the girl's grandmother. Philip seems reluctant at first to finally have a goal. Quickly annoyed by his precocious charge, Philip drops Alice off at a local police station. A Chuck Berry concert changes his mind, and he rejoins Alice who, in the meantime, has run away from the police. With a rental car, they are indeed able to find the house that Alice remembers; however, the grandmother has moved away. On a ferry, one of the police officers recognizes them and informs them that the authorities have located Alice's mother and grandmother in Munich, which, ironically, was Philip's destination anyhow. After Alice produces a hundred dollar bill that she had hidden away, Philip and Alice are able to buy train tickets. The last shot of the film looks down on the train with Philip and Alice sticking their heads out of the open window (Figure 2.1).

Falsche Bewegung/Wrong Move is based on Peter Handke's film script *Falsche Bewegung*, in turn a loose adaptation of Johann Wolfgang von Goethe's famous novel *Wilhelm Meister*.[8] The action is set in contemporary West Germany and features the trials and tribulations of Wilhelm, a man in his early thirties, in search of himself. Like the unsuccessful travel writer Philip Winter in *Alice*, Wilhelm is a writer with a writer's block. To cure his frustration and to help him find inspiration, his mother sends him on a trip to Bonn, the capital of West Germany at the time. Changing trains, Wilhelm meets Therese, a mysterious woman who is his age. On the next train, he encounters an old man, a former

Figure 2.1

concentration camp guard, accompanied by his "charge," a thirteen-year-old girl. The odd couple makes money busking. Joined by Therese, an actress, and Laertes, a hapless poet, the troupe sets out on a road trip. An encounter with a suicidal businessman interrupts their journey. The end of the film finds Wilhelm standing at the top of a mountain.

Im Lauf der Zeit/Kings of the Road—the German title would translate as "In the Course of Time"—features two aimless protagonists. Bruno Winter lives in an old moving truck, performing repairs and maintenance on old film projectors in the eastern part of West Germany. He meets Robert Lander when the latter drives his VW Beetle into a river in a half-hearted suicide attempt. Both seem to be running away from some unspecified relationship trouble in their past; however, both—especially Bruno—intend to keep their traveling companion at arm's length. Indeed, for the first hour of this three-hour movie, the men maintain the formal "Sie." After a motorcycle ride to Bruno's childhood home, now abandoned and overgrown, and an equally emotionally upsetting visit with Robert's father, the barriers come down. A soul-searching night in an abandoned checkpoint built by the American forces at the border with East Germany leads to blows. The next morning, the men part ways. The last sequence shows Bruno in his truck, driving parallel to Robert, who is riding in a rail car, pretending not to notice Bruno (Figure 2.2). Even though Bruno has torn up his itinerary, it remains unclear what and how much will change in their lives.

The genre that Wenders picked for these three films is remarkable since West Germany was certainly not a country that would lend itself to dreams of traveling on an open road. Instead of the American classic journey from

Figure 2.2

East to West, Wenders's protagonists typically travel in circles, crisscrossing Germany, traveling near the border to East Germany, finally coming to a dead end or just moving on. It is no surprise, then, that the genre-typical self-discovery is limited at best. The protagonist of *Wrong Move*, for example, does not arrive at the shores of the North Sea, or an inspiring Mediterranean beach, but finally ends up at the top of Germany's highest mountain. This movement of running in place can be found in practically all of Wenders's feature films. The critically undervalued *Bis ans Ende der Welt/Until the End of the World* (1991), an uneasy mix of sci-fi, film noir, and road movie, for example, shows an aimless scavenger hunt around the world that leads to the emptiness of the Australian Outback and Outer Space. We should also not forget the signature shot from the Road Trilogy of two parallel movements. As mentioned before, at the end of *Kings of the Road*, Bruno's truck drives next to the rail car in which Robert sits. A quite similar shot can be found in *Wrong Move*: Wilhelm and Therese look at each other from their respective compartments when the trains run briefly on parallel tracks (Figure 2.3). The final shot of *Alice* is filmed from a helicopter that at first moves parallel to the train, then flies up, while the train departs through the beautiful Rhine valley. Similar parallel movements can be found in other Wenders films.

Like other filmmakers of the German New Cinema, Wenders is keenly aware of the loss of artistic role models after the Third Reich. The heroes for his generation are the high-modernist *auteurs*: John Ford, Nicholas Ray, or emigrants like Fritz Lang, to whom *Im Lauf der Zeit* is dedicated. In this context,

Figure 2.3

Klaus Kreimeier sees Wenders's early films in particular as works of mourning. According to Kreimeier, the many references and quotations in Wenders are "remembrances of a faded, no: strangled culture."[9] The men in Wenders's cinema, it seems, search for what they lacked as children. The lack of reliable father figures leads his protagonists, like Alice in Wonderland, "down the rabbit hole" of a disorienting—that is, American—gaze.[10] In *Alice*, the monotony of the American landscape causes writer's block in Philip. And Robert, toward the end of *Im Lauf der Zeit*, utters what must be the most quoted line from Wenders's films: "Die Amis haben unser Unterbewusstsein kolonialisiert" (The Yankees have colonized our subconscious). The other protagonist of this film repairs old projectors in the countryside, keeping alive the very thing—"the old film"—that the manifesto of the Oberhausen group—of which, it should be noted, Wenders was not a member—famously declared dead in 1962.[11] I can only call this romantic irony. Bruno, who travels with an American-made jukebox in his van, is disgusted with the ware the culture industry provides; still, even a bad film deserves good projection. Tellingly, the last cinema that Bruno services is run by an old woman who refuses to show the trash that is offered—sex comedies and action flicks whose lurid posters we see displayed elsewhere. Her movie theater remains closed, the display cases empty. However, her cinema will be ready to show the "new film" once it arrives.

Gerd Gemünden makes the interesting point that in the tradition of late modernity, in Wim Wenders's cinema mass culture is associated with the feminine: "Mass culture and Americanization—employed by Wenders as two virtually synonymous terms—are overdetermined concepts that connote complex processes of political, cultural, and sexual repression and displacement in the young Americanized male protagonists."[12] In other words, Wenders's men are at once drawn to the feminine, or what they think it is, and equally repulsed by it, especially once they meet a real woman. This is perhaps best exemplified by the goalie in Wenders's 1972 adaptation of the eponymous novel by Peter Handke, *Die Angst des Tormanns beim Elfmeter/The Goalie's Anxiety at the Penalty Kick*, who inexplicably kills a cinema cashier after a one-night-stand. Bruno Winter in *Kings of the Road* makes sure that he will not have a sexual relationship with the cinema cashier, although he professes later, in quite lofty words, that he is longing for a woman even though he does not know how to live with one: "I have a deep yearning. For a woman. Any woman. Every woman makes me yearn. I think it's like this for every man. . . . Of course, I wished to be one with a woman."[13] And Wilhelm, in *Wrong Move*, who was in an uneasy relationship with—who else—a cinema cashier before leaving, clearly prefers to sleep with the teenaged Mignon instead of establishing a meaningful relationship with Therese, who is his age.

Wenders scholarship, not surprisingly, has long pointed out how much the filmmaker is indebted to the German romantic tradition.[14] His oeuvre is full of abandoned children, eerie houses, and mysterious women. His typical protagonist is *ein Wanderer*, a constant migrant, who, overwhelmed by a longing to escape the narrow constraints of his *Heimat*, roams without apparent aim. Because it is always a man who, once parted, inevitably longs to retrieve this lost unity with the feminine realm. Indeed, English has borrowed the wonderful German word "Wanderlust" for this condition of insatiable desire to travel without a destination.

It is clear, by now, that Wenders's cinema is heavily gendered, hewing to the hetero male perspective and its projections and object relations. Indeed, one would have to search very hard to find a fully fledged female character in any of his fiction films.[15] The actress Lisa Kreuzer, married to Wim Wenders at the time, plays the irresponsible mother in *Alice* and the cashier in *Kings of the Road* (she has a supporting part as Wilhelm's girlfriend in *Wrong Move*) (Figure 2.4). She also appears in a very similar role as the main character's wife in *Der amerikanische Freund/The American Friend* (1977), Wenders's next film after the Road Trilogy. Kreuzer's characters seem distanced, irritated, puzzled by, and resigned to a world where "boys will be boys." In other words, the female companion serves

Figure 2.4

as the catalyst for the main character, who needs to separate himself from this "feminine" influence. It is easy to imagine that Bruno and Robert in *Im Lauf der Zeit* left exactly "her type" behind. The more glamorous Hanna Schygulla, already famous at the time for her roles in a dozen of Fassbinder's films, plays a variation of the same strong female character in *Falsche Bewegung*. As Therese, she steadily holds Wilhelm's gaze, with a slightly mocking expression, thereby intimidating him. Although she is his age, she is certainly more mature than the protagonist. She even—inexplicably—understands why he would have sex with the thirteen-year-old Mignon instead of her. This statutory rape is an act of abuse that certainly proves Wilhelm's childish irresponsibility: a childishness that leads him to literally feel himself the counterpart of the child and that sets no bounds to irresponsible impulses.

This, then, is the crux of dealing with Wenders's movies. If we only stick to his flawed heroes, we encounter rather repulsive,[16] narcissistic child-men who appear as outright chauvinists. Those boy-men seem puerile; their mothers buy their clothes for them, or they wear flap trousers without a shirt. Worse, these chauvinists then disguise their projective fantasies about women in metaphysical ramblings, as quoted earlier. Kreimeier might be correct in diagnosing "a German addiction to being 'essential'" in Wenders.[17] But before accepting the hermeneutic suspicion that a Wenders film can only be understood as male-centered fantasy, we should acknowledge how troubled this fatherless generation of men actually is. Martha B. Helfer reminds us that we should "question whether the male romantics' wide-ranging and diffuse statements about the feminine should be read synthetically or programmatically *only* under the rubric 'theory of the feminine,' whether they should be *privileged* over the concomitant critique of the masculine formulated in many of the same writings."[18] Indeed, the Wenders *Wanderer* is not at home anywhere, especially not in his own skin. It is this displacement and restlessness that need analysis.

In this context, it is crucial to recall that Goethe's novel *Wilhelm Meister*, on which *Wrong Move* is based, is the epitome of the *Bildungsroman*, the novel of formation. At the end, notably after his underage muse has died of a broken heart, Wilhelm Meister finds his "undeserved happiness," as he acknowledges in Goethe's novel,[19] with another woman so comically perfect that she is immediately recognizable as male fantasy. Compared to this extreme "happy ending," the Handke-Wenders rewrite appears to fizzle out. Indeed, this is not the open ending so typical of new wave cinema but rather a non-ending that lacks any of the tragic heft of the work by Wenders's compatriots. Who can forget the great circle at the end of the 1972 *Aguirre, der Zorn Gottes/Aguirre, the Wrath of God*? The mad Aguirre on his raft, reigning over corpses and monkeys. Or the tragic downfall caused by a lottery win of Fassbinder's Franz in *Faustrecht der Freiheit/Fox and His Friends* (1975)? Wim Wenders's men do not trigger cathartic feelings in the audience or bring any salutary closure.

Philip, instead, is last seen on the train to Munich, where he almost certainly will not become a father figure for his young soulmate, Alice. The traveling projector repairman Bruno promises change and tears up his itinerary, but we have no idea what he will do with his life from then on. Wilhelm leaves his love interests—the singular love interest "woman" is split into the maternal actress and the beautiful, underage Mignon—in a pedestrian shopping area and ends up, with his silly little suitcase, his sensible shoes, and the coat that his mother bought for him, on an overlook at the Zugspitze. This shot is clearly an ironic reference to Caspar David Friedrich's iconic painting, *Der Wanderer über dem Nebelmeer/Wanderer above the Sea of Fog* (1818), where a wastebasket can be clearly seen in the foreground and the railing prevents any danger of falling.[20] The sublime experience is clearly lost in postmodernity. The famous Zugspitze was probably named after the avalanches that regularly come down from Germany's highest mountain. The name allows for puns that, I would argue, are intended here. The name could literally translate to "Drafty Peak." But Wilhelm, dressed by his mum, will most certainly not catch a cold there. *Zug* also means "train" in German; a *Zugspitze* generally refers to the head of a train.

Indeed, practically every fictional film by Wim Wenders contains a reference to trains: in a helicopter shot very similar to the one in *Alice,* Jonathan Zimmermann in *The American Friend* sticks his head out of the Trans-Europe Express, and his son has a lampshade that depicts the engine from Buster Keaton's famous *The General* (1926). Travis in *Paris, Texas* (1984) walks through the desert on apparently abandoned tracks. Unlike his fellow auteur, Rainer Werner Fassbinder, who constantly points to the repressed Nazi past in his *Die Ehe der Maria Braun/ The Marriage of Maria Braun* (1979),[21] Wenders avoids the sinister associations of Germany and trains almost completely. An avid fan of classic Hollywood cinema, Wim Wenders is certainly familiar with the important role traveling plays in American culture. Here, the train, as a modern rendition of the stagecoach, is associated with travel, escape, or, at the very least, a true movement over a vast landscape, from East to West. The compartment inevitably becomes a liminal space enabling impersonation, disguise, self-revelation, and a kind of shape-shifting. *Stagecoach* (1939) by John Ford, one of Wim Wenders's intellectual heroes, would be one possible example of this American figure of the compartment.[22] In comparison to American cinema, however, traveling, to Wenders, seems to mark a limitation since his protagonists do not undergo the prototypical character arc. As a filmmaker, Wim Wenders thinks in images, not in stories or in generic concepts, such as realism. He recognizes that these films from the Classic Hollywood era were, of course, shot on a soundstage, and that the compartment—the interior of the stagecoach, train, or automobile—does not move, while the landscape "moves" around this personal space by way of a back projection.

Wim Wenders employs a very similar paradox in his Road Trilogy, the still movement. Here, I would like to draw attention, again, to the parallel movements that cancel each other out. Deleuze calls them "movements of translations":[23] a train and the camera, two trains on parallel tracks, a truck and a train, a car and a boy on a bicycle. The characters now see each other through new eyes; nothing has changed, but the movement is briefly one of relative stillness. This moment turns the aimless *Wanderer* into a true nomad whose "war machine" Gilles Deleuze and Felix Guattari oppose to the "state machine" in the twelfth chapter of their *A Thousand Plateaus*. The nomad stays in the same space, paradoxically, by constantly moving. Even though the Philips and Wilhelms in these films take the train to another city, or map out the route to the next small village cinema, these points are not destinations but "relays," because the nomad is constantly on the way: "The nomad goes from point to point only as a consequence and as a factual necessity; in principle, points for him are relays along a trajectory."[24] The Road Trilogy (as well as Scorsese's *Alice* film, about which more later) saves the road movie from the teleological implications that the genre has gained, insofar as their heroes never arrive at their stated destination, thus resisting the clichéd best intentions of "finding oneself."[25] The "function of the sedentary road," as Deleuze and Guattari explain, "is to parcel out a closed space to people, assigning each person a share and regulating the communication between shares. The nomadic trajectory does the opposite: it distributes people (or animals) in an open space, one that is indefinite and noncommunicating."[26] To return to the example of *Stagecoach*, the character played by John Wayne, Ringo Kid, is exactly such a nomad. To put it bluntly, the respective incarnations of Philip/Wilhelm/Bruno in a Wenders film should not be seen as traveler but as the nomad, insofar as they stand still by constantly moving, distributed over West Germany, which is thus turned into an indefinite space. This move by Wenders bypasses politicized cinema à la Fassbinder, but significantly, it restores a political potential that is not, on the surface, identifiable as such, and which is not subjugated to any regime, except, arguably, an aesthetic one. In short, the two Germanies are liberated from their ordered "states" and to an open relation.

To return to the abovementioned "critique of the masculine" and the absence of fully fledged female characters in Wenders's oeuvre, it seems at this point that Wenders's films are a perfect illustration of Lacan's famous dictum, "woman is a symptom of man." The basic, Freudian reading perceives of any symptom as a message that needs to be deciphered in order to understand the warped desire at its core. Once this symptom that a woman represents for man is understood, it dissolves itself. When, for example, the cinema cashier meets Bruno at a county fair, she prominently carries a candle in the shape of Adolf Hitler's head, a striking image that is an obvious reference to the stifling Nazi past. Later, puzzled by a blurry spot on the screen, Bruno ventures upstairs only to find the projectionist masturbating. It turns out that the young man had inserted a small mirror into the beam, thus projecting the cheap soft porn film onto a wall. After the screening, Bruno stalls and avoids sleeping with the young woman who is clearly interested in him. Out of cast-off fragments of film he picked up from the floor of the projection booth, he fabricates an endless loop of lurid announcements and fragmented nude bodies that he screens for her until they are too tired to make love.

Here, "woman," although tempting, is clearly a castrating force, a Salome who ironically cradles the head of Hitler. She guards the entrance to the womb of cinema where men actually learn to desire. The stain in the image, as Lacan explains in his well-known reading of the Ambassadors by Holbein in *The Four Fundamental Concepts of Psychoanalysis*, refers to the Real: from a certain perspective, cinema is revealed as a machine where the image of woman serves man's masturbatory pleasure. While many examples can be found in Wenders's oeuvre, his English-language production *Paris, Texas* (1984) might provide the most stunning example for such a Lacanian reading. After wandering aimlessly for years, Travis (Harry Dean Stanton) tracks down his wife Jane (Nastassja Kinski), who performs in a peep show. She appears on a stage that resembles a kitchen. While they can communicate via an intercom, she cannot see him through the one-way mirror. Wenders's cinematography stresses the seediness of the setting, aligning our gaze with Travis's realization and, ultimately, his healing process. The domestic fantasy of the "sexy housewife" is thus revealed to Travis and the viewer as nothing but a sordid male projection. At the end, Travis turns the light in the booth toward himself, exposing his face, ravaged by years of wandering, while his wife faces away from him, staying out of sight.

These moments of healing, of almost-happiness, it should be pointed out, do not mean that Wenders's men undergo a stereotypical character arc, one that is often triggered by the pop-cultural understanding of a trauma in mainstream movies. In other words, a simplistic reading would stop at this point, misunderstanding Wenders's characters as chauvinistic, immature men. While Travis, Bruno, and Philip might now accept responsibility for their actions and, most notably, their past inactions, they do not emerge as fundamentally changed or redeemed characters. As Slavoj Žižek explains, later in his career, Lacan redefined his definition of the symptom, calling it "sinthome" (the Greek word for symptom): "'Woman is a symptom of man' means that man himself exists only through woman qua his symptom: his very ontological consistency depends on, is externalized in, his symptom. In other words, man literally ex-sists: his entire being lies 'out there,' in woman."[27] Wenders's men recognize that there will always be a sublime element that is essential and must necessarily remain unrepresentable.

The apparent unwillingness, inability—or, better, impotence—to act can also be linked to a critique of the masculine. Slavoj Žižek explains:

> Lacan says, in another provocative statement, that the only act which is not a failure, the only act *stricto sensu* is suicide, he thereby reconfirms the "feminine" nature of the act as such. Men are "active"; they take refuge in relentless activity in order to escape the proper dimension of the act. The retreat of man from woman (the retreat of the hard-boiled detective from the *femme fatale* in *film noir*, for example), is thus effectively a retreat from the death-drive as a radical ethical stance.[28]

In this light, the suicides—the industrialist in *Wrong Move* or the wife of the nameless man (played by Marquard Bohm) in *Kings of the Road*—are successful, ethical acts as opposed to the half-hearted suicide attempt by Robert, for example, who states that he is afraid that his ex-wife might kill herself. At the end of a Wenders film, his male protagonists, who took "refuge in relentless activity," can now begin to act ethically. While the Road Trilogy releases its heroes into open endings, Travis, in the abovementioned *Paris, Texas*, convinces his wife to take responsibility for their son, while he, in turn, does not attempt to recreate the false image of domestic bliss for which he is not suitable.

In this chapter, I have suggested taking a step back and looking at the films under discussion not as stories but as images. This position allows us to see Wenders as an artist who attempts to bridge the gap between nature and the self, in the best romantic tradition. As mentioned before, Wenders is the only member of the German New Cinema who actually studied filmmaking. Indeed, Wenders's films are clearly metacinematic and modern insofar as these films reflect on their own materiality as filmic texts and, furthermore, constantly remind us that, while a picture says more than a thousand words, as the clichéd saying goes, these pictures still fail miserably at capturing reality. They are either not enough or too much. The Polaroids that Philip constantly compares with drab reality at the beginning of *Alice* are strangely beautiful and, at the same time, completely ephemeral, since there is no negative to reproduce them (Figure 2.5). It is a noteworthy fact that this new technology of the Polaroid, a photo without a negative, was accessed by Wenders in advance of its official release. While providing instant gratification, a Polaroid is from the outset retrograde, a denial of reproducibility in an age of modernity, as if it were an advanced form of painting. This "image capture" that seeks to escape its modern constraints, I would argue, constitutes a kind of allegory for Wenders's films themselves: an image/negative in one excessive instance that only captures a meta-idea of its own coming into being, its own "apprenticeship" to reality, an impossible yet irresistible, even ineluctable, task.

The films of the Road Trilogy could still be compared to a novel of formation, however: the male protagonists who appear to suffer from what nowadays would be called "arrested development" go through a belated coming-of-age moment, mostly with the help of children or childlike characters and the encounter with

Figure 2.5

apparently nihilistic acts in the form of suicides and suicide attempts. This moment, undeserved as it might be, is their moment of happiness.

Again, Wenders would never attempt an ill-fated "return to" (though he does indulge in the journey that circles around such a return). His films are, definitely, not a return to the clichéd "innocent look of children." The children in Wenders's films are rather precocious it seems—more grown up, certainly, than the men who are nursing their "age-thirty-crisis." The shift in perception that Walter Benjamin locates in the early twentieth century in his famous essay "The Work of Art in the Age of Mechanical Reproducibility" cannot be undone, least of all by an attempt to make German art great again. This new perception can only be overcome in a Nietzschean sense. I believe, to put it bluntly, that the paradoxical journeys in Wenders's cinema are a search for the sublime in a post-romantic mode.

On comparing *Alice in den Städten/Alice in the Cities* (1974) to *Alice Doesn't Live Here Anymore* (1974), an uncannily similar American film made at the same time by Martin Scorsese, we can quickly see that the psychological and moral growth of the protagonist so typical of the road movie is missing in both cases. Scorsese's Alice is the mother of a troubled eleven-year-old boy. To be precise, even though she is his biological mother, she acts more like his peer and treats him like an equal, while her son attempts to assume the role of a big brother. Alienated and reified, Alice sets out in search of herself, after her oafish husband unexpectedly dies in a car crash. Just like Wilhelm, she has ill-advised aspirations of becoming an artist. Due to space constraints, I cannot point out the many surprising parallels between these films. Suffice it to say, Scorsese's Alice never makes it to Monterey, just as the search for the grandmother in the German film dead-ends in the Rust Belt of the *Ruhrgebiet*. Scorsese's Alice achieves, however, a remarkable shift in perspective, one I would like to call, for lack of a better word, "messianic." The arrival of the messiah, as Giorgio Agamben, following Walter Benjamin, explains in his *The Time That Remains*, does not mean that there will be a complete change or a new world order. On the contrary, everything is *exactly* as it was before the arrival of the messiah. But, paradoxically, everything is also utterly different, because we see everything with completely changed eyes. It is, thus, a literal "eye-opener" for Philip to travel with Alice.

From this perspective, Wim Wenders's films could be considered the product of a Deleuzian auteur, insofar as he creates "conceptual personae," as Deleuze and Guattari describe them in *What is Philosophy?*[29] Inspired by Nietzsche's Zarathustra and the Cartesian idiot, Deleuze and Guattari claim that philosophers create concepts that are, however, only accessible through an image. Such images, "conceptual personae," should be understood as true—that is, ethical perspectives, very specific, intersubjective windows to the world. Indeed, the masculine in Wenders's films—impersonated by Philip/Wilhelm/Bruno/Travis—is expressed here as the image of the roaming romantic man who learns to stand still by being constantly on the move and who gains a decisive insight through this incessant movement (cf. Figure 3.5 on page 53).

Let me sum up my points: While Wenders's protagonists start out in search of a sublime experience (e.g., finding oneself, becoming one with woman, a deeper understanding of the world), they overcome the romantic sublime and indeed arrive at the postmodern sublime, the acceptance of a lack at the heart of every representation. The coming-of-age should be understood literally as an arriving-at-the-age of postmodernity. In other words, the character itself does not change, except for a small shift in perspective that allows him to finally understand that the (impossibility of the) sublime is an essential function of ideology, the thing that, for "Roam-man-ticism," supposedly prevents full representation. In that regard, Wenders's films are very much political films in the sense of the *politique des auteurs* of the German New Cinema: every film, rather than being beholden to taking on politics in the world, establishes an aesthetic that more or less implicitly deals with ideology as *the* constituent element of politics. Wenders, the eternal apprentice of romanticism, recalls to us the ideologically ordained, implacable longing for a destination, transcendence, completion, forcing us to be satisfied instead with the circular journey, immanence, lack of closure. We are outfitted as a result with the eyes of the eternal roam-man-tic.

Notes

1 These are also among the films that I taught in my first class, "The German New Cinema: seeing *Amerika*," in my first job in the United States at Northwestern University. The "Road Trilogy" is now available in a beautifully restored Blu-ray edition, instead of the low-contrast VHS tapes that were the norm back in the twentieth century. Gracious readers will see that I am coming full circle. The Wenders conference, then, allowed me to revisit, to see again, to see anew. I would like to thank its organizers, Olivier Delers and Martin Sulzer-Reichel, for inviting me. I also thank Margaret Ozierski, Catherine Ingrassia, Shermaine M. Jones, and Brooke Newman for their succinct comments on this chapter.

2 Robert Phillip Kolker and Peter Beicken provide a succinct analysis of the role children play in Wenders's cinema. See *The Films of Wim Wenders: Cinema as Vision and Desire* (Cambridge: Cambridge University Press, 1993), 52–58.
3 The significance of windows in German romantic art is well known. Richard Littlejohns explains that "the window is significant as a threshold, the point at which those unsettled in a restrictive domestic circle or social environment can escape into visions of freedom." "German Romantic Painters," in *The Cambridge Companion to German Romanticism*, ed. Saul Nicholas (Cambridge: Cambridge University Press, 2009), 239.
4 In the same time frame, Herzog directed, among other films, *The Enigma of Kaspar Hauser* (1974), *The Great Ecstasy of Woodcarver Steiner* (1974), *Aguirre, the Wrath of God* (1972), *Land of Silence and Darkness* (1971), and *Even Dwarfs Started Small* (1970).
5 A recent *New York Times* article about the indie-rock band Dirty Projectors mentions Wenders's influence: "When they watched Wim Wenders's 'Wings of Desire' together, Longstreth asked Coffman to write down dialogue that resonated with her. These jottings became lyrics for the band's biggest single, 'Stillness Is the Move,' in 2009." Jonah Weiner, "The Dirty Projectors Go Solo," *The New York Times Magazine*, February 16, 2017.
6 An audience familiar with Wenders's oeuvre does not need to be reminded that Rüdiger Vogler reprises his role as Philip Winter in *Bis ans Ende der Welt/Until the End of the World* (1991), *In weiter Ferne, so nah!/Faraway, So Close!* (1993) and *Lisbon Story* (1994).
7 In *Angst essen Seele auf* (*Ali: Fear Eats the Soul*), Fassbinder's 1974 "translation" of Douglas Sirk's *All That Heaven Allows* (1955) to the subproletariat milieu of cleaning women and immigrants, Eugen, played by Fassbinder himself, kicks a new TV set out of anger and frustration with his obstinate mother-in-law. When Philip in *Alice in the Cities* overturns the TV set in his American motel room, apparently annoyed because a John Ford film is interrupted by cheesy commercials, the act seems immature—a boy taking out his anger on an object.
8 Martin Brady and Joanne Leal compare Handke's script to Wenders's adaptation, tracing in detail the many allusions to German literature, painting, and film, in *Wim Wenders and Peter Handke: Collaboration, Adaptation, Recomposition* (Amsterdam: Editions Rodopi, 2010), 192–239.
9 Klaus Kreimeier, "Die Welt ein Filmatelier oder: Herzkammerton Kino," in *Wim Wenders*, ed. Frieda Grafe (Munich: Hanser, 1992), 25. My translation, the original reads: "Erinnerungen an eine verblichene, nein: erdrosselte Kultur."
10 Thomas Elsaesser, in his magisterial history of the New German Cinema, points out Wenders's ambiguous relationship to this surrogate culture: "America in its dual role as resented but also emulated liberator must stand for the 'other' as opponent, rival

and father, in a double bind which in Herzog is mythologized and in Fassbinder sexually charged." Elsaesser, *New German Cinema: A History* (New Brunswick, NJ: Rutgers University Press, 1989), 231.

11 See Yvonne Franke, "Wim Wenders' *Im Lauf der Zeit*—No Place to Go," in *Heimat Goes Mobile: Hybrid Forms of Home in Literature and Film*, ed. Gabriele Eichmanns and Yvonne Franke (Newcastle upon Tyne: Cambridge Scholars Publishing, 2013), 199–201.

12 Gerd Gemünden, *Framed Visions: Popular Culture, Americanization, and the Contemporary German and Austrian Imagination* (Ann Arbor: University of Michigan Press, 1998), 208. Andreas Huyssen examines the perception of mass culture as feminine in his well-known "Mass Culture as Woman: Modernism's Other," in *After the Great Divide: Modernism, Mass Culture, Postmodernism* (Bloomington: Indiana University Press, 1986), 44–62.

13 Robert: "Ich hab' eine große Sehnsucht. Nach einer Frau. Nach überhaupt einer Frau. Jede Frau macht mich sehnsüchtig. Ich glaube, daß das allen Männern so geht.... Natürlich wünsch' ich mir, eins zu sein mit einer Frau." (my transcription/my translation).

14 See, for example, Peter Buchka, *Augen kann man nicht kaufen: Wim Wenders und seine Filme* (Munich: Hanser, 1983), 50–51; Kathe Geist, *The Cinema of Wim Wenders: From Paris, France to Paris, Texas* (Ann Arbor, MI: UMI Research Press, 1988), 79–80.

15 One exception comes to mind: Edith Farber (Jeanne Moreau), the blind mother in *Until the End of the World*, motivates the male protagonist to set out into the world and collect dream images that he has captured with a device invented by his father. Arguably, however, only the incredible screen presence of Jeanne Moreau brings depth to this under-written character. Three recent films that Wim Wenders shot in 3-D can serve as further examples: *Les Beaux Jours d'Aranjuez* (2016), his latest collaboration with the Austrian writer Peter Handke, the English-language production *Every Thing Will Be Fine* (2015), and even the acclaimed documentary *Pina* (2011), about the German choreographer Pina Bausch, do not make any attempt to take on the perspective of the female protagonists, instead approaching them as mysterious beings.

16 I always found it rather creepy that Damiel, the angel-turning-man in the Peter Handke/Wim Wenders collaboration *Der Himmel über Berlin/Wings of Desire* (1987), observes his love interest in the privacy of her room and actually enters her mind, listening to her most private thoughts, before being reborn.

17 Kreimeier, "Die Welt ein Filmatelier," 28.

18 Martha Helfer, "Gender Studies and Romanticism," in *The Literature of German Romanticism*, ed. Dennis F. Mahoney (Rochester, NY: Camden House, 2004), 237.

19 "Ich kenne den Wert eines Königreichs nicht," versetzte Wilhelm, "aber ich weiß, daß ich ein Glück erlangt habe, das ich nicht verdiene und das ich mit nichts in der Welt vertauschen möchte." ("I know not the worth of a kingdom," answered Wilhelm; "but I know I have attained a happiness which I have not deserved, and which I would not exchange for anything in the world.")

20 See Buchka, *Augen*, 70.

21 For a detailed analysis of this scene, see my *Funny Frames: The Filmic Concepts of Michael Haneke* (New York: Continuum, 2010), 103-28.

22 Preston Sturges's biting satire of the Hollywood dream factory, *Sullivan's Travels* (1941), features a hero who travels on a train first as a paid passenger and later as a hobo. Another possible intertext here would be *The Major and the Minor* (1942) by the Austrian-born director Billy Wilder. In this racy comedy, Ginger Rogers disguises herself as a child in order to travel for a reduced rate. Many thanks to Catherine Ingrassia, who pointed out this connection.

23 Gilles Deleuze, *Cinema I: The Movement Image* (London: Continuum International Pub., 2005), 101. In fact, for the definition of his central concept of the "movement image," Deleuze uses these shots as examples (22-23).

24 Gilles Deleuze and Félix Guattari, *A Thousand Plateaus: Capitalism and Schizophrenia* (Minneapolis: University of Minnesota Press, 1987), 380.

25 The prime example here would be, of course, *Easy Rider* (1969), where the nomadic heroes are killed by sedentary farmers. Wim Wenders wrote a review of this film for the German journal *Filmkritik*; see David N. Coury, *The Return of Storytelling in Contemporary German Literature and Film: Peter Handke and Wim Wenders* (Lewiston, NY: Edwin Mellen Press, 2004), 128, and Brady and Leal, *Wim Wenders*, 83. I believe that it is no coincidence that the only good—in the Deleuzian sense—road movies now come from outside the United States. For example, *Y Tu Mamá También* (2001) by Alfonso Cuarón and *Diarios de motocicleta/The Motorcycle Diaries* (2004) by Walter Salles feature characters that do not change at all. In the latter, Alberto Granado, while he returns after a road trip through South America to become a doctor, witnesses the baffling conversion of his friend Ernesto with the famous revolutionary Che Guevara, a miraculous event that the film likens to a religious awakening but does not explain.

26 Deleuze and Guattari, *A Thousand Plateaus*, 380.

27 Slavoj Žižek, "Rossellini: Woman as Symptom of Man," *October* 54 (1990): 21. See also this passage: "Symptom as sinthome is a certain signifying formation penetrated with enjoyment; it is a signifier as a bearer of jouissance. . . . The symptom as sinthome is literally our only substance, the only positive support for our being, the only point that gives consistency to the subject" (Žižek, *The Sublime Object of Ideology* [London: Verso, 1989], 75).

28 Žižek, "Rossellini: Woman as Symptom of Man," 22.
29 See especially Gilles Deleuze and Félix Guattari, *What Is Philosophy?* (New York: Columbia University Press, 1994), 73–76. For an admirably clear definition of this concept and its place in Gilles Deleuze's philosophical project, see D. N. Rodowick, "Unthinkable Sex: Conceptual Personae and the Time-Image," *In[ ]visible Culture: An Electronic Journal for Visual Studies*, 2000, www.rochester.edu/in_visible_culture/issue3/IVC_iss3_Rodowick.pdf (accessed April 14, 2018).

3

Writing in the Blood of the Past: *Wrong Move* and the Search for a Contemporary German Identity

Kristin Eichhorn

Wrong Move (1975) is one of Wim Wenders's most acclaimed early films. As the middle piece of his Road Trilogy, along with *Alice in the Cities* (1974) and *Kings of the Road* (1976), and one of the many collaborations with the writer Peter Handke, the film was highly praised by critics at the time of its release. Naturally, many scholars have analyzed Wenders and Handke's treatment of the Bildungsroman in the tradition of Goethe, in this twentieth-century adaptation of *Wilhelm Meisters Lehrjahre* (*Wilhelm Meister's Apprenticeship*, 1795–96)—the novel that inspired the project. Critics have also discussed the similarities and differences between Handke's script and Wenders's adaptation. While the dialogue of the film is obviously based on Handke's highly stylized text and has, for the most part, nothing to do with the way people normally talk, a good example of Wenders's influence is the ending of the film, when he left out the sound of the typewriter that in Handke's script is supposed to be heard in the final scene.[1]

Although commentators have thoroughly described the film's content and Wenders's artistic choices,[2] they have been much more reluctant to interpret their findings. One aspect that stands out is the strong symbolic dimension of *Wrong Move*, which has its roots in Handke's text but is significantly expanded in Wenders's adaptation. In this chapter, I focus on this element because it gives insight into the broader social and artistic context in which Wenders's work belongs. The specific historic references that the film makes to literature, art, and philosophy are as crucial to understanding its impact as the image of blood, which occurs over and over again in the film.

As I will show, *Wrong Move* is mostly a film about German identity, in the sense that it partakes in a tradition that confronts great achievements in the fields of art and philosophy, which have shaped the image of Germany as a "nation of poets and thinkers" (*Land der Dichter und Denker*), with the abysses of its recent history. It does so for two reasons. First, Wenders and Handke point out that there is a continuity between nineteenth-century philosophy and the devastating events of the 1930s and 1940s. Second, making this argument calls into question how their parents' generation has turned their focus almost entirely toward the artistic achievements of the classic and romantic period to define their own worldview during the conservative Adenauer era, thus avoiding having to confront their own participation in the rise of the Nazi Regime. In the eyes of their sons and daughters, the issue of German identity has not been sufficiently discussed. As a result, it becomes a crucial discourse in the 1960s and 1970s as those born during or shortly after the Second World War, like Wenders and Handke, come of age and start questioning their parents' choices. In short, they respond to the fact that after 1945, both East Germany and West Germany (as well as Austria) tried to move beyond "the German catastrophe"[3] by enforcing another, better, "classic" German tradition of arts and literature which is particularly associated with the names of Goethe and Schiller. As Anne Fuchs and Mary Cosgrove have pointed out, the "German *Bildungsbürger* of the postwar period sought consolation in cultural tradition."[4]

The idea of the Bildungsroman

Wenders's film *Wrong Move* is indeed an excellent example of his generation's response to people in the 1950s and early 1960s seeking comfort in the idea that true German identity was represented not by the *Third Reich* but by the *Weimarer Klassik*, trying to "get over" recent German history by referring to the cultural tradition of the century before. First, consider the choice of topic: *Wrong Move* is an adaptation of a famous novel by Johann Wolfgang Goethe, the most important representative of *Weimarer Klassik*. In this sense, the film has the potential to take the viewer back to the days of German classic literature. Of course, this is not how Wenders or Handke approach the material. It is well known that both Handke, as the screenwriter, and Wenders, as the director, took great liberties in adapting Goethe's novel, beginning with the title.

Still, Wenders and Handke not only chose a novel by Goethe but also chose a novel that is basically the prototype for every definition of the Bildungsroman: a genre that emerged in the late 1700s and became enormously popular in the nineteenth century.⁵ The concept of the Bildungsroman—for chauvinistic literary critics, a specifically German creation⁶—still shaped the understanding of German culture after the Second World War because it offered the ideals of humanism and free development of the individual. Wilhelm Meister's journey, through which he finds his true calling and becomes a useful member of society, is seen as a blueprint for educational goals in German schools. It is also how Germans like to define their identity. As with the theory of the "two Germanys," a very common notion among German writers in exile between 1933 and 1945, Goethe's humanism is the real, "good" German nature, not the "bad" ideology that led to the Holocaust.⁷

Nevertheless, as I have suggested, Wenders and Handke's film is not particularly faithful to Goethe's book, at least not in the strictest sense of the term. Despite the fact that *Wrong Move* features most of the key protagonists of *Wilhelm Meister's Apprenticeship*—namely Wilhelm (Rüdiger Vogler), Therese (Hanna Schygulla), Laertes (Hans Christian Blech), and Mignon (Nastassja Kinski)—quite a few characters of the novel are missing. The most striking example is Wilhelm's amazon and true love, Natalie, who saves his life but does not tell him her name and thereby becomes the object of a search that lasts for the rest of the book. Other film characters, like the host in the mansion (Ivan Desny), have no specific predecessors in the book, or their roles are changed in a significant way. As we will see, this is especially the case with Laertes. Since the action takes place in the 1970s, it would indeed be easy to miss the fact that the film is based on *Wilhelm Meister's Apprenticeship* at all, if it weren't for the names and a few outstanding events.

The film is more an adaptation of the concept of the Bildungsroman and its implications than of the novel itself, and sheds light on how this literary concept was used after the Second World War to define German identity based on nineteenth-century ideals. Tellingly, Wenders always refers to Goethe's *Wilhelm Meister's Apprenticeship* as a novel from the nineteenth century. This is factually incorrect since Goethe had been working on the story since the late 1770s, with the title "Wilhelm Meisters Theatralische Sendung" ("Wilhelm Meister's Theatrical Calling"), and the novel was first published in 1795–96.

Romanticism and National Socialism

The film shows its protagonist in an obvious search for German identity, having him travel all the way from the northern town of Glückstadt through the entire western part of the country, with stops in Cologne, Bonn, and Frankfurt until the final scene, which is set in the far south on the Zugspitze, Germany's highest mountain. These landscapes are often filmed in a way that resembles romantic paintings. There are numerous night shots and scenes that make use of (natural) twilight in a way that brings to mind the use of color in Caspar David Friedrich's famous works such as *Two Men Contemplating the Moon* (1825–30). In Friedrich's paintings, people are hardly ever in the foreground, and we usually see them with their backs turned to us. This perspective of a man or a woman standing on top of a hill or at a window looking into a wide landscape is commonly interpreted as a sign of the romantic *Sehnsucht* (longing) for something that is out of reach and can only be experienced outside of the everyday, for example, in dreams.[8] If we consider how Wenders stages his film, we cannot help but notice that, throughout his journey, Wilhelm again and again stands at a window, on a balcony, or on top of a mountain in slight profile or with his back turned to us, looking down on a square or on a landscape. Wenders uses this type of shot in the first scene, when Wilhelm goes to the window of his room twice to look down on the town square of Glückstadt (Figure 3.1); later we see him at the window of a hotel room in Bonn (Figure 3.2); we see Wilhelm and Laertes standing on a vineyard, looking down at the Rhine river (Figure 3.3), Wilhelm on the balcony of Therese's apartment in Frankfurt (Figure 3.4), and, finally, Wilhelm on the Zugspitze (Figure 3.5)—an image that strikingly resembles Friedrich's painting *Wanderer above the Sea of Fog* (1818).

Yet, there are other nods to romanticism and to the nineteenth century, in addition to the artistic references that I have pointed out. By listening to music by bands like the Troggs or the Kinks, the protagonist presents a modern version of

Figure 3.1

Figure 3.2

Figure 3.3

the conflict in Goethe's novel in which Wilhelm wants to be an actor because he does not agree with his father's wish for him to become a merchant. The records we see in Wilhelm's room in the beginning of the film reflect the director's personal musical taste—as Wenders explains in his commentary for a recent DVD release of the film.[9] They also signify the substantial generational rift of the 1960s and early 1970s. Bands like the Troggs and the Kinks rebelled against exactly the kind of postwar conservative morality Wenders's generation felt stuck in. This conflict becomes strikingly visible as Wilhelm's mother enters the room

Figure 3.4

Figure 3.5

while the music is still playing. The casting of Marianne Hoppe for this role adds an interesting dynamic to the scene, her first appearance on the screen, for it begins to cast the shadow of Germany's twentieth-century history over the story. Hoppe was, after all, a very successful German actress of the 1930s and managed to continue her career during the Nazi years as the wife of Gustav Gründgens— himself one of the most controversial actors of the time, whose involvement with high Nazi officials is famously satirized in Klaus Mann's novel *Mephisto* (1936).[10]

In this manner, the first scene establishes the situation Wilhelm will find himself in throughout the film. He is introduced as a rebellious protagonist seeking to break out of his home, symbolized in the act of shattering the glass of his bedroom window. But his rebellion remains strangely weak. He is not a rock star himself, he only listens to rock music, and his breaking of the window does not come with yelling and running but with silent reflection. In the subsequent conversation with his mother, Wilhelm is distant but polite—anything but a rebel in the strictest sense. This particularity of Wilhelm's character is underlined by the books he reads at the beginning of Wenders's film: His actions lack a real purpose, just like those of Joseph von Eichendorff's narrator in *Aus dem Leben eines Taugenichts* (*Memoirs of a Good-for-Nothing*, 1822), and his journey is clearly one of disillusionment like that of Frédéric Moreau in Gustave Flaubert's *Education sentimentale* (1869).

In Goethe's *Wilhelm Meister's Apprenticeship*, the initial conflict is finally solved through Wilhelm's choice to abandon his artistic aspirations in order to become a physician. In *Wrong Move*, on the other hand, there is no reintegration into society, neither in the script nor in the film. Handke's script presents the protagonist as a young man who becomes a writer because he cannot accept the bourgeois lifestyle around him, in accordance with the common sentiment of the late 1960s and early 1970s. This perspective resembles not only Goethe's first draft of the Wilhelm Meister story but a popular nineteenth-century critique of the revelation that Wilhelm is *not* an artist but merely a lover of art. This model was picked by later authors: works like Ludwig Tieck's *Franz Sternbalds Wanderungen* (1798) or Novalis's *Heinrich von Ofterdingen* (1802) are other well-known examples of the combination of Bildungsroman and *Künstlerroman* that were clearly inspired by Goethe.[11]

It is this popularity of a genre Goethe inspired that both Handke and Wenders seem to have in mind more than the actual storyline of *Wilhelm Meister's Apprenticeship*. They associate the Bildungsroman as a Künstlerroman with the nineteenth century and with romanticism, despite the fact that Goethe's novel technically is a work of the *Weimarer Klassik*. They also ignore the fact that quite a few classics that were written in Goethe's footsteps are at the very least on the verge of realism, as is the case with Gottfried Keller's *Der grüne Heinrich* (first edition 1854–55).

A pivotal scene, in which romantic philosophy comes into play, explains these references. After the group has arrived at the mansion of the industrialist whom they prevent from committing suicide (as it turns out, only temporarily), the owner of the house tells Wilhelm that there is a direct line from German romanticism to the crimes of the Nazi Regime. The industrialist makes the point that loneliness in Germany is more hidden and more painful than elsewhere because of its literary and philosophical traditions, which emphasize the necessity to overcome fear:

> Ich möchte nur noch kurz von der Einsamkeit hier in Deutschland sprechen. Sie scheint mir verborgener und zugleich schmerzhafter zu sein als anderswo. Verantwortlich dafür könnte die Geschichte der Ideen hier sein, die alle nach Lebenshaltungen suchten, in denen die Überwindung der Angst möglich wäre. Die Verkündigung von Tugenden wie Mut, Ausdauer und Fleiß sollten nur von der Angst ablenken. Jedenfalls sagen wir einmal, es sei so. Die Philosophien waren wie sonst nirgends verwendbar als Staatsphilosophien, so daß die notwendig verbrecherischen Methoden, mit denen die Angst überwunden werden sollte, auch noch legalisiert wurden. Die Angst gilt hier als Eitelkeit oder Schande. Deswegen ist die Einsamkeit in Deutschland maskiert mit all diesen verräterisch entseelten Gesichtern, die durch die Supermärkte, Naherholungsgebiete, Fußgängerzonen und Fitneßcenter herumgeistern. Die toten Seelen von Deutschland.[12]
>
> [I would like to talk briefly about loneliness here in Germany. It seems to me to be more hidden and, at the same time, more painful than elsewhere. Perhaps the history of ideas here is responsible for this, as it seeks for ways of living that might accomplish victory over fear. The declaration of moral values such as courage, persistence, and hard work were only supposed to divert people from fear. At least, let's say that's how it is. Better than anywhere else, the philosophies could be used as state philosophies, which necessarily led to legalizing criminal methods to overcome fear. Here, fear is considered vanity or disgrace. That is why loneliness in Germany is disguised in all these tellingly soulless faces that are haunting the supermarkets, local vacation spots, pedestrian zones, and fitness centers. The dead souls of Germany.][13]

Not only is romanticism the period in which the idea of German unity and nationality is first shaped, but it also produces philosophical ideas, especially those by Georg Friedrich Wilhelm Hegel, that were misused by the Nazis to legitimize their worldview.

The film works with this popular generalization a lot.[14] Once you start looking at history in this manner, however, there is no way to separate the "good" German literary tradition of the 1800s from the devastating events in the 1930s and 1940s. The attempt to redefine German identity by highlighting its classical humanistic traditions, as introduced by exiled writers during the Second World War in order to "overwrite" Hitler's reign, must inevitably fail from the perspective of the generation born in the 1940s. Not only can Wilhelm no longer find peace or meaning in his journey; behind every actual reference to Goethe's *Wilhelm Meister's Apprenticeship* lies an element of violence that is missing in the original novel.

In Goethe's book, for instance, Laertes is just one of the many actors Wilhelm encounters as he attempts to join the theater. In Wenders's film, he is introduced as a nice old man with a secret. The secret, of course, is that he was a committed Nazi. The fact is slowly revealed as Laertes keeps postponing the telling of his story several times, first promising he will talk about it after dinner, then excusing himself because of the lateness of the hour. The viewer already knows he has something to hide after he exchanges a military salute with a train conductor. As a "hint" (*Andeutung*) Laertes reveals that he was an athlete in the 1936 Olympics. Naturally, this leads Wilhelm to ask if he, like his *Führer*, refused to shake Jesse Owens's hand, and Laertes replies:

> Ich bin nur bis ins Halbfinale gekommen. Aber wahrscheinlich hätte ich damals einem Schwarzen auch nicht die Hand gegeben.[15]
>
> [I only made it into the semifinals. But back then, I probably wouldn't have shaken a black man's hand, either.]

Blood and violence as generational heritage

Laertes obviously represents the older generation that has lived through the war and therefore bears a responsibility for what happened between 1933 and 1945. This is symbolically manifest in his nosebleed that, as he puts it, is caused by "memory" (Figure 3.6). Laertes, when we first meet him, compares himself to St. Januarius of Naples:

> Sie werden wissen wollen, warum ich aus der Nase blute. Es ist die Erinnerung. Ich werde Ihnen die Geschichte mal erzählen, vielleicht morgen beim Frühstück. Sie kennen die Geschichte vom heiligen Januarius, dessen vertrocknetes Blut in einer Kirche in Neapel aufbewahrt wird. Einmal im Jahr wird es flüssig, wallt auf, an seinem Todestag.[16]
>
> [You probably want to know why my nose is bleeding. It's memory. Sometime, I'll tell you the story, maybe over breakfast. You've heard of St. Januarius, whose dried blood is kept at a church in Naples. Once a year it becomes fluid and flows, on the anniversary of his death.]

Figure 3.6

However, it is more straightforward to see the blood as a reminder of the crimes Laertes was complicit in. He embodies how his generation tries to hide their participation behind literary tradition. Neither in Goethe's novel nor in Shakespeare's *Hamlet*—the play from which Goethe borrows the character's name—is Laertes in any way a brutal or murderous character. So when we first hear the name in Wenders's film, the mental associations we make are quite different from what we find out later. The catastrophe of the twentieth century that stands behind the character of Laertes in *Wrong Move* has been overwritten by references to highly acclaimed works of world literature, but they cannot stay hidden for very long, for Laertes's nose keeps on bleeding and Wilhelm keeps on asking for the stranger's story.

Laertes's past, importantly, is not without consequences for Wilhelm and the younger generation in general. Wilhelm's path is also marked by blood, a visual element that is entirely Wenders's doing, and one that adds a symbolic impact with deep implications to Handke's text. The visual symbol of blood first appears when Wilhelm hurts his hand breaking the window in the first scene. His bleeding hand, which later operates the record player (Figure 3.7), connects him to Laertes and his bleeding nose. But there is an even more remarkable scene. As the industrialist gives his long speech on German loneliness, he picks up a pen and, while speaking, begins to turn its pointed end in the palm of his hand, cutting into the flesh. Then he puts the pen down and goes to bed. As soon as he finds himself alone, Wilhelm picks up the very same pen, opens his notebook and begins to write in it, leaving bloody lines on the page. Wilhelm is for the

Figure 3.7

third time in the film confronted with blood—the first two being his bleeding hand and Laertes's nosebleed—and for the third time his reaction is remarkably calm. Unlike the viewer, who is likely to be startled and disgusted with the fact that the industrialist abruptly begins deliberately hurting himself with the pen, Wilhelm does not in any way respond to this unusual act. He remains unfazed, almost as though he is used to seeing such a thing happen on a daily basis.

The scene, nevertheless, is not only relevant because of the protagonist's reaction or the revulsion it may stimulate. Wenders was probably inspired by an episode in the original novel by Goethe in which Wilhelm meets the mentally disturbed Aurelie. Rejected by the one she loved, Aurelie has lost all faith in men. Wilhelm is surprised to find her running around with a dagger in her hand that she calls her "dear friend." Yet he is more shocked to find her suddenly cutting his hand with its blade, saying: "Man muß euch Männer scharf zeichnen, wenn ihr merken sollt!" ("One must mark you men rather sharply, if one would have you take heed."[17])

Despite this occurrence in the book, Wenders's approach is remarkable because he exchanges not only the woman for a man but also the dagger for the pen. This choice naturally brings to mind another reference to a famous work by Goethe: Who would not think of Faust's contract with Mephisto when Rüdiger Vogler starts making lines of blood on an empty page of his notebook? This allusion implies that Wilhelm is signing away his soul, or at least considering doing so. This moment of writing in blood comes after he has already, in the first scene, tasted his own blood just before his mother, the first member of the older

Figure 3.8

generation, enters the room. The connection between the two scenes is visually emphasized as Wilhelm still has band-aids on the hand which holds the bloody pen (Figure 3.8).

Blood not only fascinates Wenders's protagonist from the beginning but is also the link between Wilhelm's generation and that of his parents. In fact, Wilhelm's subsequent behavior shows him at high risk of following in their footsteps. Since blood is clearly presented as a sign of the wrongdoings of the older generation during the Nazi years, there looms the threat that those crimes will be repeated by their sons and daughters, if only in revenge for the bloodshed that occurred three decades before. It is notable that Wilhelm, unlike Faust, does not write in his own blood but in the blood of someone who is a member of the former generation. And despite his overall restraint, Wilhelm clearly has rage in him. When the group arrives in Frankfurt, Wilhelm takes Laertes on a boat trip with the deliberate intention of killing him. He asks Laertes several times if he really does not know how to swim, and once they are on the water Wilhelm almost throws Laertes into the Main River (Figure 3.9). It is not until the very last moment that Wilhelm finally checks himself and decides to let go of the old man. It seems that distancing yourself from the crimes of the past comes with the danger of a violent revenge that is morally just as despicable.

While Handke, by writing the industrialist's speech, also points out the devastating misuse of romanticism during the twentieth century, he does not break with the ideal of seeking solace in art or in literature. In Handke's script Wilhelm is always writing—but never with a bloody pen as in Wenders's film.[18]

Figure 3.9

Wenders's view is much more ambivalent and, perhaps, more pessimistic. His Wilhelm does what was common practice for Germans after 1945. He starts reliving the educational model of the Bildungsroman he has read about, hoping that traveling the country will lead him to his life goal. In contrast to Goethe's protagonist, though, for Wenders's Wilhelm, traveling no longer provides that profound life-changing experience. In the last scene, Wilhelm is in a different geographical area, but he still has his back turned to us, looking at the world around him. The sound of the typewriter in Handke's script indicates that Wilhelm manages to find his poetic voice after all. In stark contrast, Wenders's adaptation offers no such conclusion. It ends with a voiceover confirming that Wilhelm made one "wrong move" after the other. This Wilhelm, as Kathe Geist puts it, "ends as he began: disliking people, alone, and, because of his isolation, still far from achieving his goal."[19]

On a meta-level Wenders does the same thing as Wilhelm: he tries on the model of the past by adapting a Bildungsroman. But he does not do so with the naive belief that this is the way to balance out the crimes of the Nazi Regime and replace them with a better German identity. Instead, he makes it his aim to show why that model no longer applies and why repressing the memory of recent German history has dangerous consequences. It is, in the end, not just Wilhelm's "wrong move" that the title refers to. The innocence of romanticism is clearly gone after that fatal "wrong move" in German history that Laertes stands for. Blood has both literally and symbolically been shed since the Bildungsroman reached its peak, and this is the reason why Wilhelm's journey to becoming a writer must fail. Writing in the nineteenth-century tradition of Goethe, Eichendorff, or Flaubert with a pen borrowed from the older generation is just like Faust signing the contract with the devil.

Nevertheless, there is some hidden hopefulness in Wenders's final scene even though it keeps Wilhelm's identity remarkably incomplete. Eventually, Wilhelm may not have found the peace with which the novel's eponymous character was rewarded, but he also does not have to simply pick up where the generation before him left off, either. Wilhelm has not changed or reached any kind of conclusion. Yet, the path toward violence has, at least for now, been avoided: he chose *not* to throw Laertes into the water, forgoing a revenge that would have made him just as bad as the man he was going to kill. That moment is even more crucial since Wilhelm makes the decision without the involvement of Therese, who is only passively watching from the car, in contrast with Handke's version, in which it takes an outsider's intervention to stop Wilhelm.[20] Wenders's protagonist is strong enough to suppress the impulse toward revenge, if nothing else. We are watching Wilhelm in a constant struggle to overcome his violent legacy.

Obviously haunted by the ghosts of the past he has to fight, it remains to be seen if Wilhelm manages to find the solace he is looking for. In doing nothing and ending up at no particular endpoint of his story, Wilhelm rejects adopting the identity of Laertes's generation, if only for now. In that sense, the film's main character perfectly mirrors the situation of the country he comes from: the Germany of the 1970s, like Wilhelm's and Wenders's generation, is in a transitional phase of having to find a way to irrevocably break with what it was in the past without yet knowing what the alternative, its new identity, might look like.

Notes

1 Peter Handke, *Falsche Bewegung* (Frankfurt/Main: Suhrkamp, 1975), 81.

2 See, for instance, Kathe Geist, *The Cinema of Wim Wenders: From Paris, France to Paris, Texas* (Ann Arbor: The University of Michigan Press, 1988), 43–49; Richard W. McCormick, "'Wilhelm Meister' Revisited: 'Falsche Bewegung' by Peter Handke and Wim Wenders," in *The Age of Goethe Today: Critical Reexamination and Literary Reflection*, ed. Gertrud B. Pickar and Sabine Cramer (Munich: Fink, 1990), 194–211; Norbert Grob, *Wenders* (Berlin: Spiess, 1991), 196–203.

3 Friedrich Meinecke, *Die Deutsche Katastrophe: Betrachtungen und Erinnerungen* (Wiesbaden: Brockhaus, 1946).

4 Anne Fuchs and Mary Cosgrove, "Introduction: Germany's Memory Contests and the Management of the Past," in *German Memory Contests: The Quest for Identity in Literature, Film, and Discourse Since 1990*, ed. Anne Fuchs and Mary Cosgrove (Columbia, SC: Camden House, 2010), 3.

5 Jürgen Jacobs, "Bildungsroman," in *Reallexikon der deutschen Literaturwissenschaft: Neubearbeitung des Reallexikons der deutschen Literaturgeschichte*, ed. Klaus Weimar and Harald Fricke (Berlin: de Gruyter, 2007).

6 Ibid., 232.

7 Thomas Koebner, *Unbehauste: Zur deutschen Literatur in der Weimarer Republik, im Exil und in der Nachkriegszeit* (Munich: Ed. Text + Kritik, 1992).

8 Joachim Telgenbüscher, *Die Kunst der Romantik: Europas Maler im Zeitalter der Sehnsucht 1790–1860* (Hamburg: Gruner Jahr, 2014).

9 Wim Wenders, *Falsche Bewegung* ([Munich]: Solaris Film, 1975; DVD by Zweitausendeins 2010, regional code 2), 00:02:20–00:02:25.

10 Klaus Mann, *Mephisto: Roman einer Karriere* (Frankfurt/Main: S. Fischer, 2000).

11 Erwin Neumann, "Frühromantische Künstlerromane in den Spuren des Goetheschen 'Wilhelm Meister': Ludwig Tiecks 'Sternbald,' Friedrich Schlegels 'Lucinde' und Novalis' 'Heinrich von Ofterdingen,'" in *Wilhelm Meister und seine Nachfahren: Vorträge des 4. Kasseler Goethe-Seminars*, ed. Helmut Fuhrmann (Kassel: Wenderoth, 2000).

12 Handke, *Falsche Bewegung*, 44; Wenders, *Falsche Bewegung*, 00:46:33–00:48:25.

13 All translations, unless otherwise noted, are mine.

14 See Dana Krätzsch, "Was Ist 'Falsch' an *Falsche Bewegung*? Zu Peter Handkes Wilhelm Meister-Adaption," in *Poetische Welt(en): Ludwig Stockinger zum 65. Geburtstag zugeeignet*, ed. Martin Blawid and Katrin Henzel (Leipzig: Leipziger Univ.-Verl, 2011), 38.

15 Wenders, *Falsche Bewegung*, 00:26:41–00:26:51.

16 Ibid., 00:16:53–00:17:35. In Handke's script this passage is followed by the words "So blute auch ich manchmal aus der Nase, an einem anderen Todestag" ("I, too, bleed from the nose sometimes, on another anniversary of death" [21]).

17 Johann W. Goethe, *Werke: Hamburger Ausgabe in 14 Bänden*, Vol. 7: Romane und Novellen II, ed. Erich Trunz (Munich: dtv, 2000), 281. The translation in English is from *Wilhelm Meister's Apprenticeship and Travels*, Vol. 1, trans. Thomas Carlyle (Boston: Ticknor and Fields, 1865), 265.

18 Handke, *Falsche Bewegung*, 45.

19 Geist, *The Cinema of Wim Wenders*, 48.

20 Handke, *Falsche Bewegung*, 75.

4

The Window-View and the Romantic Vision of the World: Notes on a Visual Leitmotif in the Films of Wim Wenders

Philipp Scheid

Windows and the art of seeing

In E. T. A. Hoffmann's *My Cousin's Corner Window* (published between April and May 1822 as a serial) an invalid poet, sitting in a wheelchair and suffering from severe illness, teaches his cousin the art of seeing by observing the daily bustle on the Gendarmenmarkt in Berlin with a telescope. In the course of this lesson, the chaotic setting of the marketplace becomes clearer thanks to the viewing instructions of the disabled writer. A whole set of different characters appears, and to the amusement of the two spectators, a "storyline" is devised for each person they spot.[1] Today, one might even find cinematographic potential in Hoffmann's mode of narration, for example, in the ways in which he uses point-of-view strategies, or in the arrangement of elements cut out from the larger scene. Although Hoffmann's story lacks a criminal plot, it lays the groundwork for films like Alfred Hitchcock's *Rear Window* (1954).

There is another reason why Hoffmann's text is relevant here. From the very first time he shot with a movie camera, Wim Wenders was fascinated with this visual instrument that allowed him to record the physical world as it appeared—so much so that he became obsessed with the possibility of observing reality through the eye of the camera. In Wenders's early short film *Silver City Revisited* (1968), made as a student project during his apprenticeship at the Hochschule für Film und Fernsehen (HFF) in Munich, the young artist follows in the footsteps of Hoffmann's figure of the poet who is sick but "insatiable" (in relation to the events he witnesses in the outside world). The film largely consists of different views from the several apartments Wenders inhabited at that time (Figure 4.1). His only aim was to capture what was happening beyond the range of his home: the increased traffic down the streets, the change of daylight, the changing patterns of his urban environment, and so on. Each shot lasts about five minutes, the duration of the 16-mm film reel Wenders used. This almost forced form of realism was a kind of stylistic dogma among his fellow students at the HFF—a specific style that was soon "stigmatized" by some critics as *sensibilistisch* (highly sensitive) filmmaking.[2] It is nevertheless suitable for a film student whose first efforts can now be regarded as an aesthetic survey, an exploration of the medium's limits and capabilities. Using sequence shots and a static camera, Wenders distinctly recreates a mode of early cinema particularly associated with the films of the Lumière brothers such as *Arrival of a Train at La Ciotat* (1895). On the other hand, *Silver City Revisited* reflects the formal experiments of contemporary avant-garde cinema—for example, the long and descriptive shots in the films of Andy Warhol (*Sleep*, 1963; *Empire*, 1964) or the enthusiasm for everyday life in some of Jonas Mekas's early works (*Cassis*, 1966).

The window, once defined by the Grimm brothers as the "Auge des Hauses"[3] (eye of the house) in their *German Dictionary* (1854), is in this respect equated by Wenders with the filmic vision of the world. Even more, it is connected with the act of seeing—not only technically, in the sense of defining the framing and duration of a shot but also on a personal level. The frame of the window is in a way a material marker through which the positioning of an individual is preserved in place and time, as is his way of looking at the world. These premises

Figure 4.1

are important to understanding the visual leitmotif of the window-view in feature films by Wim Wenders from the late 1960s to the 1980s.

Also critical to understanding Wenders's use of the window-view shot is addressing the romantic tradition on which it is based and its many resonances in art history. Wenders's dialogue with the romantic tradition has been addressed in other research; Peter Beicken and Robert Kolker, for example, see in the filmmaker's oeuvre a "resurrection of romanticism"[4] and remark that the experience of music—an element central to Wenders's work—as an important catalyst for romantic poetry as well.[5] One could add that music often correlates with the perception of nature, as in Ludwig Tieck's *Franz Sternbald's Travels*—a characteristic we find as well in Wenders's visual poetry. Other scholars, such as Karsten Visarius, offer us valuable hints to investigate what we might call the neoromantic features of Wenders's films.[6] What is lacking, however, is a deeper and more comparative analysis of this phenomenon as well as a focus on historical precedents and models. To my knowledge, there are only a few publications that point in the right direction.[7] The following study will therefore try to define Wenders's position toward a specific romantic theme we encounter in the window motif.

Creating imaginary spaces

At first glance, there is nothing new in the analogy between the window and the constructed image of the world. It is in fact a fairly common topos in the history of painting. The Italian humanist Leon Battista Alberti (1404–72) famously compared a picture made by means of a central perspective to an open window in his treatise *On Painting* (1435). The artists who followed Alberti's instructions managed to create their three-dimensional image spaces using vellum, a veil of translucent material with a plotted grid, stretched across a rectangular frame. In his manual *Teaching of Measurement* (1538), Albrecht Dürer (1471–1528) provided a concrete illustration of this window-like tool in his woodcut *Draughtman Drawing a Nude*,[8] and it is certainly no coincidence that Wenders refers to this drawing method in *Until the End of the World* (1991). Wenders's quoting of the image by Dürer again shows the filmmaker's ongoing interest in the history of seeing. Speaking about *Until the End of the World*, Norbert Grob once put it pointedly: "The act of seeing and the moral issue of producing images—which have been one of Wenders' central concerns all along—now become the central subject of a film."[9] Indeed, quite a few of Wenders's own writings are centered on the question of how we reflect and represent reality through different media.[10]

Furthermore, the idea of an image as a window explains why the pioneers of photography, when they first experimented with their cameras, referred to this common notion as if the new medium was capable of challenging the older, pictorial one in its mimetic claim to reproduce reality.[11] And Wenders, likely drawing on his knowledge of the early days of photography, seems to take up this visual discourse again in *Silver City Revisited*, at a time when he was trying to fathom what the essence of cinema was.

It was not until the beginning of the nineteenth century that the window became an important theme in genre and landscape painting. The German romanticists from Dresden paid particular attention to this subject and made it an emblematic element in its own right. While Georg Friedrich Kersting (1785–1847) and other artists specialized in intimate portraits of figures in an interior setting, often absorbed in creative work like painting, writing, or embroidering, some of their colleagues were concerned with the creation of an autonomous image of the window. For art historian Lorenz Eitner, there is no doubt that the "pure window-view is a romantic innovation."[12] He describes the effect produced by this type of painting in the following way:

> It brings the confinement of an interior into the most immediate contrast with an immensity of space outside, outdoors, a space which need not to be a landscape, but can be a view of houses or of the empty sky. It often places the beholder so close to the window that little more than an enclosing frame of darkness remains of the interior, but this is sufficient to maintain the suggestion of a separation between him and the world outside.[13]

Taking a closer look at two examples,[14] we find that in the cases of Caspar David Friedrich (1774–1840) and Jakob Alt (1789–1872) the artists not only contemplate their surroundings and working conditions but also locate themselves in a specific moment and in a certain space as though the painting provided some sort of coordinates for their physical existence. The arrangement suggests that the artists stepped back from their canvases for a while to turn toward the vista of the window square, which once again doubles the projected image of the painting. The window sashes are opened in these pictures to allow the eye of the beholder to roam through the depicted landscape. Thus, the perspective offered by the window provides an imaginary space for the isolated subject. In the pictures of the studios, this space becomes a kind of screen where a longing for distance can be sublimated. In the poem "Sehnsucht" ("Longing") by Joseph von Eichendorff, the writer articulates this "romantic" feeling through the famous sigh of its lyrical subject: "ach, wer da mitreisen könnte, / in der prächtigen Sommernacht!" (Oh, if only I could travel along / into the marvelous summer night!)[15]

Breaking boundaries: *Wrong Move* and *Alice in the Cities*

In the opening sequence of *Wrong Move* (1975), Wenders clearly responds to the topic of wanderlust we so often find in Eichendorff's poetry, but here the filmmaker tries to invert the stereotypical figure of the romantic traveler. Wilhelm's restless mind is no longer satisfied by the fictional journeys he can find in literature, especially in the books of Eichendorff and Flaubert, who are fictitious companions on his trip through West Germany. Wilhelm's aim is instead to write about his travel experience and thereby to articulate and even prove his own identity. In *Wrong Move* it is not the yearning for something—like the vision of the mysterious "blaue Blume" (blue flower) in Novalis's *Henry of Ofterdingen* (1802)[16]—that initiates Wilhelm's actions; it is the drabness and inertia of his present situation that can be seen as the source of his frustration. It is through a rebellious gesture that the audience recognizes Wilhelm's attempt to escape from his provincial hometown (Figure 4.2).

Figure 4.2

He smashes the glass of his (closed) window and bursts the threshold that has become a transparent wall between him and the exterior world. Through this variation on the window motif, Wenders brings us to the central question of his project: Is it even possible nowadays to go on the kind of journey the romantics celebrated? In *Wrong Move*, Wenders comes to the conclusion that this kind of romantic undertaking is doomed to failure. The landscape has visibly transformed since the nineteenth century, and so have the heroes, who are unable to sense either the inner or outer conditions of their lives.[17]

From this perspective, the world as experienced consists only of signs that hide their meaning and cannot be deciphered or "read" by the main characters of Wenders's films. Another writer figure in Wenders's oeuvre provides a comparable type of hero. In *Alice in the Cities* (1974) the protagonist, Philip Winter, also played by Rüdiger Vogler, is traveling through the United States trying to write a magazine article capturing the essence of the American landscape. Although Winter produces a large body of photographic notes on his road trip, he repeatedly laments that the Polaroid pictures do not capture what he has experienced visually. But this crisis of representation, which the photographic medium is accused of, in reality lies in the gaze of the photographer, because for Philip, what is lost is the connection between the depiction and the object it refers to. In a short scene at the beginning of the film, Wenders sums up the current problem of his protagonist. Philip has stopped at a motel and takes a rest while watching television. In one shot (Figure 4.3) that is meant to be a POV perspective, we see the window of the motel room

Figure 4.3

juxtaposed with the television set. Like a picture-in-picture, we find two different screens in comparison. The one on the left shows the parking area in front of the motel by night, a "linguistic landscape"[18] revealing the bright letters of the neon signs, while the other shows a broadcast film drama. Both offer a view of the world, but both, the view through the window and the one on the television screen, seem opaque. They appear strange to Philip, speaking to him in an incomprehensible language.

At this point it is clear that Wenders does not simply "reproduce" the visual formula of the romantic window motif; he actually seems to invert its meaning. While romantic-era paintings and poems allowed the mind of the recipient to "float" through the open window into the outside world and transform their external condition by virtue of the "inner eye," Wenders's male protagonists have lost the ability to "romanticiz[e] the world."[19] This important aspect, the struggle between the Inside and the Outside, becomes even more distinct if we take a closer look at another window: the moving window of the windshield.

The windshield between display and mirror

In spite of this predicament, Wenders's characters do not give up hope completely. They decide to move onward, even if they risk being caught in a circular or never-ending movement—a situation that Peter Handke accurately describes as a form of dynamic standstill in his novel *Short Letter, Long Farewell* (1972).[20] The cinematographic gaze through the moving window of a vehicle, a type of shot that recurs in Wenders's films, seems in this regard like a specific expansion of the visual vocabulary of romanticism. These window-views induce a new perspective: traveling creates the illusion that personal development is gaining momentum. Like in a side glance, Wenders uses these traveling shots to record the traveled distance and to scan what is seen by the side of the road. These shots create the impression that the driver, the wanderer in the automobile, is the "creator" of his own journey, as the French urbanist Paul Virilio once said, introducing the concept of *dromoscopy* to formulate a theory of automobile perception.[21] In Virilio's perspective, the vehicle can be seen as a type of visual machine producing moving images through locomotion. But unlike the romantic traveler, the driver, enclosed in the shell of the car body, lacks the physical contact with his environment. He perceives the world solely via the windshield, a window which, according to Virilio, flattens the landscape, houses, and people just like a film screen.[22] Following Baudrillard and his concept of simulacra and simulation, Alice Kuzniar comes to a similar conclusion in her study of the windshield shot in Wenders's films. She explains that as long as they are "caught" in the automobile, Wenders's protagonists are forced to "interface with their worlds through the window/mirror/screen."[23] She also highlights that they are an opportunity for Wenders to reflect once more on his own medium as well as on visual culture in general: "With their shots reflecting images in the rearview mirror or through the windshield, Wenders's road movies are quintessentially about the way we perceive 'reality' through photography, film and video."[24]

At the same time, the automobile in Wenders's films can be seen as a form of time capsule. While moving toward a vanishing point (i.e., a spatial point in the future) the characters in a way carry along their past experiences. To indicate the temporal conjunction of past, present, and future, Wenders has modified the visual relation of nearness and distance that appears in the window theme of the romantics and created an idiosyncratic picture composition. A recurring shot in Wenders's films, used enough that it has become part of his signature style, is virtually split into two parts, combining a close-up of the driver or passenger behind the windshield with the spatial corridor of a street (Figure 4.4). In this artistic manner, the filmmaker implies the isolation of the protagonist as well as their personality, split between the past (the already-covered distance of the road) and the future (the driver's focal point, which we cannot see).

Figure 4.4

I argued before that vehicles often function like a shelter or "heterotopia" (to use Michel Foucault's term) for many characters in Wenders's films. But by attempting to experience the world through these shelter-vessels, characters eschew confrontation with others as well as with their personal situation: one is even tempted to say that they are reduced to being spectators of their own lives. The windshield absorbs the feelings of the driver, reflects his wishes, and becomes in this way a mirror of his inner state of mind.[25] Along those same lines, Wenders frequently underlines the specular surface of the window, most notably in the notorious peepshow sequence from *Paris, Texas*. Here, at the climax of the story, Travis (Harry Dean Stanton) seeks his former wife, Jane (Nastassja Kinski), in a strip club in Houston. While hiding in a peep booth—another "representation of the cinematic apparatus"[26]—Travis confesses to her the sorrows and anxieties that shattered their relationship. The way in which this dialogue scene was filmed can be considered as almost exemplary with regard to the symbolic function of the window motif (Figure 4.5). The window always marks a dividing line between a character and his counterpart, whether it is a landscape or a human being. Most of the time, the communication remains limited to eye contact alone, for the "conversation partners" do not share the same space as long as they retreat into a rigid position. Overcoming this barrier—for example, by revealing true feelings in this particular sequence of *Paris, Texas*—seems to be the real romantic impulse to which Wenders alludes in his films.

Figure 4.5

We learn from these examples that Wenders has managed to adapt the romantic traditions and at the same time has updated them for his own aims and purposes. Directly linked with this practice is the project of seriously revising romantic thoughts and ideas to avoid employing romanticism as merely an instrument of decoration and idealization, a method that in relation to German film history was foremost practiced in the genre of the *Heimatfilm*.[27] The window-view helped Wenders to articulate his principles of filmmaking (*Silver City Revisited*), and it defined the precarious situation and alienation of modern individuals in the case of *Wrong Move* and *Alice in the Cities*. Furthermore, the window-shots reflected different modes of perception by examining the relation between inner and outer spaces.

Of course, Wenders's use of the window motif is not restricted to the films I discuss here. Taking in consideration feature films like *The End of Violence* (1997) or *The Million Dollar Hotel* (2000) and even his more recent productions— an example can be found, for instance, in *Every Thing Will Be Fine* (2015)— we can see that windows as screens and frames remain a recurrent theme in Wenders's body of work. Over time, romantic painting seems to have faded away as Wenders's central point of reference, replaced by an artistic dialogue with modern painters like Edward Hopper and Andrew Wyeth. Yet Wenders still uses the window motif to communicate his attitude toward filmic narrative as well as his ethical concerns about the social and political use of the image, as, for example, with the monitoring screens in *Land of Plenty* (2004). Wherever it appears, the window motif is used to bring up the question of how we look at the world and what can be revealed through certain techniques of cinematographic image-making.

Notes

1. E. T. A. Hoffmann, *Des Vetters Eckfenster* (1822; Stuttgart: Reclam, 2014).
2. Eric Rentschler, *West German Cinema in the Course of Time: Reflections on the Twenty Years Since Oberhausen* (Bedford Hills: Redgrave 1984), 94.
3. Jakob and Wilhelm Grimm, *Werke. Abt. III, Bd. 42.1: Deutsches Wörterbuch. Dritter Band: E—Forsche*, ed. Wilfried Kürschner (1862; Hildesheim/Zürich/New York: Olms, 2003), 1519.
4. Robert Kolker and Peter Beicken, *The Films of Wim Wenders: Cinema as Vision and Desire* (Cambridge: Cambridge University Press, 1993), 83.

5   Ibid., 13.
6   Karsten Visarius, "Das Versagen der Sprache Oder: His Master's Voice," in *Wim Wenders*, with texts by Frieda Grafe et al. (Munich/Wien: Hanser, 1992), 60.
7   Further steps to a critical revision of romantic stereotypes in Wenders's films were undertaken in publications by Peter Brandes ("Wim Wenders und die romantische Ästhetik des Sehens," in *Komparatistik Online*, no. 1 [2007]: 1-4) and Katharina Eißel (*Er-Fahrung neuer Horizonte: Reise und Wahrnehmung in Filmen von Wim Wenders* [Saarbrücken: VDM, 2007], 42-43).
8   Later Peter Greenaway will show the same artistic practice in his film *The Draughtman's Contract* (1982).
9   Norbert Grob, "'Life Sneaks out of Stories': *Until the End of the World*," in *The Cinema of Wim Wenders: Image, Narrative, and the Postmodern Condition*, ed. Roger F. Cook and Gerd Gemünden (Detroit: Wayne State University Press 1997), 199.
10 Wim Wenders, "Was Bilder heute bewirken," in Wim Wenders, *A Sense of Place: Texte und Interviews*, ed. Daniel Bickermann (Frankfurt/Main: Verlag der Autoren, 2005), 68-96.
11 See, for example, Louis Jacques Mandé Daguerre's famous photo of the *Boulevard du Temple* in Paris (1839), taken from the window of his local residence.
12 Lorenz Eitner, "The Open Window and the Storm-Tossed Boat: An Essay in the Iconography of Romanticism," *The Art Bulletin* 37, no. 4 (1955): 285.
13 Ibid., 285-86.
14 Caspar David Friedrich, *Blick aus dem Atelier des Künstlers, rechtes Fenster* (*View from the Artist's Studio, Right Window*), 1805/1806, drawing, sepia on paper, 12.2 × 9.3 inch, Vienna, Österreichische Galerie Belvedere; Jacob Alt: *Blick aus dem Atelier des Künstlers in der Alstervorstadt gegen Dornbach* (*View from the Artist's Studio in the Alstervorstadt toward Dornbach*), 1836, watercolor, 20.1 × 16.3 inches, Vienna, Albertina, Collection of Prints and Drawings.
15 Joseph von Eichendorff, "Sehnsucht," in *Deutsche Gedichte. Von den Anfängen bis zur Gegenwart*, ed. Benno von Wiese (1834; Berlin: Cornelsen, 1993), 376.
16 Novalis, *Heinrich von Ofterdingen: Berlin 1802*, ed. Joseph-Kiermeier-Debre (1802; Munich: DTV, 2014), 12.
17 Peter Handke and Wim Wenders, "Die Helden sind die Andern," in Wim Wenders, *Die Logik der Bilder: Essays und Gespräche*, ed. Michael Töteberg (Frankfurt/Main: Verlag der Autoren, 1988), 18.
18 Catherine Russell, "The Life and Death of Authorship in Wim Wenders's *The State of Things*," *Canadian Journal of Film Studies / Revue canadienne d'études cinématographiques* 1, no. 1 (1990): 22.
19 *Novalis: Vorarbeiten zu verschiedenen Fragmentsammlungen*, in Novalis, *Schriften, Bd. 2: Das Philosophische Werk I*, ed. Richard Samuel (1798; Stuttgart: Kohlhammer, 1960), 545.

20 Peter Handke, *Der kurze Brief zum langen Abschied* (Frankfurt am Main: Suhrkamp, 1972), 95: "Ich spürte eine Unlust bei unserer Bewegung, ein Gefühl, als seien wir mit laufendem Motor stehengeblieben."
21 Paul Virilio, "Die Dromoskopie," in Paul Virilio, *Der negative Horizont. Bewegung—Geschwindigkeit—Beschleunigung* (Munich/Vienna: Hanser, 1989), 134.
22 Ibid., 136.
23 Alice Kuzniar, "Wenders' Windshields," in *The Cinema of Wim Wenders*, ed. Cook and Gemünden, 223.
24 Ibid., 224.
25 For Malte Hagener and Thomas Elsaesser, the window as a metaphorical circumscription for the cinema's mode of operation (and here they meet with Wenders's own idea of the medium) can also be seen as a "showcase" or projection surface for the spectator's desire and therefore function like a mirror. See Malte Hagener and Thomas Elsaesser, *Filmtheorie zur Einführung* (Hamburg: Junius, 2007), 47.
26 Thomas Elsaesser, "Time, Place, and Self in the Films of Wim Wenders," in *The Cinema of Wim Wenders*, ed. Cook and Gemünden, 252.
27 Elisabeth Eisert-Rost et al., "Heimat," in *Der deutsche Heimatfilm. Bildwelten und Weltbilder. Bilder, Texte, Analysen zu 70 Jahren deutscher Filmgeschichte*, ed. Wolfgang Kaschuba (Tübingen: Tübinger Vereinigung für Volkskunde 1989), 21–25.

Part II

Reimagining Cinema and Photography with Wenders

5

As If It Were for the Last Time: Wim Wenders—Film and Photography

George Kouvaros

In a million years,
when no one will be around any more
to even remember us faintly,
some of these places will.
Places have memories.
They remember everything.
It's engraved in stone.
It's deeper than the deepest waters.
Their memories are like sand dunes,
wandering on and on.
I guess that's why I take pictures of places:
I don't want to take them for granted.
I want to urge them
not to forget us.

—Wim Wenders, *Pictures From the Surface of the Earth*

1

In Wim Wenders's photographs, the camera is an instrument not simply for seeing but also for registering different gradations of time. During a visit to the Toshodaiji Temple in Nara, Japan, the photographer's attention is caught by a mound of moss growing at the foot of the temple wall (Figure 5.1).[1] The forces of time and weather that gave birth to the moss have covered a section of the adjacent wall with a golden-brown patina that competes with the moss for ownership of the wall's surface. Another photograph taken during the visit to Nara shows

Figure 5.1 Inside the Toshodiji Temple, Nara, Japan 2000. © Wim Wenders.

the cross section of a large rock. The countless fine lines and indentations that decorate the rock's surface also testify to the forces of weather—this time over a period not of years or decades but of centuries. A third image from the same trip recalibrates our sense of time yet again. It shows a tiny praying mantis perched near the edge of a void. In contrast to the vast expanse of time inscribed on the rock's surface, the image of the magnificent insect suggests a parcel of time that barely registers.

Wenders's concern with using photography to document the passage of time can be traced to an earlier set of images that were taken during the preparation for his 1984 film, *Paris, Texas*. In an interview with the French critic Alain Bergala, Wenders recounts how the experience of taking these photographs helped to familiarize him with the light and landscape of the American West. During the months he spent crisscrossing the country, Wenders found himself drawn to particular types of surfaces, both natural and man-made, that testify to the passage of time: billboards, cinema facades, and abandoned shop fronts worn away by the elements. These weathered surfaces clarified photography's documentary purpose. "The way I see it," he tells Bergala, "it's a vital part of photography, seeing something and recording it as if it were the last possible chance to do so. To my mind, that's the 'end of the world' side of photography."[2] But during the same discussion he also acknowledges another side to this sensibility—namely that, once taken, the photograph serves to perpetuate the existence of things even after their extinction.

To look at something as if it were for the last time, as if the thing being looked at was in the process of disappearing. In this chapter, I want to consider what this attitude reveals about Wenders's work in both film and photography. For Wenders, photography has a number of overlapping functions: it is a medium with its own aesthetic requirements and demands, a means for reflecting on the nature of cinema, and, most challenging of all, a form of temporal experience in which we confront the ending and surviving of things. With these functions in mind, I will trace a series of connections between photography and cinema. My aim is to shift our understanding of Wenders's career from that of a filmmaker who also takes photographs to someone for whom the photographic image—its history and temporal implications—plays a central role in his creative practice.

2

In the interview with Bergala, Wenders recalls a piece of advice the American director Nicholas Ray gave to his actors: "Even if you're only asking for a light, even if you're only saying good day, you have to do it as if you thought it could be the last time" (10). In practice, we know that the action performed by the screen actor can be repeated again and again. But what Ray's statement alludes to is the fact that what can never be repeated is the moment in which the action is performed. Uniquely among the arts, film and photography preserve this unrepeatable moment. "All films are ultimately documentaries," Wenders extrapolates, "because in passing, unintentionally, they record the clouds crossing the sky or a flock of birds somewhere in the background or someone walking by who doesn't notice he's being filmed" (10). In an appreciation of Ray's 1952 film, *The Lusty Men*, Wenders reaffirms this view of film's documentary qualities. He recounts how Ray began the shoot with a script of just twenty-six pages.[3] Each night, Ray worked with his screenwriters and actors to prepare material for the next day's shooting. The outcome of this method is exemplified by a sequence near the start of the film in which a lone figure (Robert Mitchum) hobbles away from an empty rodeo arena. Arriving at a dilapidated farmhouse and finding the front door locked, he walks around to the back and retrieves from under the house an old rodeo program, a six-shooter pistol without handle-grips, and a small tobacco tin. The unhurried manner in which these activities unfold opens the door for a relationship to the film in which the documentary status of the images assumes equal weight to the fiction:

> Without any pressure, without any sense of haste, every shot gradually becomes a sign in some sort of runic script, that you slowly see and hear. A song. Mitchum's slightly limping gait. A landscape opening up. Trees standing alone. A wavy line of soft hills on the horizon. A remote farmhouse without even a path leading up to it. The short shadows of the midday sun.[4]

In Wenders's description of the film's opening moments, it is not just a character that we see but also the actor, Robert Mitchum. It is not just a location that we remember but also the geography of an actual place. Overall, it is not just a story that we recall but also an event whose existence, captured by the camera, is projected on the screen. This insistence on the film's "eventness" lies at the heart of the photographic attitude that pervades Wenders's work. We can trace its impact by turning to another occasion when Wenders pays tribute to Ray. In *Kings of the Road* (1976), he replays the scene of Mitchum's return to his former home. But whereas the homecoming in *The Lusty Men* only takes a few moments of screen time, Bruno's (Rüdiger Vogler) return to his childhood home in Wenders's film, first by motorcycle and sidecar and then rowboat, is in keeping with the film's digressive approach. Even when Bruno arrives at the house, the drama is slow to emerge. As we watch the character take stock of the abandoned house, it's unclear what types of emotions are being stirred. That powerful emotions have indeed been triggered is evidenced by Bruno's action of throwing a heavy object through one of the windows. No explanation is given for this act, nor are we told the reason for the tears that he wipes from his face later the same night. By withholding these explanations, Wenders ensures that the focus of the drama extends beyond character psychology to incorporate other scenic elements such as the space in which the actor moves, the material objects in that space, and the actor's gestures perceived as gestures rather than simply external manifestations of an inner life. Underpinning all this is the director's insistence on keeping two ways of treating the cinematic image alive: on the one hand, the image as part of the telling of a story and, on the other, the image as the record of a particular time. Across Wenders's films, this approach gives birth to stories in which narrative movement and character development are prone to suspension, stories in which nothing seems to happen except the passing of time.

Near the end of *Kings of the Road*, Bruno reflects on the impact of the journey to his home on the Rhine. "I'm glad we went to the Rhine," he tells his traveling partner, Robert (Hanns Zischler). "For the first time I see myself as someone who has gone through a certain time, and this time is my history. The feeling is quite comforting." Rather than some childhood trauma, the thing that Bruno confronts in the house is time. The abandoned rooms of the house embody a parcel of time that is over and cannot be revivified. He calls this encounter comforting, but his actions suggest that, at a deeper level, it is also disturbing. This disturbance lends weight to the conclusion that what Bruno confronts in the house is the same thing that Wenders confronts in his written reflections on *The Lusty Men*: a sense of time specific to cinema. That this encounter is not only comforting but also disturbing tells us a lot about the photographic attitude that pervades Wenders's work. Bruno's homecoming affirms a view of cinema as a type of memento mori. Remember this, Wenders insists. Remember both the film from which Bruno's actions are taken and the cinema's capacity to give us an image of time that sweeps away all traces of human life. For Wenders, the places and events that we remember and manage to return to through the cinema have the capacity to reciprocate this investment. They do so by speaking to us of our own passing.

3

To look at something as if it were for the last time, as if the thing being looked at was in the process of disappearing. Tracing the history of this attitude leads back to the films of Ray. Pursuing a different course, we arrive at another figure that can also clarify the photographic attitude informing Wenders's work: the American photographer Walker Evans. In the interview with Bergala, Wenders sums up the significance of Evans's photographs: "The photos Walker Evans took in the Depression were just that: preserving something that was going to disappear in three or four years' time, in your eye and in your memory" (10). The affinity between Wenders and Evans is evident in their mutual fascination for images of ruin and decay. In 1935, Evans accepted a commission from New York industrialist Gifford Cochran to document surviving examples of

Greek Revival style architecture in the South. The photographs were intended as illustrations for a book on the architecture of the South that never made it to print.[5] Despite their concern with the remnants of a once grand lifestyle, the dominant tone of the images is not nostalgia but rather a disquieting sense of time's passing. The dilapidation that marks the structures photographed by Evans indexes a movement of time that is unstoppable. Looking at these images, we register what it means for people and things to get older, to lose their sheen. The depredations that accompany the passing of time are evident in a photograph taken during a visit to the Belle Grove Plantation in White Castle, Louisiana (Figure 5.2). The details on the Corinthian columns that stand at the entrance to the abandoned room reveal the level of care and expense that went into the room's construction. At the same time, the watermarks, exposed woodwork, and crumbling plaster are sure signs of impending dilapidation. Soon enough, the plaster will completely fall away, and the intricate carved details on the capitals will start to dissolve. The power of Evans's photograph resides in the coexistence of this accretion of decay with the fading signs of a once grand past. Writing in the third person, Evans provides his own summation of the significance of this photograph: "Evans was, and is, interested in what any present time will look like as the past."[6]

Figure 5.2 Room in Louisiana Plantation House, 1935. The Metropolitan Museum of Art, Gilman Collection, Purchase, Ann Tenenbaum and Thomas H. Lee Gift, 2005 (2005.100.322).

Evans's concern with evoking different registers of time is not restricted to his photographs of once grand estates. It is also evident in his images of places with no such pretensions. One of his most well-known photographs from the 1930s shows the interior of a Negro barbershop in Atlanta (Figure 5.3). Although the shop is empty of people, the towels draped across the arms and headrests of the chairs wait in readiness for the next person to walk through the door. The towels, the worn leather chairs, the lanterns lined up on a shelf, the hat resting on the bureau: these things wait for us. But they also speak of a life that happens without us, a life that happens after we have left—or are yet to arrive. These objects are, in other words, emblems of photography itself. They affirm the medium's capacity to induce what Miriam Bratu Hansen eloquently describes as "an awareness of a history that does not include us."[7]

In his prose poem "Places," Wenders explains why he takes pictures of places: "I don't want to take them for granted. / I want to urge them / not to forget us."[8] To press the point, urging places "not to forget us" is not about personification. Rather, it involves a type of inversion whereby human existence is looked at from the point of view of a material realm that does not include us. The histories evident in these places are histories in eclipse. This is the photographic vantage point that underpins the work of both Wenders and Evans. But the question we

Figure 5.3 Barber Shop Interior, Atlanta Georgia, 1936. The Metropolitan Museum of Art, Walker Evans Archive, 1994 (1994.258.353).

have yet to deal with is: How does Wenders deal with the dilemma of coming *after* Evans, in other words, the fact that when he looks at a billboard, a shop front, a road sign in the American West, he is also looking at a photograph by Evans of a billboard, a shop front, a road sign in the American West? This question aligns with what Gerhard Richter refers to as "a general and expanded concept of afterness in which what has superseded or outlived remains intricately indebted to the very thing it has outlived or overcome." Richter goes on to stipulate: "There can be no after without a debt, an unsettled relation, a haunting."[9] Our question then becomes: How does this "unsettled relation" leave its mark on Wenders's photographs and films?

In 2001, Wenders spent a week in the coastal town that serves as one of the principal settings in Yasujiro Ozu's masterpiece *Tokyo Story* (1953). The photobook that documents the visit frames the dilemma of coming after as a matter of seeing things that one already has in mind:

> Onomichi showed me once again
> that we don't just "see."
> We recognize what we already "have in mind."
> We have learned to appreciate certain things,
> want to see them all over again
> and in the process disregard others.
> We find (so often) the very thing we were looking for.[10]

This is another aspect of the photographic attitude pervading Wenders's work. His awareness of recognizing things already "in mind" positions the films and photographs as part of a continuum of approaches and carries with it certain obligations. Thomas Elsaesser describes the nature of these obligations:

> To make films is for Wenders in a sense to watch once more and remember the films one had already seen. Action could only be the retelling of action. The point was not to film something that had never been shown before but to show something in such a way that it appeared to be a memory of something one had already seen.[11]

Following up this suggestion, we can say that, for Wenders, taking photographs is not a matter of seeking to photograph something that has never been shown before but rather of photographing something so that it appears as a memory of something already seen. In Wenders's photographs, memory and the effects of time passing operate side by side. Walter Benjamin outlines a similar interaction in his essay on Proust. He describes Proust's "true interest" as "the passage of time in its most real—that is, space-bound—form, and this passage nowhere holds sway more openly than in remembrance within and aging without."[12] Benjamin's summation crystallizes a question that is as important to Wenders's photographs as it is to the design of Proust's monumental work of literature: How to remember well? How to do justice to the memories that inform and help shape one's own viewpoint? For Wenders, this question defines the historical dilemma of coming after.

One way that he negotiates this dilemma is through writing. In *Journey to Onomichi*, for example, Wenders's written text emphasizes the impossibility of separating his vision of Japan from the vision of others:

> The Japan I perceive through my camera
> is strictly my very own sight.
> (Or "insight"?)
> It is shaped by the history of Japanese Cinema,
> (that I got to know in Paris and New York,
> long before I ever set foot in Japan for the first time,)
> but also by Caspar David Friedrich, Vermeer, and Hopper,
> by Walker Evans, Sebastiao Salgado and Joel Meyerowitz,
> by Van Morrison, Dylan and Lou Reed,
> by Peter Handke, Walker Percy and Bruce Chatwin
> by my wife's black and white photography
> and by everything else I ever saw, read, heard and loved. (62)

This recitation of names provides Wenders with an opportunity to place Ozu's influence in the context of other influences that have shaped his photographic approach. At the same time, it serves another purpose that is also directly related to the recognition of coming after. "My stories always start from images," Wenders wrote in 1982. "My stories always begin with places, cities and landscapes or roads."[13] Through their integration of image and text, Wenders's photobooks represent a continuation of these founding principles. The stories they tell are dispersed across a vast range of places: Cuba, Australia, the United States, Japan, Russia, and Israel. But each story is grounded in a single defining experience—the experience of arriving at a place one has never been to before and finding in that place traces of a story that has already been told. Even before we take our first step, memory arrives in advance, populating the world with everything we have seen or heard.

Walking through the streets of Onomichi, Wenders struggles to master the basic requirements: "I buy unidentifiable refreshments from vending machines. / At a fast food stand I point at dishes / for which I have no name. / In the streetcar or bus I hold out / my handful of coins to the driver" (59–60). Gradually, he comes to understand this unfamiliar place through his memory of Ozu's film:

> It was all there:
> The coastal waters with the nearby offshore islands,
> (one could take this for the mouth of a big river,)
> the flat houses, built against the hills,
> the temples nestling among tall trees in vast parks,
> and most of all: the railroad line
> winding its way down along the coast.
> (The trains play a big part in the film . . . .) (61)

Even though Onomichi had become unrecognizable from the city depicted in Ozu's film, just enough remains for Wenders to catch sight of "the old days" of Onomichi. Rounding a corner, he asks himself: "Those men casting their lines on the quay walls / and the smoking onlookers around them, / didn't I see them in black and white?" This is what it means to tell stories from the point of view of images: to wander through a world that is unfamiliar, yet also inhabited by the phantoms of stories and figures that have come before. Wenders's account of his journey to Onomichi affirms that coming after is not simply about being at the end. It is also about things continuing and the struggle to understand what this unsettling continuation means for the present. For Wenders, photography aligns our existence with the existence of things that have passed; at the same time, it imbues these things with an afterlife that calls us to account as temporal beings.

"This is how it is. Nothing else, says the picture of the empty red bench in front of the camouflage colors of a large warship. Nowhere the hint of an affect, the mirroring of a strange aesthetic. No afterimage of the picture. No connotations. Nameless" (10). In a short accompanying essay, Heiner Bastian claims that Wenders's images of Onomichi mirror Ozu's refusal to aggrandize the details of the material world. On one level, this is true. But it does not rule out the suggestion of other figures and influences positioned just over the photographer's shoulder. This is evident in Wenders's creation of a sense of place through the traces and marks people leave behind. *The Sofa* shows a tatty grey sofa pushed up against the wall of a restaurant (Figure 5.4). Although nobody is sitting on the

Figure 5.4 The Sofa, Onomichi, Japan 2005. © Wim Wenders.

sofa, the signs of wear and tear testify to years of occupancy. Nobody is sitting on the sofa, but, soon, somebody will be. Like the chairs in Evans' photo of the Negro barbershop in Atlanta, the sofa waits for us; perhaps it even waits for Evans, or his memory, at least, to find its way back to this unfamiliar city located between the past and the present.

4

To look at something as if it were for the last time, as if the thing being looked at was in the process of disappearing. We now know that this also involves acknowledging the figures and influences that have brought us to where we are. In *Journey to Onomichi* this occurs through a combination of still images and written text. In his films, Wenders has other resources at his disposal. Slowing things down, allowing the narrative to digress, and ensuring that place is as important as character—these are some of the means by which Wenders draws out the implications of Ray's legacy for his own approach to cinema. Just as significant is his employment of gesture. Again, I am thinking of Bruno's action of throwing the heavy object through the window of his former home. Up to this point, everything about the homecoming scene has been about the past: the actor's slow movement through the rooms of the house, the dust and debris that cover the remaining pieces of furniture, the dim light filtering through the windows. Smashing the window serves to "change the beat": its violence demands a new set of responses from the actor and audience. Acting coaches employ these sudden changes to ensure that the process of performance does not solidify into a replaying of predetermined emotions and meanings. This does not prevent the actor from utilizing skills learnt through training, habit, and memory. But it does ensure that these things do not hinder what Lee Strasberg and others refer to as "the illusion of the first time."[14]

"Fifty years ago," Benjamin wrote in the third version of his essay "The Work of Art in the Age of Its Technological Reproducibility," "a slip of the tongue passed more or less unnoticed."[15] All this changed with the publication of Freud's *On the Psychopathology of Everyday Life*: "This book isolated and made analyzable things which had previously floated unnoticed on the broad stream of perception" (265). Benjamin claims that the arrival of cinema brought about a similar deepening of "apperception":

> On the one hand, film furthers insight into the necessities governing our lives by its use of close-ups, by its accentuation of hidden details in familiar objects, and by its exploration of commonplace milieux through the ingenious guidance of the camera; on the other hand, it manages to assure us of a vast and unsuspected field of action. (265)

Immediately after this passage, Benjamin provides his famous image of the "prison-world" of taverns, metropolitan streets, offices, furnished rooms, railway stations, and factories burst asunder "with the dynamite of the split second, so that now we can set off calmly on journeys of adventure among its far-flung debris." (265)

The purpose of this detour to Benjamin's canonical essay is to draw out how Bruno's violent action exemplifies the photographic attitude central to Wenders's work. In his draft notes for "The Work of Art," Benjamin describes Chaplin's capacity to integrate his gestures with the discontinuous nature of filmic movement. "Each single movement he makes is composed of a succession of staccato bits of movement. Whether it is his walk, the way he handles his cane, or the way he raises his hat—always the same jerky sequence of tiny movements applies the law of the cinematic image sequence to human motorial functions."[16]

Chaplin's jerky movements suggest both the interpenetration of the performer's physiological impulses with the apparatus and a playing with the structures and rhythms that are part of the alienation of everyday life. Jumping forward nearly four decades, Bruno's unexpected smashing of the window in *Kings of the Road* represents another instance in which an actor's physical actions take on a founding principle of the medium itself. This is the principle of "the split second" that bursts asunder the prison-world of the everyday. At the heart of this principle is a twofold process in which movement is, for a split second, arrested and calibrated differently.

In photography, the dislocating effects of this principle are held fast for our contemplation. In narrative film, the unfolding of images tends to fabricate an experience of the present that is seamless. But it doesn't take much for the originating disturbance to surge back to life: a sudden look or gesture on the part of the actor that breaks the confines of character, an element of decor or setting that is present or visible beyond its scenic requirements, a moment of immobility when the unfolding of images appears to stall. Regardless of how it occurs, the outcome is a reengagement with the camera's dislocating effects. In *Kings of the Road*, Bruno's violent gesture is geared to the accomplishment of this outcome. Its disruption of the scene aligns the continuation of Ray's legacy with the emergence of something new, something whose significance remains uncertain or yet to be determined. The dilemma of coming after—of finding one's place and history already circumscribed and indebted—is thus not just about comprehending the legacy of the past but also about creating the possibility of a future. We can now nuance our understanding of Ray's advice to his actors about approaching each action as if it were the last time. To see or do something as if it were for the last time: finally, we can see that, for Wenders, this is synonymous with seeing or doing something as if it were for the first time. The astonishing thing about film and photography is that everything we see has happened for the first and last time.

Notes

1 Wim Wenders, *Pictures from the Surface of the Earth* (Munich: Schirmer Art Books, 2003), np.

2 Wim Wenders, "Wim Wenders in Conversation with Alain Bergala," in Wim Wenders, *Written in the West* (New York: Neues Publishing Company, 2000), 10.

Further references to this interview are included in the text as page numbers in parentheses.

3 Bernard Eisenschitz provides a slightly different account of the production circumstances. He notes that, about a month before shooting started, the production department had fifty-five pages of "final" script: "This was not enough to prepare a breakdown and shooting schedule, since the 'second act' had not yet arrived." Eisenschitz also quotes Ray's statement during a talk to Vassar students: "We had about twenty-five or thirty pages of script. . . . I like it that way. Keeps the show fresh and spontaneous. And your imagination works overtime. We wrote every night. So there wasn't much beside instinct and the reactions of my actors to what we had done the day before." Bernard Eisenchitz, *Nicholas Ray: An American Journey*, trans. Tom Milne (London: Faber and Faber, 1993), 179–80.

4 Wim Wenders, "The Men in the Rodeo Arena: Lusty," in *Wenders: On Film: Essays and Conversations*, trans. Michael Hofmann (London: Faber and Faber, 2001), 122.

5 A selection of these images is included in Gilles Mora and John T. Hill, *Walker Evans: The Hungry Eye* (London: Thames and Hudson, 2004).

6 Walker Evans, quoted in Walker Evans and Jerry L. Thompson, *Walker Evans at Work: 745 Photographs Together with Documents Selected from Letters, Memoranda, Interviews, Notes* (New York: Harper and Row, 1982), 151.

7 Miriam Bratu Hansen, Introduction to *Theory of Film: The Redemption of Physical Reality*, by Siegfried Kracauer (Princeton, NJ: Princeton University Press, 1997), xxvi.

8 Wenders, *Pictures from the Surface of the Earth*, np.

9 Gerhard Richter, *Afterness: Figures of Following in Modern Thought and Aesthetics* (New York: Columbia University Press, 2011), 6.

10 Wim Wenders, *Journey to Onomichi* (Munich: Schirmer/Mosel, 2010), 62. Further references to this book are included in the text as page numbers in parentheses.

11 Thomas Elsaesser, "Spectators of Life: Time, Place, and Self in the Films of Wim Wenders," in *The Cinema of Wim Wenders: Image, Narrative and the Postmodern Condition*, ed. Roger F. Cook and Gerd Gemünden (Detroit, MI: Wayne State University Press, 1997), 248.

12 Walter Benjamin, "The Image of Proust," in *Illuminations: Essays and Reflections*, ed. Hannah Arendt, trans. Harry Zohn (Suffolk: Fontana, 1982), 213.

13 Wim Wenders, "Impossible Stories," in *The Cinema of Wim Wenders*, ed. Cook and Gemünden, 33–34.

14 Lee Strasberg, "A Dream of Passion: The Development of the Method," in *Star Texts: Image and Performance in Film and Television*, ed. Jeremy Butler (Detroit: Wayne State University Press, 1991), 44.

15 Walter Benjamin, "The Work of Art in the Age of Its Technological Reproducibility: Third Version," in *Selected Writings*, vol. 4, 1938–1940, ed. Howard Eiland and Michael W. Jennings, trans. Edmund Jephcott (Cambridge, MA: Belknap Press of Harvard University Press, 2006), 265. Further references are included in the text as page numbers in parentheses.

16 Walter Benjamin, "The Formula in Which the Dialectical Structure of Film Finds Expression," in *Selected Writings*, vol. 3, 1935–1938, ed. Howard Eiland and Michael W. Jennings, trans. Edmund Jephcott, Howard Eiland and others (Cambridge, MA: Belknap Press of Harvard University Press, 2002), 94.

This article originally appeared in *New German Critique* (125, Vol. 42, No. 2, August 2015). Reprinted with permission of Duke University Press.

6

Wenders–Salgado: Space, Time, and Transformation in *Salt of the Earth*

Darrell Varga

Wim Wenders's documentaries have always been opportunities to explore the artistic process and the idea of image-making; that is to say, the form, materiality, and ontological nature of cinema. These concerns are also present throughout his fiction films, but in the documentaries, they are less hindered by narrative or, more specifically, by the commercial forces that tend to structure narrative films and elide questions of process. The documentary *Salt of the Earth* (2014) begins with a reflection on the medium that is characteristic of Wenders documentaries, reminding us that photography is the drawing of the world with light and shadow. With the metaphor of drawing, Wenders is situating his film within an art world context, but not just any context: it is one associated with the body and with a direct tactile engagement with the process of representation. Indeed, these are central concerns of documentaries he made in the 1980s, at a time when he was working in America and dealing with the complex financial and interpersonal machinery of commercial feature filmmaking. Among these titles are *Lightning Over Water (Nick's Film)*, made in 1980 amid the disappointment of working for Francis Ford Coppola on *Hammett*; followed by *Chambre 666*, his lament for the future of cinema, released in 1982, the year that *Hammett* was finally completed; *Tokyo-Ga*, released a year after the success of *Paris, Texas* in 1984 (though filmed a few years earlier); and *Notebook on Cities and Clothes*, made in 1989, between *Wings of Desire* (1987) and *Until the End of the World* (1991). In all cases, these documentaries not only celebrate the creative eye of the film director but, I would go so far to say, that they also work to exonerate auteurism at the very moment the commodification of the cinema image begins to accelerate with the rise of the blockbuster and the veneration of the producer.[1] Robert Kolker and Peter Beicken put it this way: "Almost as often as he makes fictional films about young men attempting to sort out their existence, Wenders makes quasi-documentaries about himself in which he attempts to authenticate his belief in cinema and his own stake in it."[2] That description was written in the early 1990s, when Wenders was at the high point of his career; by now, neither the filmmaker nor his subjects are young men, and the redemption is the focus of the quest. Considerable time has passed from that period of artistic ferment and the making of *Salt of the Earth*, but I maintain that the early period of documentaries provides the framework for understanding the later work.

This period of the 1980s in Wenders's career has been characterized as that of the individual artist struggling against the blunt forces of the studio system, where greed and ego supplant art or, to put it more bluntly, where "art" has only ever been a marketing device for mass-produced entertainment. This self-mythologization is most evident in Wenders's *The State of Things* (1982) and in the film's critical reception as well as in the filmmaker's own contemporaneous commentary.[3] Kathe Geist describes the film as "a vehicle for exploring European versus American values for filmmaking," asserting that America represents a debased "coarseness" and emphasis on money.[4] Kolker and Beicken affirm the consensus:

> This film is a cry of anger at an unresponsive industry and at an artistic temperament that cannot yield to that industry; it is both an image of the director's martyrdom and an act of redemptive suicide, the adult's desire to kill the child who wants to maintain an imaginary simplicity and self-possession— the child who believes that the accurate, adequate, and valid image can redeem loss, absence, and amnesia.[5]

If "martyrdom" is a bit of an overstatement, it does reflect the filmmaker's existential dilemma of working within and against the constraints of popular culture. The subjects Wenders finds for his documentaries embody this struggle. In particular, the two films shot in Japan, *Tokyo-Ga* and *Notebook on Cities and Clothes*, follow the New German Cinema practice of essentializing Japan as other to Europe and focus respectively on a cinema "father figure," Yasujiro Ozu, whose work encompasses the technological and commercial history of cinema in the twentieth century, and Yohji Yamamoto, an artist "brother" in the parallel industry of fashion design and, like Wenders, an oedipal child of the disaster that is the twentieth century. The title *Salt of the Earth* recalls the radical classic made by blacklisted filmmakers (directed by Herbert Biberman) released in the dark days of McCarthyism in 1954. Biberman's film brought the subject of labor and racial relations to the big screen in a way unlike anything in Hollywood's history. In fact, the apparatus of the studio system and its avatars in politics and media regulate the system in order to deflect from politics inasmuch as it may interfere with the flow of revenue and the broader function of mass entertainment as the soft power of American imperialism.

Wim Wenders is not a radical political filmmaker but, in his *Salt of the Earth*, he is met with a subject who has gazed directly into the horror of twentieth-century history in a way that is at once political, personal, and deeply embedded in the question of image and identity. Wenders has always been outspoken, especially early in his career and, notably, in the narration for *Tokyo-Ga* and *Notebook on Cities and Clothes*, on the colonizing effect of American media, but his films avoid anything approaching analysis of what that may mean on a social or a political level. His criticism typically accommodates the use of popular culture for play and personal expression. In this respect, he is less Frankfurt School and more Raymond Williams.[6] Robert Cook points out that "as his criticism of the colonizing American culture industry becomes more deliberate, Wenders does not dismiss all its products out of hand and continues to incorporate various forms of popular culture into his films."[7] To be sure, there is little room for rock and roll in *Salt of the Earth*, and documentary always exists at the margins of mainstream cinema, but Cook's comment does accurately describe the overall thrust of these films. The implicit question asked of Sebastião Salgado, and one that runs parallel with Wenders's own existential angst as filmmaker, is of the possibility for photography (or film) as meaningful intervention in the world. Nora Alter suggests that Wenders's silences in his documentaries, and specifically the absence of any probing of Ozu's wartime politics in *Tokyo-Ga*, can be seen as "symptomatic," in Althusser's terms, of ideological complicity.[8] On the other hand, Thomas Elsaesser suggests that the "introspective and melancholy" male characters in his films offer a radical undermining of prevailing political orthodoxy, if not in any directly self-conscious political way.[9] In my view, all media texts are political, and it is overly prescriptive and unproductive to demand that a filmmaker's work fit within and explicitly express a desired perspective. We can, however, determine an overall political disposition through analysis of a body of work and measure the work against the dominant forces of power active in the same time period. If anything, we can expect, as in life, to find contradictions and inconsistencies, but that should by no means hinder our experience of the work and its potential to enrich our understanding of the world. Wenders will not, however, take up the ethical question, following Susan

Sontag, of what it means to photograph the suffering of others for a Western audience.[10] To point this out does not diminish the work of either Wenders or Salgado, but does raise otherwise unanswered questions.

In *Salt of the Earth*, the story of the Brazilian photographer Sebastião Salgado is presented as nothing less than a mythic journey as described by Joseph Campbell in his book *The Hero with a Thousand Faces* (1949).[11] This classic study of mythology, influenced by structuralist anthropology and the psychoanalytic concept of a collective unconscious articulated by Freud and Jung, identifies patterns of mythical character and narrative across dominant mythic stories from many cultures from around the world and observes a recurring narrative. Campbell determined that a hero's journey would include travel away from the security of home, into an external world of adventure where he would be challenged by powerful and even supernatural forces, facing struggle and loss before his eventual victory. He returns home not only transformed but also able to transform his world. From the perspective of ideological and feminist critique, this schema is limited, but I mention it here because of its pervasive influence on narrative cinema.[12] The idea has been codified in the influential screenwriting book, *The Writer's Journey* first published in 1998, and is highlighted in the opening chapter of *The Complete Idiot's Guide to Screenwriting*, where George Lucas and the original *Star Wars* trilogy is cited as having been strongly influenced by Campbell.[13] The latter book is typical of popular texts claiming to unpack the secrets of successful mainstream filmmaking for those who hope to enter into the industry.

The mythic journey, in Wenders's film, has a young Salgado travel away from his small and remote home village to learn about the ways of the world. He intends to work in the field of global finance in hopes of contributing to the betterment of humankind, but his journey detours from this path as he takes up the camera and heads into dark places. This journey almost destroys him, but he is able to repair his vision and find redemption through a renewed engagement with nature. I mention this narrative form because one function of the institutionalization of Joseph Campbell's framework is to deflect radical alternatives within narrative cinema—Hollywood producers want a system that helps mitigate risk, and this takes two forms: a conscious tendency to deploy techniques that are demonstrably successful and an unselfconscious tendency to limit the representation of social and political alternatives. These tendencies have influence over non-Hollywood practices by their global and hegemonic pervasiveness. In the film, Salgado is aged and weary over what he has witnessed, but continues to explore the landscape and the idea of home with his camera. The film is codirected with Juliano Salgado, the photographer's son, who is on the journey to get to know his father, who was absent for much of his childhood. It is a mirror of Wenders's own yearning for fathers in such figures as Yasujiro Ozu and Nicholas Ray. These are Wenders's central concerns throughout his films: home, son and father (or absent father), belonging, *Heimat*, and homeland, all concepts that can be taken up in progressive or reactionary ways. One impulse for this cinematic journey with the "good" father-figure Salgado is that it is redemptive of the search for the father in Wenders's own wayward attachment to Hollywood. As Robert Kolker and Peter Beicken describe his work on *Hammett*: "Seeking the completion of his oedipal journey, he went into the heart of the cinematic patriarchy, which repaid the favor by forcing on him the language of the American father figures he emulated."[14] Is it "father" that he desires or the image of father within a cinematic frame?

In Wenders's *Salt of the Earth*, the concept of home manifests in tropes of presence and belonging and in the question of how what we see in front of us relates to the idea of "home" that is in our heads. In this way, home is something that is lost, or that only exists in the fleeting glimpse, as Proustian madeleine recalled in dream (or nightmare). For Wenders, it manifests in a sense of longing and existential loss, the image of the lost soul wandering the desert; for Salgado, it is the experience of devastation in looking directly into the monster that is the modern, as Adorno describes the Enlightenment as a trajectory beginning with the slingshot and ending with the atom bomb. This film asks whether images in the world can be found to replace that which has been destroyed. Can belonging only ever be shaped by exile, whether that exile is self-imposed or forced by political circumstances? This is the persistent question of the postwar German filmmakers, and it is one of the links between Wenders and the subject matter of Salgado's photographs. The idea of home is, needless to say, all the more relevant today—the displacement of people by the machinations of capital, war, and the destructive path of climate change are, altogether, the major plight of our time.

Salgaldo's story is one of returning to a home that has been made into a desert by the combined forces of capital and the environment, and it is through the process of unmaking this trajectory through the act of seeing that the film emerges. This is the story of image-making, of the wreckage of human history not as a chain of events but as one spectacular catastrophe, as if viewed by Walter Benjamin's angel of history, but it is also the story of the dignity of ordinary people, the Salt of the Earth. Wenders has great affection for the simple dignity of labor, as represented by the team of workers in Yohji Yamamoto's Tokyo studio in *Notebook on Cities and Clothes*, and in the photographs of ordinary people, especially those by August Sander in his book *People of the 20th Century*, a title first published in 1927 and also inspiring to Yohji for his fashion designs. However, one gets the sense, via Wenders's camera, that the workers in Yamamoto's studio function as tools in the hands of the master, though this may be a consequence of the organization of labor in the analogous industries of fashion and cinema and unlike the solo journeys of Salgado. What Wenders sees is an organization of labor where there is a place for everyone, and where everyone remains in their place. There are no questions put to this social order, no scenes of radical resistance in his films, no claim to disrupt the vertical and hierarchical organization of labor.

August Sander was associated with a movement called "new objectivity"—a reaction against expressionism that combined romanticism with a desire to engage ordinary people. With Yamamoto, Wenders is yearning for a sense of community and belonging, one he hopes to glimpse in the faces of the people in these photographs. The people in the Sander photographs would have been destroyed by the Second World War, whether as victims or as murderers, along with the humanist ideal behind the photographs; symptomatic of that destruction is the fact that the Nazis confiscated the book because Sander included marginalized peoples alongside pictures of the German folk. I think that this relationship to images connects with *Salt of the Earth* in another way, the alternative meaning of the title, that of the earth salted by claims to power and the madness of war, greed, and capital. In this sense, there is an echo of Herzog's *Lessons of Darkness* (1992), on the oil field fires of the first Gulf war, an event that is also photographed by Salgado, but that Herzog uses as a landscape for the narration of an alien visitor. We need to see these different representations together in order to understand alienation not as science-fiction speculation but as consequence of specific economic and social organization structured by language and power.

Salgado's father's farm was once a rich forest, but the lumber was cut to earn the money to send the children to school. This is the logic of the free market, which can accumulate vast wealth while turning its back to the violence of the real costs to the environment. It is to this cost that Salgado is witness in the world. "Cost" is the correct metaphor not least because Salgado, at his father's prompting, trained as an economist and was headed for a career at the World Bank, one of the major structuring forces of globalization. He knows well the cost of power and finance and came to witness that cost in the man-made famine in Ethiopia where government deliberately withheld food from part of the population, in the genocide in Rwanda, in refugees fleeing Slovakia, and in 1994 in the Congo through images of bodies heaped together, recalling the Jewish Holocaust. The film's structure may be a mythic journey, but what it shows us is not myth; it is our human history. Some of the footage from the Congo was filmed by Hubert Sauper, the director of *Darwin's Nightmare* (2004), another film informed by a global collaborative sensibility, and one that is also a journey into the darkness of human impact on the environment under the madness of globalization.

The film opens with Wenders speaking over black on the origin of the word photography: "A man writing and rewriting the world with light and shadows." In this way, he situates the story that is to follow in romantic terms, with the process of representation performing as the dawn of creation. It is up to Salgado to ground the images in their social reality, but his approach is to frame images that evoke the grand narrative. The first of these images is from Brazil's Serra Pelada gold mine, described by the photographer as representing "the babble of 50,000 people in one huge hole"—for him, a picture of all of human history. We see masses of people moving up and down ladders into a deep open area, all in search of gold. What is especially powerful here is the image of Salgado's face superimposed over the photograph as he says, "I had returned to the dawn of time." The bodies of the workers are written on his face, like the lines we get from old age, like the memory of the struggles and the violence he has witnessed. While photography may be described as drawing with light, filmmaking is drawing with time and thus with history. In this respect, it is not enough to say that the image is written with light; it is written, following Marx as he turned Hegel on his head, in the blood of ordinary people who are making history even if not in conditions of their own choosing.[15] Salgado's career and life is shaped by the fact that he has witnessed vast suffering. The image of the Brazilian mine layered over Salgado's face evokes the fact of time's passage as well as the ability of the artist to take us into a distinct temporal zone and to remind us that time and space are not coherent in Euclidian terms, that multiple experiences of time and space exist simultaneously, and that this is what the photographer experiences as he travels the world.

Salgado is looking at us, through the picture, and through the film camera. At this early stage of the film, the photographer expresses a sense of wonder, a sentiment that also characterizes the filmmaker's approach, one that allows for unexpected ways of seeing, but that also resists analysis. Here, it is echoed in the desire on the part of the miners, who come from all walks of life, to strike great wealth. But who really benefits from this labor? Wenders is fond of images of hands, as I discuss later, but we also need to ask the question that the film avoids: In whose hands does most of the gold end up? Later, we see Salgado reviewing projections of his own images, altogether Wenders is signaling a set of relationships toward the image where the responsibility of seeing is in dialectical relation to the image and to the world. Let us not forget, however, that this is an image of labor for the treasure of gold and that the image is an allegory for the underlying violence in the global struggle for riches. By beginning the film here, Wenders is at least setting up the opportunity for an understanding of the image in the political-economic context, and this is distinct from the approach of his other documentaries.

The story of human labor is later echoed in Salgado's series begun in the late 1980s and published in book form in 1993 with the title *Workers: An Archeology of the Industrial Age*.[16] We are introduced to this section in the film with an image of Salgado's hands opening the book, gesturing in front of the images as if to demonstrate the specific nature of the work shown in each photograph to Wenders, whose hands are, at the beginning of the scene, folded in the lower right of the frame. The movement of hands, along with the soundtrack evoking the noise of a factory, helps to bring us into the reality within the frame as well as to remind us of the distance, of the frame itself, between us and the workers who are the photographs' subjects. It is important that these are prints, physical objects, not data bytes on the screen. Their handling recalls similar shots in *Notebook on Cities and Clothes* discussed earlier. With Salgado, through Wenders, the images are a demand to look, to see, and to touch the world for what it is. As he tells the filmmaker regarding his return to Rwanda, "You felt the whole planet was covered with refugee tents." We see death in churches, in schools, in the institutions of civilization. The act of looking is linked with sorrow, and Salgado is left with the sad belief that human beings do not deserve to live on this planet. Wenders narrates this section using the analogy of "seeing into the heart of darkness." On the one hand, it is clever wordplay, but, on the other hand, it references Joseph Conrad and the long history of Europeans' viewing of Africa as barbaric. What is witnessed is indeed barbarity, but we have to more properly see this horror not as innate to the African landscape, as the Conrad reference suggests, but as a consequence of the violence of global geopolitics.

Wenders establishes Salgado as a heroic adventurer in the European tradition by following the black-and-white introductory images from Brazil with those of Salgado among the Yali people of the West Papua Highlands in Indonesia. The scene conveys the fact that Salgado has traveled widely in his career, and it may also fit with the idealization of "innocence" characteristic of Wenders. The setting is beautiful but one may also see it as the kind of exoticization of the other that is marketed in the West. It could be that the photographer is entangled in this system of economic and image relationships irrespective of his intentions. What is important, however, is the fact of human life in an environment free, for the moment, from external strife. This is how we are first introduced to the subject, and with the brief narrative description of his early journey away from home to attend school, this future economics professional was too innocent to even know how to exchange money for food since he had grown up on a farm where everything the family needed was produced on the land. The images of trains are important here: those carrying the minerals out of the land and away to market, and the one that carries Salgado as we learn of this history before the fall. The train he is riding plunges into a tunnel, and out of that blackness comes modern human history and, not incidentally, the cinema. These technologies of vision and mobility have, after all, accompanied the colonial plunder of the world.

For Salgado, what is important is the enormity of experience contained (and offered to the world) in the fraction-of-a-second shutter click. His first major series of images, "Other Americas," takes him to countries surrounding Brazil, to indigenous people living as if untouched by the forces of modernity. This is, however, a pretense that in cinema was exploited by Robert Flaherty and has long been associated with anthropologists and outside "experts" to legitimize a particular narrative of the so-called new world from the perspective of European settlers. As Charles Mann extensively documents, the indigenous peoples throughout North and South America had built complex societies and were involved in trade long before European colonization.[17] A scene of Salgado in the Arctic photographing a walrus is a reminder of Flaherty's *Nanook of the North* (1922), famously constructed by the filmmaker's urging that the Inuit use traditional spears, even though they wanted to reach for a rifle. Here, it is a persistent polar bear that interrupts the picture-taking. Nonetheless, the images from the "Other Americas" series offer a profound essay on the human face and its relation to community and landscape. Salgado tells the story while looking directly into the camera lens, and it is clear that he was much more than a taker of images on these journeys; these were profound experiences. If a photograph moves us emotionally, it is because it somehow reveals something of the relationship at play in a privileged moment, but for the photographer, these are the experiences that come to shape his sense of place in the world. Later, images of famine and disaster push Salgado to the breaking point, and we have to see these moments not as discrete images but, following Walter Benjamin, as the accumulated disaster that is history.

Disaster is both world-historical and local-environmental. We see video of Salgado's father describing his farm as once being rich and abundant, but now barren. The history of the environment follows from the history of colonialism: a trajectory of plunder and exploitation. The description of the farm is met by images of the famine in Ethiopia. In both cases, these are human-engineered disasters, but the wealth of the farm was plundered so that Salgado and his siblings could experience material affluence. All of that is far removed from the images in Ethiopia, where the starving use precious water to wash the bodies of the dead. These deaths are a direct consequence of the withholding of food, an inverse of the desertification of the land for material gain.

Redemption is in the return to the father's ranch—a desert restored as a place of life, now called the Instituto Terra and held as a public trust. In this way, the film returns to that image at the beginning, of the dignity of simple human labor, but now the gold is not of capital and commerce but of the life of the earth itself. Even here, though, the filmmaker remythologizes this history by describing, even if just in passing, this act of labor as "a miracle." It is better understood not as a miracle, even if that was meant metaphorically, but as a place transformed by the work of human hands; it is a landscape shaped by human history, just as this landscape has shaped the eye of the photographer. In both instances, the landscape is never neutral or separate from human action, even if the film is returning its hero to the Garden of Eden. Salgado is seen in this place still taking pictures; here the image-making is tangibly linked with the responsibility of being and acting in space. When we make pictures, we are giving shape to the spaces in which we live.

Salgado's return home and eventual recovery from having been witness to the violence and suffering of the world provides him with the inspiration to set out on what may be his final photographic journey. Here, the socially engaged photographer now wants to frame the beauty of nature, motivated by his curious claim that half the planet is still as it was at the time of creation, as if creation occurred in one singular moment. This is the starting point for his *Genesis* project (2013).¹⁸ He has witnessed the violent fall of mankind and, it seems, has to believe in this fantastical ideal of a resurrection. He then sets out to prove it by taking startlingly beautiful images whereby the world is framed to meet the ideal in what Wenders calls "a love letter to the planet." Perhaps this final movement of the film can be understood as the story of human resilience, that we have to tell ourselves that there is beauty, and set out to find it, as a way of living past the horror. Scientists now refer to our epoch as the Anthropocene as a way of describing the fundamental and full-scale transformation of the planet by human intervention. Yes, there are still animals to photograph, but this is a period of mass extinction. There are places of beauty and wonder (that word again), but the oceans are warming and dead zones have taken over parts of the sea, the icebergs are melting, and the deserts are expanding. One gets the sense that the photographer and the filmmaker *have* to believe in the resilience of beauty, now set free from the European idea of the sublime, even if they have landed amid the spectacle of destruction that is twentieth-century capitalism. I can only imagine that these artists are compelled to do so, simply so that they can keep breathing; as Wenders continues to search for images that offer up an ideal of redemption and, in a more grounded way, as Salgado makes possible the restoration of the forest around his childhood home, planting the trees that produce oxygen and breathe life into the planet.

Notes

1. This is not to idealize any one period of feature filmmaking as if outside of the conditions of the marketplace but to indicate a notable shift in the conditions of production. I examine this shift at length in my essay "The Bones of Reagan; Or, The Ruins of Art Cinema in Contemporary American Film," *CineAction* 75 (Winter 2008): 4–19.
2. Robert Kolker and Peter Beicken, *The Films of Wim Wenders: Cinema as Vision and Desire* (Cambridge: Cambridge University Press, 1993), 87.
3. This sensibility runs through Wenders's interviews in the 1980s and is also present in his own collection of writings, *Emotion Pictures*, trans. Shaun Whiteside (London: Faber and Faber, 1989).
4. Kathe Geist, *The Cinema of Wim Wenders: From Paris, France to Paris, Texas* (Ann Arbor: UMI Research Press, 1988), 91, 95.
5. Geist, *The Cinema of Wim Wenders*, 95. This would certainly be the general direction of the filmmakers associated with New German Cinema, as illuminated

by Thomas Elsaesser's *New German Cinema*, a book that remains useful even though it was published just prior to German reunification.

6   The thinkers associated with the Frankfurt School of Critical Theory, especially Theodor Adorno and Max Horkheimer, discuss popular culture as the transformation of expression in service of the regimentation of the capitalist economy. Thinkers associated with British Cultural Studies, including Raymond Williams and, later, Stuart Hall, consider the potential for political expression and agency, especially on the part of marginalized groups, through engagement with mass entertainment. See Theodor Adorno and Max Horkheimer, *Dialectic of Enlightenment*, trans. John Cumming (1944; New York: Herder and Herder, 1972); Raymond Williams, *Problems in Materialism and Culture: Selected Essays* (London: Verso, 1997); and David Morley and Kuan-Hsing Chen, eds., *Stuart Hall: Critical Dialogues in Cultural Studies* (New York: Routledge, 1996).

7   Roger F. Cook, "Postmodern Culture and Film Narrative," in *The Cinema of Wim Wenders: Image, Narrative, and the Postmodern Condition*, ed. Roger F. Cook and Gerd Gemünden (Detroit: Wayne State University Press, 1997), 122.

8   Nora M. Alter, "Documentary as Simulacrum: *Tokyo-Ga*," in *The Cinema of Wim Wenders*, ed. Cook and Gemünden, 140.

9   Thomas Elsaesser, "Spectators of Life: Time, Place and Self in the Films of Wim Wenders," in *The Cinema of Wim Wenders*, ed. Cook and Gemünden, 245.

10 A. O. Scott makes this reference in a review of the film, "The Eyes of the Beholder of Hardship", *The New York Times*, December 11, 2014, www.nytimes.com/2014/12/1 2/movies/wim-wenders-on-sebastio-salgado-in-the-salt-of-the-earth.html.

11 Joseph Campbell, *The Hero with a Thousand Faces* (New York: Pantheon, 1949).

12 I acknowledge the irony of discussing this framework for narrative while also claiming Wenders's documentaries as a movement away from Hollywood influence. I suggest that the aesthetic desire of the filmmaker may not be consistent with the actual patterns at work in his films. In any case, this is a filmmaker who has been very explicit about the influence of classical Hollywood and American popular culture, especially rock music, on his work.

13 Christopher Vogler, *The Writer's Journey: Mythic Structure for Writers* (Studio City, CA: Michael Wise Productions, 2007); Skip Press, *The Writer's Journey* (Toronto: Alpha-Penguin, 2008), 12.

14 Kolker and Beicken, *The Films of Wim Wenders*, 94.

15 In brief, Hegelian philosophy posits that meaning arises from preexisting universal categories as if handed down from the heavens while Marx declares that history is made by human action within the material conditions of everyday life. In *The Eighteenth Brumaire of Louis Bonaparte*, Marx says: "Men make their own history, but they do not make it as they please; they do not make it under self-selected circumstances, but under circumstances existing already given and transmitted

from the past" (*The Eighteenth Brumaire of Louis Bonaparte* [1852; Beijing: Foreign Languages Press, 1978], 9). Walter Benjamin follows this in his "Theses on the Philosophy of History," noting that "Whoever has emerged victorious participates to this day in the triumphal procession in which the present rulers step over those who are lying prostrate" (in *Illuminations*, ed. Hannah Arendt, trans. Harry Zohn [New York: Schoken Books, 1968], 256). The question for the filmmaker raised by Benjamin is the degree to which the work can resist becoming another "document of barbarism" within a triumphalist view of history. In my analysis of Wenders, he fully rejects triumphalism even if that does not translate into explicit political statements.

16 Sabastião Salgado and Eric Nepomuceno, *Workers: An Archeology of the Industrial Age* (London: Phaidon, 1993).

17 Charles C. Mann, *1491: New Revelations of the Americas before Columbus* (New York: Random House–Vintage, 2005).

18 Sabastião Salgado, *Genesis* (Köln: Taschen, 2013).

7

Wim Wenders's *Pina*: A Cinematic Homage to Pina Bausch

Peter Beicken

Pina: Dance, Dance, Otherwise We Are Lost (2011) is a remarkable cinematic homage to the late Pina Bausch (1940–2009) and the Wuppertal Dance Theater. As a resourceful experiment in the 3-D technique and as a methodological departure in Wim Wenders's documentary style, the film is unique in the director's oeuvre. Wenders saw 3-D as a new language capable of radically changing cinema, and in creating *Pina* he used this cinematic technique and machinery to great effect, employing conceptual innovations and a newly developed technical apparatus to capture the visuality of dance in unprecedented ways. Pina Bausch's untimely death, which almost resulted in the film never being made, ultimately led Wenders to adopt the choreographer's gaze and employ her concepts and methods of choreographing her revolutionary dance theater. The result is a singular homage that also breaks new filmic ground.

Upon Pina Bausch's untimely death on June 30, 2009, two days before shooting was to begin, Wenders was shocked to have lost his personal friend and collaborator on the intended film project. The film had been in the making for almost a quarter of a century. However, with the death of the admired choreographer, their "common project suddenly came to a harsh stop," and to "continue on with it in any way seemed unthinkable"[1] to Wenders who, since 2007, had seen in the 3-D technique a synergistic means to document Pina Bausch's exceptional dance art. Having canceled the project upon Pina's death, Wenders changed his mind and resumed it a few months later, after the dancers had pleaded passionately with him and offered to collaborate on "a film *for* Pina,"[2] their beloved choreographer.

The film that almost did not come about was originally conceived by Wenders as "a film *with* Pina,"[3] after he met the choreographer in Venice in 1985 at a retrospective showcasing several masterpieces of her dance theater. Wenders happened to be attending a film festival in Venice. His girlfriend at that time, Solveig Dommartin (1961–2007), almost literally had to drag the filmmaker to a performance of Pina Bausch's dance theater, as Wenders describes vividly in a 2011 interview about his film *Pina*.[4] As he relates the story, Dommartin had seen the dance theater before at a performance in France. She had been very impressed and wanted to see the dancers again, while Wenders had no understanding of and no real appreciation for dance at all. He knew about Pina Bausch and her dance theater, but he was not curious to learn more. Dance was something that he did not care for. But upon Dommartin's insistence, Wenders caved in and attended one of the performances at the retrospective.

Café Müller and *Le Sacre du Printemps* were the two pieces presented that evening. Being "forced" to watch these two Bausch signature pieces, Wenders was rather apprehensive and not expecting much at all. What happened then, as he confessed, gave him the shock of his life. The first dance, *Café Müller*, had originally been created in 1978, as one of the very few pieces in which the choreographer danced a leading role herself. Ten minutes into the performance, Wenders, sitting on the edge of his seat, burst into tears, and wept through the remainder of the performance. All of a sudden, intense emotions overwhelmed him and totally changed his view of dance. Wenders relates that the dance

> had knocked me out completely and that had me coming back for more. Somebody was telling me something essential about men and women that the entire history of cinema had not shown me, at least not so clearly and so purely. With these six people on stage humanity stood in front of me in its entirety that told me about longing, love, hate, loss, attraction and rejection, despair, bliss, apathy, carrying you or dropping you and all of that without a word. Only by gestures and movements, by body language, by dance. Pina had made me experience that as a language of its own that spoke to me, belonged to me, and that I was capable of understanding.[5]

Watching the second feature of the evening, *Le Sacre du Printemps*, Pina's stunning version of a modern classic, Wenders felt again the overpowering emotional impact of the dance art that he had ignored for so long. Through his "Pina experience," he became truly initiated, absorbed, and transformed. Dance as the art of moving in space touched the human soul.

Extending his stay in Venice, Wenders attended all the other performances of the retrospective. He also met Pina Bausch at a café. Sitting at a table, Wenders for the first time felt her eyes on him: "Pina's look was really extraordinary. She saw right through you. You were an open book to her; but it wasn't unpleasant; you felt recognized by a penetrating, yet kind look."[6] Wenders could relate to the exceptional personal "look" that informed Pina's choreographic art and that her dancers have addressed in so many ways. As someone focused on image-making, Wenders could easily appreciate the importance of the gaze, himself being an unusually visual person who is always working with exceptional cinematographers to realize his distinct vision. Back in the Venice café, Pina Bausch sat there, smiling enigmatically. She remained silent, while Wenders, enthused, let slip that he wanted to do a film with her. He did not get an answer, and he initially thought she had not heard him. But a year later, meeting in Wuppertal, she asked him about his idea of filming the dance theater, and the collaborative project was agreed upon.

While this collaboration *with* Pina was more than twenty years in the making, in the end the original plan was never realized. Time and again, Wenders felt that he was incapable of finding an appropriate way to film dance, let alone to capture the magic of Pina's intricate work. Finally, in 2007, he found a cinematic method, the 3-D technique, that he saw as the one and only way to film dance. At last the start date for the principal shooting was set—but then Pina Bausch's unexpected death put a sudden end to their collaborative project. After the grieving members of the dance theater succeeded in making Wenders return to the project, the concept of the film changed. Replacing the original project, the "film *with* Pina," with the "film *for* Pina," Wenders worked with the dancers both in mourning Pina and in paying homage to her legacy by filming her art before it would vanish. The final film's subtitle, "dance, dance, otherwise we are lost," is a phrase that Pina had adopted after hearing it from a little gypsy girl in Greece many years earlier. The girl had been pleading with Pina to join her family in dancing, at first to no avail. Finally, she was able to coax the shy and reluctant choreographer to take part in the dance by telling her, "dance, dance, otherwise we are lost."[7] These words became a fitting artistic credo and existential motto for Pina, and Wenders used them as a haunting subtitle to his film.

Wenders's film *Pina* transcends conventional documentary styles by eschewing the traditional interview method and using the moving camera very innovatively. The film is unique not only for the 3-D technique and its visual depth but also for its creative energy and ingenious ways of filming dance. Wenders succeeds in mesmerizing the viewer, as the film captures movement in space with a fluidity and plasticity that is both novel and emotionally stirring.

Like Pina Bausch's exceptional art, this cinematic homage offers powerful images that are sutured into a visual narrative of grief and admiration, lament and exultation. Pina Bausch turned motion into emotion by creating a universe of feeling and desire that was both raw and refined, violent and sublime. Exploring his many affinities with Pina's art, Wenders sets out to replicate the choreographer's "look," while also recapturing the creative vision and intense emotion that mark his earlier films, notably the highly improvisational *Im Lauf der Zeit* (*Kings of the Road*, 1976).

Philippina Bausch was born in Solingen on July 27, 1940. Called Pina, the child experienced traumatizing bombings of her hometown during the war years, as she recalled in her 2007 Kyoto speech.[8] By the end of the war, she was almost five, a hyperactive child who danced for guests in her parents' restaurant. Finding encouragement, she desired in her teens to become a dancer. Her parents relented and let the fifteen-year-old attend the Folkwang School in Essen, where Kurt Jooss (1901–79) was the director. He had been an innovative practitioner and promoter of modern German dance in the 1920s, the expressionist *Ausdruckstanz* mediated by the concepts of the influential dance theorist and pedagogue Rudolf Laban. Born in Bratislava in 1879, Laban championed *Bewegungskunst* and *Freier Tanz*, leaving Nazi Germany for England in 1936, where his work and influence continued until his death in 1958.[9] While Pina Bausch was educated in modern dance with elements of the theater style, she also got a solid foundation in classical ballet. After graduating in 1958, she received a stipend enabling her to continue her studies at Juilliard in New York City, starting in 1959. For two years she danced for various companies, among them the Metropolitan Opera Ballet. In 1962, Jooss lured her back to the Folkwang School, where she became both a soloist and an assistant, succeeding her former teacher as artistic director in 1968. Then, in 1973, she accepted the directorship of the Wuppertal Opera Ballet.[10]

In Wuppertal, Pina Bausch had a very rough start. But undeterred by an often hostile audience, underappreciated performances, negative reviews, and an uncooperative opera orchestra and chorus, she endured. For her stunning staging of *Le Sacre du Printemps* in 1975 she had to pipe in the recording of Stravinsky's music by Pierre Boulez because the orchestra pit was too small for all the musicians. As she developed her dance theater together with Rolf Borzik (1944–80), her ingenious, minimalist stage and costume designer and her companion as well, Pina Bausch mainly relied on recorded music, sometimes also using live music on stage or singing by the dancers, both as a solo and as a group. After years of scandal-ridden evenings, audience appreciation of her began to increase, and so did critical acclaim and success. Guest performances, notably in other European countries and overseas, made the Wuppertaler Tanztheater a high-in-demand, celebrated hit. Pina Bausch and her ensemble became synonyms for avant-garde dance theater, celebrated in Germany, in Europe, and across the world.

When Wenders initially proposed the collaborative film to Pina Bausch, he did not realize that he would struggle for over two decades to find a convincing method of filming dance. He saw other films devoted to Pina's pieces, but found them lacking. For example, he described the 1985 film version of *Café Müller* by Rudolf Rach as "exemplary," but limited, like most existing approaches, in capturing events and choreography on stage.[11] Wenders was looking for something radically new. After years of inactivity and delay, Pina started pushing Wenders to come up with a solution for their common project.

It took another transformative event for Wenders to find a breakthrough. At the Cannes Film Festival in 2007, Wenders happened to attend a screening of a U2 concert film in 3-D. The experience of a new, third dimension was another epiphany and completely changed his view of the cinema. Effusively, Wenders noted:

> The screen disappeared and became a huge window through which one could peer into depth, or in front of which things emerged. *Space* actually opened up! And wasn't that exactly what we had been lacking: the ability to penetrate the dancers' very own element: SPACE? Here was the solution! The scales fell from my eyes. Only a three-dimensional film could do justice to Pina's art.[12]

Realizing that he had found the "solution" to his decades-long search, Wenders immediately called Pina from Cannes and told her what luck he had struck. He portrayed 3-D as an absolutely felicitous way to film dance and finally initiate, undertake, and complete the project. Happy to oblige, she adjusted her schedule to stage anew the four pieces both agreed should be at the center of the film, *Café Müller*, *Le Sacre du Printemps*, *Kontakthof* (1978), and *Vollmond* (*Full Moon*, 2006). In the final film, Wenders has also incorporated brief scenes from other pieces, such as *Nur du* (*Only You*, 1996); *Für die Kinder von gestern, heute und morgen* (*For the Children of Yesterday, Today, and Tomorrow*, 2002); *Ten Chi* (2004), *Danzón* (1995), and notably, *Nelken* (*Carnations*, 1982). He also included, sparingly, earlier documentary material, photographs, and film clips, but his intention remained not to make a biographical movie/documentary but to create a very different film about Pina Bausch in collaboration with her dance theater.

Having chanced upon 3-D, which he thought "thrives on space,"[13] Wenders perceived the technology as cutting-edge: a thing of the future—though he knew very well that 3-D had been around since the Lumière brothers. Through a neighbor, François Garnier, Wenders learned about and consulted with Paris-based Alain Derobe (1936–2012), an inventive stereographer and 3-D expert who provided him with exceptional expertise and state-of-the-art equipment to film three dimensionally. While Wenders thought that 3-D would revolutionize the flat screen and 2-D cinema by capturing movement in space with an extraordinary sense of depth, a prospect thrilling to the filmmaker, the first trial shots in Paris gave Wenders such a shock that he did not dare to show them to Pina. As he noted a "highly distressing shortcoming of the medium became apparent. It could manage 'space' [and] create the illusion of great depth," but the depiction of "motion" was clearly unsatisfactory and a filmed body in motion "looked like a Hindu deity, with numerous arms and legs! His movements were jerky, and the stroboscopic effect was extremely unpleasant to the eyes. A fiasco!"[14] Wenders realized that the equipment at hand was not able to "capture the elegant und fluid movements of Pina's dancers."[15] Rigorous testing continued for another year. Derobe improved both technique and apparatus to achieve a better depiction of fluid motion in 3-D. Finally, everything seemed ready, the trucks in Paris loaded with the enormously bulky and heavy equipment and about to depart for Wuppertal, when Pina's death made Wenders abandon the project. Yet the "film *for* Pina" did come about, though with many discoveries that transformed Wenders's filmmaking.

While Wenders was shooting in the fall of 2009, he became aware that James Cameron had used the technique very successfully in his blockbuster science-fiction epic *Avatar* (2009). When he viewed the film later in the year, after most of his shooting had been done, Wenders deemed Cameron's film masterful because of its superb 3-D quality, particularly in the animated figures in the foreground, but he found the 3-D quality lacking in depicting the real human figures in the background.[16] There were other directors working in 3-D around that time as well, such as Werner Herzog with *Cave of Forgotten Dreams*, a 2010 documentary; Martin Scorsese with *Hugo*, a 2010 feature film; and Steven Spielberg with *The Adventures of Tintin*, a 2011 3-D computer animation.

While the concept for their common project had aimed at capturing the dance theater in its delicate and ephemeral aspects, Wenders wanted a different approach for the "film *for* Pina."[17] Pina Bausch had adamantly rejected a biographical film, but wanted instead to document her ensemble in a language that would preserve the dances she had chosen to be featured in the film.[18] Following her death, however, Wenders focused on Pina's gaze, trying to find how she was able to see so differently, how she watched with such precision, patience, and persistence this one thing: the language of dancing bodies. Citing Pina's famous statement, "I'm not interested in how people move, but in what moves them,"[19] he turned his cinematic homage into a search for the secret of Pina's art.

At the outset of shooting in 3-D, Wenders was both anxious and enthused about the new technique. Searching for Pina's distinctive gaze, he turned to the dancers and noticed: "Pina's look [was] still on them."[20] Commenting on the opening of *Le Sacre du Printemps*, Wenders describes one of his "favorite shots," which shows "this figure of a woman in the foreground lying there in such a corporeal sensual presence, and all the other women one by one appearing in the background. It's how they're staggered in space, that's what is giving the image such depth."[21] While extolling the unparalleled depth of the 3-D image, Wenders admitted that the film can be seen on the flat screen as well, though it is not such a "physical experience," and as a "consolation" he acknowledges that the 2-D film image has more definition and a sharper, crisper quality than the 3-D one.[22] Two-dimensional film also seems to have an edge in capturing the moving body, although Wenders claimed that the body gains enormously in volume when filmed in 3-D. Pleased about the great plasticity achieved, he stated that the body in front of the camera appears much more present and real in 3-D. But Wenders conceded that the stage in the Wuppertal Opera house where Pina's four pieces—*Café Müller*, *Le Sacre du Printemps*, *Kontakthof*, and *Full Moon*— were filmed was a rather shallow space, only 20 meters deep from the front to the back of the stage, which significantly limited the 3-D illusion of depth. The shooting on location around Wuppertal, as Bausch had done in her only film, *Die Klage der Kaiserin* (*The Lament of the Empress*, 1989), proved much more 3-D-friendly and conducive to creating the desired illusion of depth and reality.

Considering the new technique, Wenders was thrilled that, unlike conventional documentary filming, 3-D allowed him to be "in the realm of the dancers with space, the space between people, the space between men and women . . . and witness the core, the essence of her [Bausch's] work in an appropriate way. . . . Dancing and 3D are made for each other. I don't think there is any other thing that is so appropriate in 3D than dancing."[23] Wenders reveled in the unique opportunity afforded by 3-D to enter the dancers' space cinematically. Crucial to his aesthetic approach was his willingness to abandon the usually controlling role of film director by putting himself into Pina's place. While he was trying to adopt her gaze, he also followed her method of dealing with her dancers by asking questions.

Pina's gaze was fully audience-oriented, and her dance aesthetics directed the dancers to present themselves to the spectators for the greatest artistic and emotional impact possible. Positioning the 3-D camera where Pina was seated during rehearsals and performances, Wenders privileged her role as the gazing artist, choreographer, and spectator in the house. After a short section of opening credits, Wenders begins the film with a full proscenium view, paying tribute to the audience view that Pina embraced. The look from the back of the auditorium reveals the very stage that was transformed by Bausch's revolutionary dance theater. In reverence, a portrait of her appears at the back of the stage, filmed in a long shot, a typical cinematic establishing shot.

To enter the dancers' realm, Wenders focused on the "most filmic part" of *Le Sacre du Printemps*, which "Pina had directed and choreographed . . . so graphically" that he "just had to shoot it differently . . . in a lot of set-ups much more like in a movie."[24] The crucial difference affecting the film was the use of the huge Derobe-designed 3-D techno crane, the "dinosaur,"[25] which needed to be placed on one side of the auditorium during live performances. However, the crane did not stay put. Its mobility allowed two cameras that were connected with a mirror to reach onto the stage and come near the dancers, both for medium shots of the ensemble and close-ups of individual figures and faces. Wenders was amazed by how the dancers looked straight into the zooming camera, without blinking an eye, which he knows is very difficult even for experienced actors. He then realized that this unflinching gaze was achievable because Pina had prevented all role-playing on stage. She had ensured that the dancers were "truly resting in themselves."[26] In filming a pivotal scene of *Le Sacre*, Wenders made an exception to Pina's strict audience-orientation rule by including a close-up of the male dancer (Andrey Berezin), who selects the sacrificial female, in a reverse angle shot from the stage toward the audience. Specially drawn "flow charts"[27] directed the crane's mobility to make elaborate camera movements rhythmically and cinematically in sync with the dancers' movement in space. While the 3-D technique provides depth, Wenders's moving camera enters the dancers' realm, captures the magical movements in space, and congenially visualizes the secrets of Pina Bausch's art.

The other crucial aspect Wenders adopted was Pina's unique working method of asking her dancers for suggestions to be presented in body language, in movements, and gestures as a way of communicating their feelings and ideas. Pina relied on this communication to transform the autobiographical and elevate the personal into dance art. Supporting and respecting the diverse individuality and aura of her dancers, Pina fostered each dancer's expression of self and made self-presentation the crucial element of collaboration within her ensemble.

On occasion, though, Pina would direct a soloist in an entire dance, such as Lutz Förster's solo dance from *For the Children of Yesterday, Today, and Tomorrow* (2002), a rare departure from her listening and receiving a dancer's ideas and input.[28] Wenders conveys the concept of self-presentation by montaging, intermittently, brief episodes where the camera focuses on individual dancers who look into the camera, but their speaking comes from the off, either in their mother tongue or sometimes in German as a tribute to the language that Pina spoke to them. Wenders wanted these self-presentations to be like the dancers' "inner voices," so that one "could listen to their thoughts"[29]—as does Lutz Förster in reminiscing about an encounter with Pina, who was known for her fastidious staging. After a badly danced rehearsal of *Iphigenie en Tauride* by Gluck, Pina came to his dressing room on the day of the premiere. She did not address the weak dancing. Rather, calling Förster by his nickname "Lüttchen" (a diminuitive of Lutz), she wished him well, whereupon he answered mockingly: "Pinchen, have fun." As Pina left his dressing room, she told him: "Don't forget, you have to scare me!" Förster describes how Pina's words made his head spin, because he felt that the comment was much more to the point than talking for hours about the terrible rehearsal.[30]

The concept of giving space to individuality and self-presentation is something that Wenders employed in his first full-length documentary, *Buena Vista Social Club* (1999), a film about Cuban musicians whom he filmed with a steadycam, often encircling the subject at hand to present him- or herself as storyteller of a life rather than being a mere respondent to an interviewer. *Buena Vista* is enlivened by a rapid film montage that creates a vivid collage of the musicians, colorful Cuban life, and entrancing music-making.

Montage and collage were major methods in Pina's dance theater. What makes Wenders's film so fascinating and visually absorbing is the softening of the cinematic montage that enhances the fluidity, beauty, and elegance of the dances, even when sudden and abrupt movements or repetitive motions seem to counteract the larger flow.

The way Wenders captures the spectrum of movements in the performance of *Le Sacre*, from petrified stillness to ecstatic motion, from fearful expression to calming beauty, is a stunning feat of his cinematic art. As mentioned, much of this spectacle was filmed live in the opera house during regular performances with the heavy techno crane. The two cameras angled at 90 degrees from each other were filming in the same direction via a semi-transparent mirror and synchronized in all functions by eight motors. Despite the detailed flow charts that Wenders designed in advance for the crane and camera movements to create panning, tracking, and zooming shots as well as close-ups, more flexible shooting resulted from 3-D steadicams newly created by Derobe, which facilitated the filming of individual self-presentations or small groups on locations around Wuppertal and the region in 2010. Because 3-D is unforgiving when the slightest mistakes occur, the two cameras have to be in absolute sync down to the pixel. While 3-D simulates what the human eyes are doing, the imitation of human seeing using lateral movements and changing angles requires the 3-D apparatus to accomplish very complicated technological processes. For example, to film natural movement really fluently, the use of fifty frames per second instead of the standard twenty-four frames would improve image quality enormously. But, as Wenders laments, commercial cinemas worldwide and the industry do not provide the projection facilities to accommodate fifty frames per second because of the enormous cost involved. Nevertheless, Wenders believes that "no other film has such a natural, spatial look" as his homage to Pina.[31] Extolling the special depth of 3-D in his film is perhaps too self-serving an assessment.

Pina is a fascinating film because it is a one-of-a-kind moving dance spectacle. There are rich layers of meaning, much beauty, symbolism, and expressions of love and despair, of tenderness and alienation. And the work achieves a rare congruence between film and dance by showing the filmmaker in sync with Pina Bausch's creative depiction of motion and emotion and her search for redemption through dance.

One other creative highlight of Wenders's is his exhortative use of Tanztheater images and scenes as leitmotifs. At the film's beginning, following the homage paid to Pina with the abovementioned photograph at the back of the stage, a fade-in shows Julie Ann Stanzak standing in her underpants, covering her naked upper torso with an accordion. Upon her cheerfully reciting by words and signing by gestures the four seasons—spring, summer, fall, and winter—from *Carnations*, the other dancers appear in a line that snakes across the stage, at times separated by transparent curtains. The pace is *schreiten*, a German word for a solemn, deliberate, and parading gait that is celebratory in its slowness. As the dancers sign the seasons with their arms and hands and smiles on their faces, their pace follows the measured rhythm of Louis Armstrong's revered *West End Blues* (1928). The blues has often been played at funeral processions in New Orleans. Here in *Carnations*, the association with funeral music suggests grieving in what the film calls "mourning work." Appearing several times throughout the film, the moving line of dancers also concludes it. In the very last scene, the entire ensemble walks along the rim of a former mining pit, finally snaking through a long row of totem poles. A memento mori, the scene also gives solace to us with the comforting notion that the dead are not forgotten. As certain as there are the seasons and the cycle of life, human life is continuing even after great losses. Pina's tombstone in Wuppertal bears a memento as well: *Media vita in morte sumus*. A film like *Pina* is reassuring that art creates an afterlife for the artist whose legacy we celebrate.

Notes

1. Donata Wenders and Wim Wenders, *Pina: The Film and the Dancers* (Munich: Schirmer/Mosel, 2012), 245.
2. Wenders and Wenders, *Pina*, 245.
3. Ibid.
4. Wim Wenders, "Wim Wenders über seinen Film *Pina*," interview by Matthias Greuling and Alexandra Zawia, March 30, 2011, *celluloidVideo*, https://www.youtube.com/watch?v=rvsWg4_b9zI. A different version appears in Wim Wenders, *Pina: Dance, Dance, Otherwise We Are Lost*, dir. Wim Wenders (Road Movies, 2011), DVD (The Criterion Collection, 2011), disc 1, audio commentary featuring Wenders, 4:45–6:38.
5. Wenders, *Pina* audio commentary, 26:20–27:20.
6. Wenders, *Pina* audio commentary, 6:20–6:35.
7. Pina Bausch, "Etwas finden, was keiner Frage bedarf. Rede beim '2007 Kyoto Prize Workshop in Arts and Philosophy' am 12. November 2007 in Kyoto," in *O-Ton Pina Bausch. Interviews und Reden*, eds. Stefan Koldehoff and Pina Bausch Foundation (Wädenswil, Switzerland: Nimbus, 2016), 317.
8. Pina Bausch, "Was mich bewegt. Rede aus Anlass der Verleihung des 'Kyoto Preises' am 11. November 2007 in Kyoto," in *O-Ton Pina Bausch*, ed. Koldehoff and Pina Bausch Foundation, 295.

9. Valerie Preston-Dunlop, "Rudolf Laban," *Trinity Laban Conservatoire of Music and Dance*, https://www.trinitylaban.ac.uk/about-us/our-history/%20ivili-laban.html (accessed September 11, 2017).
10. Anne Linsel, *Pina Bausch. Bilder eines Lebens* (Hamburg: Edel Books, 2013), 12–56.
11. Wenders and Wenders, *Pina*, 246.
12. Ibid., 247.
13. Quoted in Jonathan Kahana, ed., *The Documentary Film Reader: History, Theory, Criticism* (Oxford: Oxford University Press, 2016), 995.
14. Wenders and Wenders, *Pina*, 248.
15. Ibid.
16. Ibid., 251.
17. "Wim Wenders Explains the Making of His Film *Pina* (2011)," interview by Zoila Clark, February 12, 2012, *Coral Gables Art Cinema, Florida*, https://www.youtube.com/watch?v=tAtPS2n3tVc.
18. For the following see Wim Wenders, *Pina* disc 1, audio commentary, 57:50–58:44.
19. Wenders, *Pina* disc 1, audio commentary, 57:50–58:44.
20. Wenders, *Pina* disc 2, audio commentary, 5:50–5:51.
21. Wenders, *Pina* disc 1, audio commentary, 4:00–4:19.
22. Wenders, *Pina* disc 1, audio commentary, 4:20–4:28.
23. Wenders, *Pina* disc 2, audio commentary, 12:08–12:55.
24. Wenders, *Pina* disc 1, audio commentary, 10:52–11:10.
25. Wenders and Wenders, *Pina*, 249.
26. Wenders, *Pina* disc 1, audio commentary, 12:30–12:32.
27. For one example see Wenders and Wenders, *Pina*, 250.
28. Wenders, *Pina* disc 1, audio commentary, 41:20–41:22.
29. Wenders, *Pina* disc 2, audio commentary, 15:55–15:57.
30. Wenders, *Pina* disc 1, audio commentary, 40:50–41:19.
31. Wenders, *Pina* disc 2, audio commentary, 17:49–17:50.

Part III

Transnational Wenders

8

Multitrack and Transcultural Narratives in Wim Wenders's Works

Simone Malaguti

"Ah, if I could be all the people in all the places."[1]

From intermediality to interculturality and beyond

Many studies have theorized the central characteristics of Wenders's image-making; his commitment to real and artisanal practices; the relationship between image and storytelling, film and literature, film and the arts; autobiographical influences; ways to preserve a sense of authenticity and autoreferentiality; and the ease with which he is able to handle images, even those that are full of affliction. Frequently, Wenders theorizes these practices in his own publications or interviews. This chapter proposes an analysis of Wim Wenders as an itinerant author from the point of view of transcultural practices. Wim Wenders's films, photos, and writings are shaped by multitrack narratives and have been capturing the interest of researchers in various disciplines as operating increasingly intermedially, transmedially, and multidisciplinarily. In addition to those central characteristics, his early films already contained specific features that are now clearly visible throughout his entire body of works, including mobile subjects; wandering characters; traveling men and women; a juxtaposition of places, cultural awareness, comparisons between landscapes, reminiscences of visited places; and so on. Through these elements, Wenders directly draws our attention to his own biography since he is known for often changing his residence while working in different languages and places. His films and personal journey clearly move beyond what Jan Blommaert called the "one language—one culture assumption"[2] and reveal an openness and success in operating not only across media but also among different places, languages, and social groups. In many films by Wenders, the unsettled way of living is closely connected with medial competencies. In fact, his works are largely as multimodal as they are transcultural.

Wenders summarizes his love of filmmaking in the following way: "The wonderful thing about filmmaking is not only that you are practically in touch with all forms of art, but that you can express experience."[3] As I have asserted elsewhere,[4] he outlines two main approaches that help us to understand his filmmaking and his general artistic position. First, he highlights the fundamental dialogue between film and "all forms of art," suggesting that film is a comparatively more open medium that borrows from and transforms art of all types. Secondly, Wenders sees film as a medium that records one's experience in a certain manner, time, and place. By recording experiences with all their pictorial energy, film saves cultural representation, storing *and* forwarding "culture" in the process. And these two approaches are interlinked: as Wenders's interest in "all forms of art" crosses spatial borders, the intermedial transformation is accompanied by transcultural elements and intercultural reflection. In fact, considering his filmography and preferences comprehensively, it is hard to say what comes first in his works: intermediality or interculturality.

The material culture of any given place may offer Wenders a substrate or a central theme for his work and can sometimes serve as a unique starting point for one of his films, photos, or writings. Wenders's work often reaches "other" places and then collects them, reflects on them, and shows them in a dislocated way. This dislocated viewing leads to a more dynamic viewing experience of the work since it shows other places in a manner that is drastically different and more fragile than originally conceived. Spatial references and places play a great role in his films that foreground not only physical locations (Paris, Texas; Berlin; Tokyo; Palermo) but also more symbolic locations (*Schauplätze*, the "room" of *Chambre 666*, the end of the world, or Aranjuez). His fictional narratives cover a great deal of spatial dislocation: in *Until the End of the World*, for example, Claire and Sam travel around the globe, passing through Berlin, Lisbon, Moscow, Tokyo, San Francisco, and Australia. In *Alice in the Cities*, Philip Winter is in the United States, and in Holland before later arriving in Germany. Later, in *Lisbon Story* (1994), the same character travels from Frankfurt to Lisbon, learns Portuguese while driving, and is surprised by his new experiences there. In this sense, a privileged portion of Wenders's works is devoted to developing an understanding of the sense of place.[5]

Cinema and the sense of place

In his role as a visual critic, Wenders takes great care to ensure that his depictions of a given place capture the unique texture of that place. This is meant to stand in opposition to a tendency in contemporary visual culture to sanitize local differences through cheap reproduction. His vision of places emits a peculiar aura which can trigger emotions that he feels are worthy of eliciting.[6] Wenders is thus engaged with a sense of place, understood as people's feelings and beliefs toward a place. Since the physical landscape can also affect how people organize their way of living, habits, and interpersonal communication, one might associate individuals and groups with a particular locality or place.

Even beyond these definitions, Wenders recognizes the important role that places play in cinema. For him, storing the physical reality of a given place is as much a distinctive characteristic of cinema as mixing media is.[7] Cinema is viewed as a form of archive of real places and of the elements belonging to them at that time: it stores the history of a place, its geography, and its material culture, including its archaeology, topography, monuments, memory, preserved or destroyed areas. Cinema can also recreate a place and keep it alive.

Wenders illustrates this clearly in *Lisbon Story*. Zé, a Portuguese boy, explains why Fritz, the filmmaker, is working in an area where houses might be demolished soon: "He [Fritz] says, these houses down there, when they are all swiped away, disappearing, the stories that they are hiding, they have to come then in the light."[8] If Fritz had not filmed theses houses and their people, this place would have remained anonymous and nonexistent. Humanity would have had one less story to tell, and, worse than that, humanity would have had one less story from which to draw more understanding about its own existence. Consequently, storytelling is necessarily place-bound, both socially and culturally, and influenced by media.

A recent essay by Pablo G. P. de Campos Martins contemplates the perception of places and spaces in *Slow Homecoming*, Wenders's unpublished screenplay and literary adaptation of Handke's text.[9] The essay highlights Wenders's phenomenological ability to describe landscapes extensively in such a way that the main character, the scientist Sorger, seems to disappear or to be just a detail. Sorger observes the nature and landscapes around him with different equipment and media. Although each piece of equipment evokes a different feeling in Sorger, the camera's main target is the places around Sorger: "If we had to resume *Slow Homecoming*, we could argue that this is a history of an absent character between present places and spaces."[10] For instance, the opening scene of the screenplay is long, with the locations or places involved in the film explored by the camera in some detail before the camera finally reaches the main character. By taking this approach, Wenders intends to capture images with the camera in order to translate the sense of those places and he can consequently generate an aesthetic experience of those locations. Since each medium (e.g., radio, photo camera, book, telescope) translates a situation or a place differently, using a variety of equipment renders the sense of place even more complete. Wenders's adaptation embraces so many different media and locations—urban spaces, natural parks, small cities from Alaska, other places in the United States as well as in Europe—that it brings "subtle perception" to the fore.[11]

When considering Wenders's photobooks, picture-stories, essays, and conversations, we can call his body of work a transcultural journey of sorts. Starting in Munich, his very early films bring viewers to a European city while simultaneously making very clear musical and pictorial references to America—so much so that one might almost believe they were seeing American landscapes. Sometimes the German backland is put in conversation with American culture, which might create a kind of cultural contrast or even culture shock. This dynamic way of showing places side by side becomes a common theme throughout his later works. Spectators are taken to several destinations inside Germany, Europe, and the United States, and then continue onward into other countries and continents including Australia, Japan, the Soviet Union, Armenia, Jerusalem, Canada, Cuba, and Brazil. At this point, we can consider that Wim Wenders's sense of place is connected with individuals moving through different places, countries, and continents and involved with several different communities. By doing this, Wenders develops multimodal settings and explores multitrack narratives, for example, multilingual and multimedial.

If we want a deeper understanding of Wenders as a multimodal author, it is important to analyze his films from the transcultural perspective suggested by language ecologists and intercultural film studies. This approach argues that the constant uprooting and changing of places by authors and writers can often leave different marks in their works. It also reflects upon personal interaction with the social environment affecting the body of works of artists when they move from one place to another and are confronted with multiple codes and cultural identities as well as their struggle with different social values, cultures, and memories.[12] Gesine Schiewer sees particularities in their styles in three ways: First, they often express thoughts through options, referred to in German as "optionales Denken."[13] Next, there is a refusal to practice one-dimensional thinking and a tendency to embrace a plethora of perspectives in works, or "Denken wie üblich und eindimensionales Denken werden vermieden."[14] Finally, they share a sense of change and displacement because of their moving around, or "Ortswechsel des Denkens."[15] Claire Kramsch also believes that the increasing circulation of people among different places on the globe has impacted multidimensional communication: "The twenty-first century is all about meaning, relations, creativity, subjectivity, historicity and the trans- as in translingual and transcultural competence."[16] According to Kramsch's concept of "symbolic competence," subjects who are used to these changes and mixtures of language and culture display the ability to (1) deal with various linguistic codes and spatial and temporal resonances, (2) associate emotions with the use of a given language, (3) perform and construct various historicities while in dialogue with others, (4) manipulate conventional categories by creating and performing alternative realities, and (5) reframe human thoughts and actions in order to change the social context. Recent approaches to film have also begun proposing looking beyond the specificities of the medium and into what has been deemed "lived realities"—that is, the reality of life itself and the corporeal, personal engagement on the part of individuals (crew, cast, director) as a means to "bridge the divide between studies of aesthetics and culture."[17]

Given the fact that Wenders himself and his body of work have both made a journey around the globe and tend to operate—*diegetically* or not—among several places, I find it empowering to investigate particularities explored by the abovementioned language ecologists and film interculturalists in Wenders's works. I have charted at least three different ways in which narrative in Wenders's body of work can be analyzed, and below I offer interpretations by applying aspects of the theoretical framework to some of his films, photos, and picture-stories.

Overcoming a one-dimensional way of thinking

The film *Alice in the Cities* (1974) follows Philip and his struggles to break with his one-dimensional way of thinking. He is so encapsulated in his own world that he cannot establish contact with others or things that could bring him to write. Philip is also incapable of "hearing" or paying attention to what someone has to say. This glaring incapability becomes more evident when he meets his ex-girlfriend in her apartment. His inability to hear her is also his inability to develop a feeling for her place or for the outside. Although he has left his place (Germany), he has just "transferred" his beliefs and attitudes to the new land (the United States) without reflecting on them and their worth. The scenes showing Philip using his Polaroid camera and his constant peering through windows (car, hotels, bars) is a metaphor for the cultural process going on in Philip during his travels. He takes many pictures of the American landscape and the objects in it not because he is interested in engaging with another place but because he wants immediate confirmation of his way of thinking. The sheer number of those shots points to a kind of profusion of this dimension that inhibits him and his tendency not to care about what is outside his dimension.

This unresolved tension is culturally and historically explained as a metaphor for postwar European history, and specifically the generation of Germans searching for a new identity in the years after the Second World War. The difficulty of being productive is somewhat justified by the difficulty of finding some form of identification in the world outside. The postwar European generation's new project was also to break with the romantic ideal, which held a "one language—one culture assumption."

In *Once*, Wenders describes *Alice in the Cities* as about "a man who had set out in search of the world, all the while protecting himself from the world with the help of polaroids."[18] Philip can only break his trance once he meets Alice, to a large extent because he has to take care of her. After taking up the mantle to support Alice, he is stripped of his ability to protect himself from the outside world and finally learns a new way of expressing himself, which frees him to finally write again. Throughout the film, the characters constantly move and exchange places, languages, and roles in order to solve their problems. While the search for a place is important, the search for a position in that place seems to be the most significant one taken. The protagonists engage not only in a change of place but also in a longing for old places and the emotions that come with each of those places. The travels of Philip and Alice have them practicing their sense of place, particularly for Philip since traveling reminds him that the self is not a sole unit. It has to be at least two: his own eyes and the more objective eyes of others, in this case, Alice. Philip's destiny is changed as soon as he activates his dialogical imagination. A similar approach is used in *Wrong Move* (1975), *Palermo Shooting* (2008), and, more recently, *Every Thing Will Be Fine* (2015). These films also showcase how a planned or unexpected change of place can impact the destinies of individual people.

Lisbon Story is an impressive variation of this topic, taking the romanticized, German Philip in *Alice in the Cities* and transforming him into a postmodern European figure. The Phillip (with a letter added to his name) in *Lisbon Story* is a sound engineer capturing impressions of Lisbon. Along the journey, Phillip is again confronted with kids, yet this time he can hear and is much more receptive to what is going on around him. Yet still, the traveling scenes in America are important as they highlight a latent violence simmering within the original Philip, for instance, when he hits and screams at the radio or destroys a TV. Many wide shots on the way to Portugal exemplify an oversensitivity in Phillip and his relationship with spatial dislocation. Whereas the Philip in *Alice* does not really care about what is going on around him in America, he (the Phillip on his way to or in Lisbon) enjoys sensing the new, united Europe. He also reflects about the possibilities of this new place, concluding that it is unfortunately founded on an "old place" (Europe). Yet in *Lisbon Story*, we see a new Phillip, with a mind open to rediscovering this old place by learning Portuguese during the road trip and even starting small conversations with people around him.

Portugal was once seen as a symbol of prosperity to other European nations, but in recent years, the country and its language have fallen into relative obscurity. In spite of this, Phillip decides to go there because he feels that his friend, Fritz, and the country itself are representative of a new situation inside the European Union. The understanding of Portugal as a new place represents the generation that could completely dismantle and replace the old one as a promise to develop a new citizenship based on the union of several languages, cultures, and economies. It is a promise of more social support, welfare, social mobility, and lower taxes, too. For this new European project, the people and places inside of the European Union should all stand up for one another so that citizens can always feel at home even when outside of their native countries. Pessoa's writing on the wall of Phillip's bedroom *Ah, não ser eu toda a gente e toda a parte* (Ah, if I could be all the people in all the places) succinctly depicts the essence of this new project.

However, this quote also represents Wenders's concern about this project in a very poetic way, highlighting a doubt that people are capable of leaving their comfort zones in order to understand one another. Is there a way to solve one-dimensional thinking and our own sense of place in the eyes of others? Wenders's body of work at least makes an attempt to deal with this question and reflect on it meaningfully.

Multiple scales

The lessons learned from that isolated self in *Alice in the Cities* are echoed in the picture-stories of *Once* as what Wenders himself has dubbed "double evidence."[19] "Double evidence" represents Wenders's aesthetic efforts to operate on multiple levels and scales while expressing himself by showing different viewpoints of the same experience. For instance, the line "Alice wanted to give me double evidence that I, too, was still around"[20] is followed by pictures shot during the production of *Alice in the Cities*. One of them is a close-up of Wenders looking directly into the camera. The next photos show Yella Rottländer, who plays the girl Alice, displaying the exact same photo as Wenders did to the camera in reverse angle. By approximating fictional and real elements, such as Philip's comment "Polaroids do have something to do with proof" or Alice's dialogue with Philip about taking pictures, this picture-story exemplifies how Wenders operates through images and language on "multiple levels of reality and fiction."[21] This strategy is also used in another picture-story: "Once . . . I went to a screening of *Paris, Texas* together with Harry Dean Stanton in an awfully long limo. Even in the middle of New York, Harry was still Travis, sitting in the back of his brother's car and travelling through the desert in silence."[22] The picture in this story shows Harry Dean Stanton sitting inside the limo and looking through the window, just the same way as he was shot in a few scenes of *Paris, Texas*.

This way of operating through pictures and language on many levels of reality and fiction serves as an introduction to exploring Wenders's ability to construct multiple scales of space in which dissimilar—and sometimes distant—places are somehow connected with one another. *Once* has several different examples:

> "I entered Australia via Thailand and Indonesia, through the backdoor, so to speak."[23]
> "I flew from Paris to Tokyo. At the time there were no direct flights yet, you had to stopover in Moscow."[24]
> "I walked all the way from Salzburg to Venice, across the Alps."[25]

These quotes almost distract our attention from how cartographical they are because of the way they are expressed. The surplus of places mentioned in these short sentences seems to approximate them when they are uttered in this unusual manner. Wenders deviates from the final destination in each, challenging us to think about the places in-between.

According to an ecological view of language usage, such optional and multiple practices mean not only what is in fact expressed but also an elision—a lack of information. In other words, such utterances embody remembered or projected verbalization kept only for the subject—in the sense that mentioning these places only brings up feelings and ideas about them to the people that have been there.[26] The sentence "I entered Australia through the backdoor" highlights this practice: it sounds like a not-so-explicitly stated critique of the sociocultural status of the Asian-Australian border, satirizing the idea that it has a front door and a broadly spread skyline in the south. Such multiple scales of space are also common in *Alice in the Cities* and *Until the End of the World*, where protagonists travel and move from one city, country, or continent to another a great deal.

The display of multiple scales of space is not exclusively used in fiction or in memories. In the documentary film *Salt of the Earth*, several places are connected through Salgado's biography and photographic works. Since Salgado's photos and film scenes are revisited in the documentary film, the viewer is taken on a trip around the world. The film not only shows Salgado's masterpieces from different continents but also translates the social structures and historical dimensions of Salgado's relocations and work sites (Brazil, Paris, England, Africa, Balkans, the Russian Arctic, Asia, and then back to Brazil). The constructed scale of places is not about a simple journey around the globe; it is an allegory for a journey around a world in crisis. It also stands for political resistance, the refusal to accept social spaces and societal norms, the repudiation of business motivations, and environmental protections.

In opposition to this overwhelming and exotic world journey in the film about Salgado, the main location in *Pina* (2011) remains Wuppertal, a small German city close to where the dancer Pina Bausch was born. The multiple scales are now constructed by different people who travel to one specific place. Despite the remote location, Bausch maintained her company in Wuppertal and insisted in engaging dancers coming from different parts of the world "to avoid anything explicit" and as a principle of "semiodiversity and untranslability."[27] Diversity, a principle of Bausch's dance and work, is also the main basis for Wenders's project about Pina. In the film, the dancers are the main characters. They pay homage to their teacher in their mother tongue (in nine different languages) and in their own body language. The soundtrack is performed in various languages and styles. The book about the film is also available in different languages.

Whereas Salgado, the main "character" of *Salt of the Earth*, had to leave his home country located in the periphery of the world in order to "conquer" it from another position and place, *Pina* shows how a European woman brings "allegorical multilingualism"[28] to her new place of residence. In *Salt of the Earth*, the Brazilian photographer narrates his biography in French and Portuguese accompanied by close-up photos of him. The film matches this with images and a harmonic narration. *Pina*, in contrast, is narrated by several different media and modes—bodies, movements, dances, music, places, stage, pieces of clothing, colors, noises, and so forth. David Gramling explains that *Pina* is "a disorientingly multimodal film. . . . Such hybrid, multimodal linguistic landscapes throughout the film obfuscate viewers' decoding effort—not only by aesthetic design, but also by virtue of the recalcitrant and multiscalar indexicality of semiotic diversity in public space."[29] These ways of showing space on multiple scales in association with cultural memories brings me to the last type of method through which Wenders operates in between places.

Reframing contexts and changing one's position in the world

Wenders's photo-poems, "Meteorite Crater, West Australia, 1988"[30] and "Ferris Wheel, Armenia, 2008,"[31] illustrate how one place becomes another as soon as the subject changes his position in the world. The crater was no longer a crater as soon as the photographer and writer walked over it. In the same way, the big wheel in Armenia, apparently a sign of fun and freedom, turns out to be a contradiction in the reverse angle since it stands near the quarters of the Soviet occupying force. This kind of juxtaposition refers to the relativity in the meaning of cultural memories embodied in places despite their nature—landmarks, skylines, squares, parks. By moving, Wenders reframes the previous pattern, dissolves its meaning, and changes the reality of a place.

The title of the film *Paris, Texas* is another attempt at reframing the context of a place. In the film, Paris is referred to as the location from a photograph of a vacant lot in Texas owned by a man named Travis. His obsession with the town is based on the notion that he may have been conceived there. In this sense, *Paris, Texas* synthesizes Travis's loneliness and desire to come to terms with himself. However, it can also be a metaphor for so many of Wenders's physical and imaginary relocations as well as of his transatlantic reflections about the differences between the European and American ways of life—a perspective he often mentions in his interviews.

On the other hand, in his photo-poem "Once . . . I spent some time in Pittsburgh, Pennsylvania," Wenders equates his hometown to that American city, saying, "it smelled exactly like in the city of Oberhausen, in the Ruhr district where I grew up."[32] He follows up this poem with black-and-white pictures of inexpensive buildings made of brick and stone, ads for Coca Cola, coffee, beer, pizza, and donuts similar to what we see in *Alice in the Cities*. Through the socio-ecological view of language, this way of sensing places could be an example of expanding or evolving symmetry, meaning the ability to develop place patterns which are self-similar on different scales. This pattern is also found in the picture-poem "Once . . . Potsdam reminded me of Lisbon"; "and Lisbon of the Germany of my childhood."[33] This story is followed by several pictures of Lisbon and Potsdam, which again look like the brick walls and buildings seen in Oberhausen.

We see more recent examples of this way of thinking about places in *Inventing Peace*—Wenders's publication with Mary Zournazi.[34] In the text "on a train of thought," Wenders is completely aware of where he is physically and geographically, sitting in a train in Australia. However, as soon as he senses where he is, as soon as he feels movement in space, he starts reflecting about his former stays and experiences in Berlin, the Congo, and Cuba. The texts in this book are particularly expressive because in most of them Wenders also performs his own social and cultural background, demonstrating his understanding of others in their own places and positions as well.

Conclusion

In a world characterized by the increasing movement of people as a result of decreased economic opportunity, political tension, work demands, or lifestyle, the way that people and groups feel or sense new places in a more globalized, multilingual, interconnected space is relevant. If we consider Wim Wenders a representative of this new world, the analysis of his body of work gives us some insight about narrative practices formed by spatial dislocation. The socio-ecological language approach helps us to explore the cultural and aesthetic experience of transnational authors like Wenders and to find answers to questions such as: How do such authors, who shift from one language or place to another, describe their worldview? What is particular in their works? On the one hand, we have a cultural generation project: Wenders's postwar generation wishes to break with the "one language—one culture assumption" and does this by vigorously experimenting with languages and cultures, crossing any border that can be surpassed. On the other hand, this project has aesthetic implications, mixing all forms of arts and innovating into the postwar period.

If we pursue the "intercultural project," we will indeed find out that Wenders's works are concerned with matters of cultural understanding, *Landeskunde* (or what French people call *cours de civilization*, i.e., the people and culture of a place), cultural or intercultural shock, language learning, and multilingualism. The Pessoa quote "Ah, if I could be all the people in all the places" in *Lisbon Story* reflects the extent of such a project—that is, if only we are given the possibility of reaching all people in their own places personally, we can understand them (better). Being everywhere physically is almost an impossible mission, but could texts and media help us to be in all the places and learn what places have to tell us?

Considering Wenders's spatial way of thinking, we might also find in him a critic of places, a thinker concerned about the general importance of places for humankind. For Wenders, places have stories waiting to be "captured." In *Lisbon Story*, the philosopher says that humans are different from animals because humans can "capture" stories and tell them. Places embody stories, and film is a tool for storytelling. Cultural understanding also depends on stories. Wenders transposes mere "cultural awareness" in his body of work by operating between and among places, with multiple scales and optional ways of thinking. By connecting places and showing them in relation to each other or side by side through intermediality and a complex "multiscalar indexicality of semiotic diversity," as Gramling put it, Wenders reflects on and shows how permeable and connected places indeed are (in opposition to ideologies based on nations, frontiers or political-economic spaces which still give the impression that the world is disconnected).

Salt of the Earth and *Pina* are emblematic examples of multitrack and transcultural narratives and to some extent of how one tries to be in all places. The subjects of these films also have their lives threaded together by dislocation, code switching, and interculturality. Thus, this chapter has implications for sensing places as a communicative strategy and for the combination of intermediality and interculturality as a means to "bridge the divide between studies of aesthetics and culture."[35] No matter whether we are analyzing films, picture-stories, or conversations, the many examples of films or photos discussed earlier call for a vigilant attitude toward one's movements between and among places. These examples also propose instances of sensing places (lack of, surplus of, reflectivity about, searching for) and of what Pierre Bourdieu called the "sense of one's place" as a "sense of the place of others."[36] With this in mind, Wenders offers examples of how he uses his resources for making and communicating meaning in a postmodern world. When Wenders changes his position in the world or when he changes media, he considers his entire repertoire. Is this possibly the starting point for talking about intermediality or image-making in his works? Instead of putting aside languages, cultures, identities, memories, knowledge, acquaintances, and experiences, Wenders considers them and lets his body of work be shaped by them.

Notes

1 "Triumphal Ode" by Álvaro de Campos (Fernando Pessoa's heteronym) quoted in *Lisbon Story* (1994).
2 Jan Bloommaert, *Discourse: A Critical Introduction* (Cambridge: Cambridge University Press, 2005), 216. With the expression "one language—one culture assumption," Bloomaert means the belief of "the radical version of relativism or Herderianism. All cultures are equal; but all cultures function perfectly only within the confines of their historical region of origin. Transgression of cultural boundaries, for instance through migration or intermarriage, leads to the distortion of a natural order and therefore to conflicts" (199). The "one language—one culture assumption" suggests that any given culture is homogenous, uniform, and territory-bound. For instance, one language belongs (only) to one culture (or vice versa). This expression rejects the possibilities of cultural mix, cultural change or coexistences of languages or cultural practices.
3 Wim Wenders, "In Defense of Places," in *Wim Wenders: A Sense of Place*, ed. Daniel Bickermann (Frankfurt/Main: Verlag der Autoren, 2005), 176.
4 Simone Malaguti, *Wim Wenders' Filme und ihre intermediale Beziehung zur Literatur Peter Handkes* (Frankfurt/Main: Peter Lang, 2008), 77.
5 At least since his essay "In Defense of Places," Wenders has been known not only as a defender of images but also as an intentional researcher and defender of places. This might be one of the reasons why he is an itinerant author and self-described "traveler and globe-trotter." Moreover, Wenders does not confine his experiences as a globe-trotter to his private life: his body of works also narrates his several trips around the world.

6 Wim Wenders, "Auf der Suche nach Bildern. Orte sind meine stärksten Bildgeber," in *Iconic Turn: die Neue Macht der Bilder*, ed. Christa Maar and Hubert Burda (Köln: DuMont Literatur und Kunst Verlag, 2004), 285.
7 Wim Wenders, *The Act of Seeing: Texte und Gespräche* (Frankfurt/Main: Verlag der Autoren, 1992), 53.
8 *Lisbon Story* [00:46:21].
9 Pablo G. P. de Campos Martins, "As Espirais dos Arquivos: Lento Retorno e as Paisagens de um Filme sem Telas," *Galáxia* (São Paulo) no. 33 (2016): 94–106, doi: 10.1590/1982-25542016225353.
10 de Campos Martins, "As Espirais dos Arquivos," 96.
11 Ibid., 97.
12 Einar Haugen, "The Ecology of Language," in *The Ecology of Language: Essays by Einar Haugen*, ed. Anwar S. Dil (Stanford: Stanford University Press, 1972); Modern Languages Assocation Ad Hoc Committee on Foreign Languages, "Foreign Languages and Higher Education: New Structures for a Changed World," *Profession* 12 (2007): 234–35. www.mla.org/Resources/Research/Surveys-Reports-and-Other-Documents/Teaching-Enrollments-and-Programs/Foreign-Languages-and-Higher-Education-New-Structures-for-a-Changed-World
13 Gesine Lenore Schiewer, "Interkulturelle Philologie am Beispiel der Interpretation von Chamisso-Literatur—Ansätze der Linguistik unter Berücksichtigung der Mehrsprachigkeitsforschung," in *Literatur interpretieren. Interdisziplinäre Beiträge zur Theorie und Praxis*, ed. Jan Borkowksi, Stefan Descher, Felicitas Ferder, and Phillipp Heine (Münster: Mentis, 2015), 371.
14 This phrase was used by Gesine Lenore Schiewer in an unpublished call for papers for a 2013 conference, "Chamisso-Literatur: eine 'Nomadisierung der Moderne?' Interdisziplinäre Perspektive der Interkulturalitätsforschung," http://www.chamisso.daf.uni-muenchen.de/index.html
15 This final point is relevant to French scholar François Jullien and his exploration of changes in attitudes and points of view accompanied by one's change of geographical place. François Jullien, *Ein Umweg über China. Ein Ortswechsel des Denkens* (Berlin: Merve, 2001); see also Ulfried Reichardt, *Globalisierung: Literaturen und Kulturen des Globalen* (Berlin: Akademie Verlag, 2011), 64.
16 Claire Kramsch, "Ecological Perspectives on Foreign Language Education," *Language Teaching* 41, no. 3 (2008): 405, 400.
17 Kramsch, "Ecological Perspectives on Foreign Language Education," 400.
18 Wim Wenders, *Once: Pictures and Stories* (Munich: Schirmer/Mosel and D. A. P., 2010), 168.
19 Wenders, *Once*, 168.
20 Ibid., 128–29.
21 Kramsch, "Ecological Perspectives on Foreign Language Education," 391.

22 Ibid., 128–29.
23 Ibid., 18.
24 Ibid., 36.
25 Ibid., 92.
26 Kramsch, "Ecological Perspectives on Foreign Language Education," 392.
27 David Gramling, "Seven Types of Multilingualism: Or, Wim Wenders Enfilms Pina Bausch," in *The Multilingual Screen: New Reflection on Cinema and Linguistic Difference*, ed. Tijana Mamula and Lisa Patti (New York: Bloomsbury Academic, 2016), 49.
28 Gramling, "Seven Types of Multilingualism," 49.
29 Ibid.
30 Beat Wismer, "Wim Wenders, Photographer: Some Introductory Remarks," in *4 Real & True 2! Wim Wenders: Landscapes, Photographs*, ed. Wim Wenders and Beat Wismer (Munich: Schirmer/Mosel, 2015), 74.
31 Wismer, "Wim Wenders, Photographer," 273–83.
32 Ibid., 172–77.
33 Ibid., 240, 244.
34 Wim Wenders and Mary Zournazi, *Inventing Peace: A Dialogue on Perception* (London: I.B. Tauris, 2013).
35 Lucia Nagib, *Impure Cinema: Intermedial and Intercultural Approaches to Film* (London: I.B. Tauris, 2014). Back cover.
36 Pierre Bourdieu, "Social Space and Symbolic Power," *Sociological Theory* 7, no. 1 (1989): 19.

"I Can Imagine Anything": The European Project in Wim Wenders's *Wings of Desire*

Mine Eren

> When the child was a child,
> Berries filled its hand as only *berries* do,
> and do even now,
> Fresh *walnuts* made its tongue raw,
> and do even now,
> it had, on every mountaintop,
> the *longing* for a higher mountain yet,
> and in every city,
> the *longing* for an even greater city,
> and that is still so,
> It reached for *cherries* in topmost branches of *trees*
> with an elation it still has today,
> has a shyness in front of strangers,
> and has that even now.
> It awaited the first *snow*,
> And waits that way even now.
> —Last strophe from "Song of a Childhood" by Peter Handke (emphasis mine)

Before stepping into time, Wim Wenders's angel Damiel in *Wings of Desire* (1987) reveals to his companion angel Cassiel how he imagines the first day of his worldly *Dasein*.

> "First I'll take a bath," he says, "Then I'll get a shave from a Turkish barber, if possible, who'll also massage me down to the fingertips. Then I'll buy a newspaper and read it from headlines to horoscope. . . . I'll be familiar to everyone and suspect to no one. I won't say a word, but I'll understand every language. That will be my first day."

This scene, shot in black and white, switches then to color when Damiel finally takes the plunge. The bodily sensation of gravity is foregrounded when a piece of Damiel's bronze angelic armor falls with a thud on his head. Tasting the blood on his fingers and noticing the color red, he later points at the graffiti on the Berlin Wall, blanketed with painted human faces, asking a stranger to help him identify all the other colors. Damiel, who seems to be reverted to a childlike state, enjoys this game of learning and discovery. It is as if he has stepped into a whole new world, experiencing Berlin's culture anew, almost a cathartic moment, when the artsy background with the colorful faces reveals itself as a world of plenitude. No longer stuck in black-and-white eternity, Damiel finally experiences the taste of coffee and the feeling of rubbing his hands together.

The next long take, a minute and a half long, is emblematic of the theme established at the end of Wenders's film. In this single street-tracking shot, initiated by the line "When the child was a child," the last strophe of Peter Handke's "Song of Childhood" (see above), the fallen angel has now taken on the role of a flâneur, wandering on foot through the city's streets. The camera follows Damiel, still carrying his armor under his arm, as he enters the *Oranienstraße*, a street located in the Kreuzberg district (Figure 9.1). Damiel passes an ordinary "Berliner," a Turkish migrant, who is helping his child out of the car, taking the child into his arms, and then looks toward Damiel and the moving camera. While the (male) voiceover reads Handke's poem and dominates the film's visual, the encounter with the Turkish father is marked by the use of nondiegetic sound. Here, the film draws the viewer's attention to the interaction between the sonic

Figure 9.1

image and the visual one. In the background plays "Karlı Kayın Ormanında" ("In the Snowy Night Woods"), a piece composed by Zülfü Livaneli, a popular Turkish musician, composer, and writer. Regarded as a "lefty" cult song within Turkish culture, the song was composed for a poem of the same title by Nazım Hikmet which begins with the line "The beeches deep in snow, I walk the dark woods."[1] In the center of the poem are feelings of loss, mourning, and sorrow. Described as the first modern Turkish poet and a "loving" and "romantic revolutionary,"[2] Nazım Hikmet was frequently arrested for his political beliefs and spent much of his life in prison.[3] He wrote "In the Snowy Night Woods" in the writers' colony of Peredelkino in Moscow in 1956, where he died in exile in 1963. The poet, who said that he would like to be buried under a tree in an Anatolian village, turns his aching nostalgia for his native land and long-lost youth into a distant dream: "Is my country farthest away, or my youth or the stars?" In Wenders's Kreuzberg scene, Peter Handke's poem, with its imagery of snow, trees, cherries, walnuts and longing, offers literary allusions to Hikmet's poetry in exile years.[4] This sonic reference becomes a metaphor for Berlin's own history of exile and displacement—as well as for Turkish immigrants, for whom Turkey still holds the "status of a geographical origin myth," to use Jenny White's phrase, that is "kept alive through the dream of final return."[5]

Wenders's early work was influenced by America, and although he lived there more than a decade, it was never, as the director explains, an exile for him.[6] Considering himself "purely [an] image maker" at the beginning of his career,[7] uprootedness becomes a dominant theme in his films of the 1970s.[8] His characters are permanently in search of something, a "lost homeland," as Daniela Berghahn explains.[9] In the footage described earlier, aided by the utopian power of Hikmet's lyrics, Wenders frames "a city in exile," and guides the viewer's eye, to reiterate the director, to "something that seems so palpably there when you arrive in Berlin: a feeling in the air and under your feet and in people's faces that makes life in this city so different from life in other cities."[10] Divided and held captive in the ideological confusion of the Cold War, when the world was trying to understand the past and the Holocaust, 1980s Berlin became, as Thomas Mohnike proposes in his study of Nordic literature, an "island of subversiveness" for the artistic imagination, and its alternative culture and art offered "laboratories for new post-capitalist utopia."[11]

When I first encountered Wenders's *Der Himmel über Berlin* (which translates literally as *The Sky over Berlin*, although it was given the English title *Wings of Desire*), I was fascinated and puzzled: How does the director playfully connect national and diasporic identity without favoring one over the other? What was it about Wenders's film that allowed me, from the position of a (female) nondominant viewer, to participate in the film's renegotiation of national identity? Why was I less critical of Wenders's imagery of traditional Turkish femininity despite its visual similarity to representations that constructed the image of the oppressed and victimized migrant woman in pre-1989 German cinema?[12] And, what made me think that Wenders's film consisted of moments that allowed spectators to step into the film's diegesis so that they could envision themselves as part of Wenders's "imagined community" and hence of a "post-capitalist utopia"?[13]

Wenders's film would seem like an odd choice of text for a postcolonial feminist reading. Yet *Wings of Desire* is unique in its experimentation with point of view. My intention here is to discuss how the European project emerges in Wenders's preunification film. The film's release coincides with the era of Helmut Kohl—Germany's chancellor from 1982 to 1998—who declared that Germany was not a "country of immigration" and was renowned for his restrictive minority policies.[14] Read within this context, *Wings of Desire* seems radical in offering a convincing transnational narrative of German identity. This is achieved by what I will call Wenders's *fluid* and *inclusive cosmopolitan gaze*. Wenders's cosmopolitan vision resembles the ideas of philosopher Kwame Anthony Appiah.[15] Appiah proposes that cosmopolitanism is to be conceived of neither as liberal universalism (i.e., the idea of imposing one's values onto others) nor as cultural relativism (i.e., the belief that cultural differences cannot be bridged).[16] For Appiah, our responsibilities for others extend beyond those people who are connected to us through kinship and citizenship. Wenders's cinema, as I shall demonstrate, endorses this idea without imposing a set of values on others. Rather than working with a simplistic model of monolithic German identity, his film proposes the idea of *Heimat* as inclusive concept. A close look at certain scenes will illustrate the director's use of a variety of cinematic techniques to offer a distinct viewing experience for the spectator, allowing him or her to perceive in Wenders's presentation *a culture of coexistence*.

Wenders's Berlin: "*Schau*-Platz der Begegnung" (Theater of Encounter)

The English translation for *Schauplatz* is "location," although the word's literal translation from German is "showplace," implying an invitation for an outside viewer to look and see the particularities of a given place. In *Wings of Desire*, Berlin signifies this meaning: the film showcases Berlin by putting it and "the world in a box" so that the peculiarities of angelic and circus life, as well as the everyday life of ordinary people, can be uncovered.[17] The filmgoer becomes part of Wenders's *Stammpublikum*, like the regular audience of the Alekan circus, their minds and senses navigated by Wenders's imagination.[18] From this position, spectators are invited to step out of the ordinary and into the magic world of cinema. The continuous change in the nature of the film's cinematography—from bird's-eye view to frog's-eye view, high to low angle shots, unhurried to abrupt zoom-outs and zoom-ins, subjective to objective point-of-view, from a roaming, hovering, and drifting camera to "grounded" tracking shots—defines Wenders's narrative itinerary. The feeling of letting oneself go—*das Sich-fallen-lassen*—is achieved with this aesthetic, allowing the spectator to experience visual dizziness. Within that context, the viewers' experience oscillates between steadiness and motion, illusion and disillusion, realism and enchantment. Wenders's angels, who serve as the camera's eye, invite the spectator not only to "watch" from a position inaccessible to human beings[19] but also to explore Berlin's spaces with delirious lucidity. Robert Kolker and Peter Beicken suggest that Wenders's camera becomes an "instrument of affection," "the feeling eye" that "caresses the things it perceives" through its "desiring," "accepting, loving gaze."[20] Wenders's "horizontal and vertical road movies," as Daniela Berghahn points out, in a way seek to provide instructions for a proper way of looking ("*versuchen eine Anleitung zum richtigen Sehen zu geben*").[21] Whatever would lead to utopia in Wenders's film world, it is always correlated with the search of what Berghahn calls the *modified gaze* (*die "Suche nach dem veränderten Blick."*)[22]

I propose to expand this discussion and suggest that the moving pictures that once fascinated early audiences form the subtext for Wenders's narrative. It has been suggested that Wenders's interpretations of Berlin allude to Walter Ruttmann's *Berlin, Symphony of a Big City* (1927).[23] Ruttmann's seminal silent film opens with a steam engine ride, bringing the audience by train into Berlin. Early cinema was fascinated with the train. Moviegoers were intrigued by cinema's new feature, the *phantom ride*, which allowed them to journey seamlessly through reality. Technically, these were films shot from the very front of moving trains, capturing the approaching tracks and the passing landscape, establishing a first-person perspective for the viewer while recording the journey from the train's perspective. The perceptual field was established through this movement, without showing the train itself. From this viewing position, as Christian Haynes points out, "the film would appear to be moving by aid of an invisible force." Indeed, writes Haynes, "it was the speed, motion and unique perspective that were the primary pleasures of the phantom ride." It provided the spectator with not only a visual experience but also "the unique sensation of traveling while sitting still."[24] What wowed audiences in the silent era was the unique perspective that these films introduced—a more exciting and sensational piece of realism. Many shots in *Wings of Desire* appear to evoke the visual and bodily sensations of the phantom ride: by tracking or by ghosting effortlessly through the streets, the air, into the houses and through windows, while showing glimpses of the celestial plane and reality, of places and no-places, the film seems to be moving as if by an invisible force. In this light, Wenders reinvents cinema and the cinematic experience for his audience. Through vertical, horizontal, and diagonal phantom rides, viewers figuratively visit both actual and imagined landscapes of Berlin, experiencing, simultaneously, a new sense of seeing and feeling as well as time and space. Wenders aptly describes this sensation. "If you like roaming about in order to lose yourself," he says, "you can end up in the strangest places."[25]

Wings of Desire is Wenders's first German film after *Paris, Texas* (1984), marking his homecoming to German cinema, and it offers the perspective of "a truly globalized filmmaker."[26] It is a testament to its time. Wenders's invisible angels Damiel and Cassiel are faced with the "complex topographies of West Berlin" in preunification Germany[27]—or the "strange place" that the director wants his viewers to visit/revisit. We see Berlin mostly from the angels' perspective as they drift over, cruise, and swoop across the divided city. The slow and floating camera shots, orchestrated by cinematographer Henri Alekan, achieve a gentle and lyrical view of urban space, allowing the spectator to perceive West Berlin as a cultural island. Damiel and Cassiel listen to the inner thoughts, fears, hopes, and dreams of anonymous Berliners, often resting their weightless hands on them to ease their pain and suffering. Although invisible, they can only be seen by children and their presence can also be felt by other former angels, such as the character of Peter Falk, who is making a detective movie set in Nazi Germany. While Wenders's film remembers Berlin's history, it is also an attempt to understand its unique present status. When Damiel stumbles on the Alekan Circus, he falls in love with the French trapeze artist Marion, who feels at home precisely because she is a stranger in the city. Wandering the streets, subways, buildings, and the public library, Damiel and Cassiel encounter Berlin as a space of deterritorialized people. It is through these images that Wenders's narrative resists the idea of separation and segregation in everyday life. It implies that Berlin has become home to dreamers, drifters, strangers, and migrants in search of a sanctuary as well as economic and political liberation.

In the wake of Germany's postwar economic miracle, West Berlin had become a magnet for migrants who participated in the domestic labor market. Germany called its labor recruits *Gastarbeiter* (guest workers), underlining the temporariness of their stay.[28] The Turkish writer Aras Ören in his 1972 epic poem "Was will Niyazi in der Naunynstrasse?" ("What does Niyazi want in Naunyn Street?") uses the term *Schauplatz der Begegnung* ("theater of encounter") metaphorically and as creative impulse to "reshape the boundaries of public debate about the guest worker after 1970."[29] With his Berlin trilogy (1973–80), as Rita Chin argues, Ören established "a fundamental rethinking of what constituted German identity."[30] One finds the same dramatic shift in the concerns of German cinema with Wenders's film: when compared to his predecessors, *Wings of Desire* constitutes the first explicitly cosmopolitan and transnational narrative film produced by a West German director. In Wenders's account, coexistence is no longer presented as a clash of cultures and civilizations.[31] Instead, Berlin is home to Germans, Americans, French, Japanese, Iranians, Turks, and other migrants who participate in national and transnational spheres. Through layering of stories of pain and suffering, intergenerational conflict, depression, marital relations, loneliness, financial problems, and alienation, Wenders depicts, as Les Caltvedt suggests, a "solidarity with the masses ... as part of a new beginning."[32]

Capturing a non-monolithic view of German culture

> She was tragic because there was no place in the cinema for her, no loving pictures. She too was absent image. It was better then, that we were absent, for when we were there it was humiliating, strange, sad. (bell hooks)[33]

Pre-Wenders German cinema is marked by an absence of minority representation. Representations of Turkish women in television and film, when they existed at all, were rigidly organized around biased ethnic stereotypes. In the (male-)dominant media culture, the Turkish woman came to symbolize the quintessential Other,[34] particularly as she appeared in the image of the oppressed Turkish/Muslim woman. Objectified through the orientalist gaze, not only was she imagined as intellectually inferior to men; her negative image as victim placed her in a position of inferiority in relation to the West and German women. In terms of female spectatorship, these constructed images of ethnic womanhood favored what Toni Morrison calls the masochistic look of victimization.[35] In films such as *Shirin's Wedding* (1975), *Melek Leaves* (1985), and *40 Square Meters of Germany* (1986), spectatorial pleasure aligns with a hierarchical system of sexual difference. Moreover, such modes of representation privileged veiled (Turkish) women, while negating the existence of diasporic women who favored the practice of non-veiling.[36] Until the mid-1990s and the emergence of what came to be known as the Turkish German cinema,[37] there were no counternarratives to challenge the prevalent (male) fantasies about Turkish women's diasporic lives. But most of all—to draw an analogy to bell hooks's recollections above—there were no loving pictures of Turkish women in cinema. They were "scapegoated on all sides"—and when their images did appear, they were "humiliating, strange, sad."[38]

In "The Oppositional Gaze: Black Female Spectators" (1996), American feminist and cultural critic bell hooks discusses black women's movie-going practices in connection with female spectatorship. Hooks offers an alternative theory in response to Laura Mulvey's ideas in "Visual Pleasure and Narrative Cinema" (1973), in which Mulvey argues that visual pleasure in narrative cinema is derived from women's objectification to the male gaze.[39] Observing that she grew up with cinematic images of black women that "made [her] stop looking," hooks argues that the paralyzing phallocentric gaze that fixes the woman's body as an object, fetish, or spectacle can be negated by watching films with an oppositional gaze.[40] Hooks recognizes in the "gaze" the potential for a (political) site of resistance allowing (black) women to become active spectators with critical agency. To find pleasure in cinema, women must "resist identification," writes hooks, and view films for the pleasure of deconstruction. Within this context, hooks calls attention to Manthia Diawara's work on Black British Cinema (1992) and his notion of "rupture," the moment of the (black) spectator's anti-identification with and disavowal of hegemonic representations.[41] Hooks develops Diawara's concept and suggests that black women watch films with an oppositional gaze and hence challenge dominant ideology. If these moments of rupture do not occur, then the female spectator decodes and accepts the connotative meaning of the screen image as truth. What makes hooks's formulation intriguing is not only how cinema can transmit ideas around identity and ethnicity but also how it articulates a space from which the female spectator is able to resist power in discourse. However, filmmakers, too, can practice the oppositional gaze, says hooks, and create a space for "new transgressive possibilities for the formulation of identity."[42] The gaze provides a means through which transformation can occur. While spectators can truly oppose and critique what they watch with their gaze, filmmakers can create a "realm" of gaze where the oppositional gaze can exist and invite audiences to look differently.[43]

In *Wings of Desire*, one encounters Turkish migrant women outside the domestic sphere. For example, there are two images of head-scarf-wearing women who appear in Wenders's presentation of the public library. In one depiction, she is shown at night, vacuuming the floors of the empty library (Figure 9.2). In another, she is depicted in the crowded library sitting at a desk and reading from a book while the film discloses her inner thoughts (Figure 9.3). In both instances, she is surrounded by Wenders's angels. These shots stand out because of the looking relations that are set up in these scenes. While it has been argued that some scenes in *Wings of Desire* position the angels as voyeurs,[44] I suggest that each scene offers a moment of "rupture," when it returns the gaze, in a sense suggesting "I see you seeing me." In the first example, a female angel stands in close proximity to the working woman, gazing back into the panning camera. In the other scene, the angel leans over the book-reading migrant woman, gazing and smiling back at the audience (Figures 9.2 and 9.3). In both cases, the gaze within the filmic frame reorients the look as a response to the paralyzing orientalist gaze that fixes the other (ethnic) woman as a spectacle. The returned gaze manages to undo the voyeuristic visual pleasure in the spectacle and to create an exchange of looks between the camera's gaze and the spectator. These shots are an instant reminder about the "power of the image,"[45] allowing the critical (female) spectator not only to read against the grain but also to experience the pleasure of resistance in looking. It is in these moments of rupture, as defined by Diawara and hooks, when Wenders's film contests, resists, and interrogates dominant filmic looking relations in culture.[46]

Playing with layers of representation, another scene possesses not only poetic value but also a postmodern perspective on migrant life. Established through a rapid zoom-in and a hand-held movement, the shot frames a woman with a head-scarf from behind, sitting alone in a public laundromat and with several suitcases standing in front of her. The camera lingers for a brief moment on this perspective, guiding the viewer's attention to the glass window and the details in the mise-en-scène. Then, it cuts to the interior and

Figure 9.2

Figure 9.3

pans back to her, while first showing washing machines in a row, all working simultaneously and rhythmically. When the camera returns to the woman after the pan, Cassiel is sitting next to her. Both gaze at the floor. At this moment, the film shifts our attention from the visual to the sonic image when we become aware of her voice and its particularities. Speaking in Turkish, the female voice represents an inner monologue about the chores for which she must take responsibility. As there are no subtitles, non-Turkish-speaking viewers have access only to the sounds of her language, not the content of her thoughts.

The camera concentrates on her voice, the sonic image, rather than the visual one or the meaning conveyed in her speech. And all along, the angel's act of listening as well as his curiosity to learn about the "Other" is foregrounded—an image that fosters the idea of alliance and a rejection of the objectifying orientalist gaze. From a spectator's perspective, the gaze oscillates between a stream-of-consciousness voice and silence, between sameness and difference (Figure 9.4). The scene switches to color and frames her body again from the front window of the laundromat, alone, and with the washing machines in the background. In a way, she no longer seems to be the center of the image: the arrangement distracts our gaze away from her and to the machines. The fluidity established in this constructed image dissolves center and periphery positions. It is, as Robert Kolker and Peter Beicken suggest, the "'tenderness' of [Wenders's] camera, the loving stance of the cinema that foregrounds all details in the mise-en-scène."[47]

This presentation allows for a separation between the image and the ethnic female Other.[48] These scenes are an intervention through the way they reenact and mirror the erasure of ethnic womanhood prevalent in film.[49] Wenders reworks the image of the veil so that it does not carry a meaning of oppression and victimization, but illustrates how it is shaped into an emblematic symbol in the representation of minority culture, reinforcing (Turkish) migrant women's cultural and social exclusiveness within Germany. One could say that the film directs our attention to how postwar German society unwittingly sustains

Figure 9.4

practices of ethnic and sociocultural exclusions. The film speaks to the women's diasporic visuality, not rendering it as a separate discourse but rather inviting the viewer to partake in the process of rethinking national identity. Rather than evoking ethnic negation, this presentation suggests an inclusive, cosmopolitan look onto German culture. In a way, this cinematic practice creates new realms of the gaze that allow, as bell hooks suggests, the formation of "new transgressive possibilities of identity."[50]

Dreaming beyond barriers and borders

Another striking feature in *Wings of Desire* is how Wenders engages the viewer's imagination through the metaphoric use of sound—his alternating use of sound and silence, for example, or the "gaps" or "perceptual tensions," to use Michel Chion's phrase, between sound and image.[51] Through the superimposition of sound, such as the vocal flow of his characters' internal voices, Wenders frames different perspectives on *audible* pasts in his narrative, and by doing so, he invites the listener to imagine the possibilities of sociopolitical and cultural change. The images of the Berliner *Himmel* heighten the desire to see beyond the material world and "to define oneself in relation to something larger than the individual."[52] Wim Wenders has been influenced by Japanese filmmaker Yasujiro Ozu and his utilization of intermediate spaces,[53] which I will refer to here as a "twilight zone." By capturing the sights and sounds of a twilight zone, in which Wenders's guardian angels live and observe mortal life, the filmmaker invites the audience to experience Berlin—a metaphor for Germany[54]—as a transnational space. The city's cultural marginality and physical inaccessibility are contrasted by shots of passengers, vehicles (such as cars, buses, metro, trains, airplanes, helicopters, bicycles, a circus trailer) that indicate the flow of people (Figures 9.5–9.8). The shots of migrating birds, the advertisements on bulletin boards for car tires or written on walls ("*Reifen*"), the whirling machines in laundromats, the circus, and a rotating camera take of the "*Funkturm*" (radio tower) indicate circularity, movement, and the flow of mediated culture across nation-states. It is in these visual and sonic images that the concept of national identity is dissolved into a fluid category. In his portrayal of German identity (and counter-identity) and how it is experienced under the pressures of the Cold War, Wenders subverts fantasies of cultural homogeneity by creating a collective "we" that challenges traditional concepts of home, belonging, and citizenship. Hence, *Wings of Desire*

Figure 9.5

Figure 9.6

presents more than an aesthetic intervention into German public and political discourses on memory.

The close-ups and extreme long shots of the *Siegessäule*, the golden massive statue of an angel, are intended to create intertextuality with symbolism of the American Statue of Liberty, the "Mother of Exile," a reassuring sign for thousands of immigrants that they had arrived in their country of dreams. It is this enthusiasm for a united Europe, a Europe without geographical, political, or cultural divisions, that manifests itself in *Wings of Desire*. In Wenders's presentation, diasporic cultural spaces are not marked as borderlands consisting

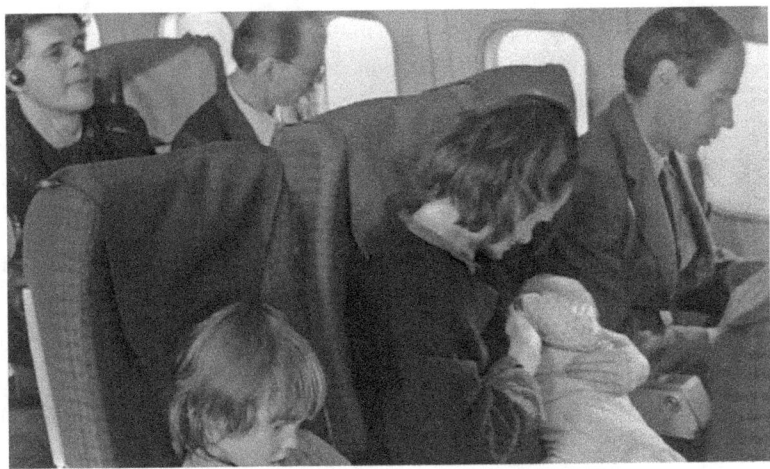

Figure 9.7

Figure 9.8

of minority ethnic communities. The black-and-white cinematography not only presents the angels' perspectives of the world but also raises concern about the lack of political and activist engagement toward struggles against racist, anti-migrant, and anti-refugee politics. In a sense, the existence of the black-and-white binary points to the contemporary concept of Europe and how it perceives itself and its "others."

The angels in *Wings of Desire* evoke, as scholars have noted, Rilkean themes and Walter Benjamin's allegorical interpretation of Paul Klee's picture *Angelus Novus*.[55] In Benjamin's famous description of the "angel of history," the angel is "confronted with history as a self-perpetuating catastrophe."[56] Wenders has acknowledged Rainer Maria Rilke's *Duino Elegies* as an inspiration for *Wings of Desire*. It is noteworthy that Rilke's engagement with Islamic culture and his travels within the Islamic world allowed the German poet, as Karen Campbell suggests, "to assimilate certain features of [Islamic] angelogy into his writing."[57] Although scholars have avoided relating Wenders's angels to religion, one could argue that the reference to the *Siegessäule* points to the problematic identification of Europe with its Christian heritage to the extent that it is a tradition of universalizing that perpetuates an existing East-West dichotomy. To overcome Eurocentrism as a dominant perspective on the world (exemplified by Damiel or Cassiel sitting on the golden angel and looking down at the urban landscape), Europe has to build a future that avoids the approaches that led to war, destruction, and displacement.

In an interview with Omid Nikfarjam, Wim Wenders shares memories about his childhood and growing up in Germany. The director remembers how the number of borders in Europe made travel within the continent difficult. "The friendship between Germany and France, and the even more utopian vision of a United Europe, set my imagination soaring more than anything else.... When I was a boy, [traveling without papers] was an absolutely unbelievable prospect."[58] The idea of change is exemplified in Damiel's decision to forgo eternal life and his transition from the twilight zone to human existence. His desire to experience love and to become a "world" citizen manifests as the leitmotif of the film as it ultimately shifts the film's focus from the philosophical to the practical realm. This shift is exemplified in the change to Technicolor, signaling the possibility for positive change. Moreover, the polyphony of voices, supported by a free stream-of-consciousness technique, presents Berlin as a cosmopolitan and borderless space. The aerial shot of the radio tower accompanied by the sounds of "a shifting, kaleidoscopic melange of stations"[59] reminds the viewer of the power that language has to divide nation from nation. As Walter Murch notes in his foreword to Michel Chion's *Audio-Vision: Sound on Screen*, "In 1927 there were over twenty different languages spoken in Europe by two hundred million people in twenty-five different, highly developed countries. Not to mention different dialects and accents within each language and a number of countries such as Switzerland and Belgium are multilingual."[60] With this visual and sonic image, the viewer is reminded of the magnitude of the loss of such cultural treasures when Wenders embeds into the "frantic cacophony of human thought and feeling," as Adam Bingham describes it, a storyteller in "the ragged person of an old man named Homer," to whom the angel Cassiel repeatedly returns to listen.[61] The old man laments the loss of grand storytelling traditions, "noting at one point that mankind's loss of its storytellers equates to the loss of its childhood."[62] Along these lines one could argue, then, that it is the power of stories to refresh and to create a new world—a desire that carries particular meaning for Wenders's idea of a European dream.

Thus, the film is a constant recourse to the viewer's "inner child." Most of the frames are populated by children, especially when the film presents them as the regular audience of the Alekan circus. Many scenes contrast the angels' perspectives with a child's "unmodified" view from below, switching between low- and high-angle shots, between a frog's-eye and bird's-eye perspective. Children address or speak to the angels, gaze at the camera, run into a scene and disappear, creating at times a moment of irony, an interruption in the flow of time and space. It is the children's fascination for exploring their surroundings that models Wenders's approach to life in the metropolis. In order to put the past behind us, as suggested in Benjamin's model, melancholy should not lead to passivity and resignation but rather function as a creative force for a new beginning. Damiel's fall signifies a utopian impulse in the film that wants to motivate activism and change. Pessimism, as Benjamin has illustrated in his discussion of art and literature, makes fundamental change impossible and takes away the power of utopian dreams. Only in sharing in the creation of new stories and in working together, says Benjamin, can society be restored. Benjamin's "angel of history," as presented in *Wings of Desire*, is still waiting for us, as Raymond Barglow puts it, to create relationships across generations, cultures, or any kind of difference.[63] Dreaming of a new continent and its new image will enable the angel at last to take wing.

Wings of Desire reveals itself as an unfinished story about love and reconciliation. It was produced at a time when hardly anyone in Germany, as political scientist Herfried Münkler puts it, could anticipate that the rigid political constellations in Cold War Europe would dissolve, the Wall disappear and Germany reunite.[64] If read within this context, Damiel's euphoric statement "I can imagine anything" is an invocation to the audience inviting them to do the same, namely, to let themselves fall so that in this delirious state they can imagine a borderless Europe and a culture of (peaceful) coexistence. While the utopian idea of a united Europe has been accomplished since the film's release, the quest to give Europe a new "soul"[65] remains a project to be explored and defined by European cinema. "Europe's soul is old," says Wenders. "It simply wants to continue telling its story in all of its languages; it wants to continue singing its song in all of its tones. Otherwise, it will wither and die."[66]

Notes

1. Négresse Verte, "Nazım Hikmet Ran—Zülfü Livaneli: 'Karlı Kayın Ormanında' ('In the snowy night woods')," *Négresse Verte* (blog), August 16, 2007, http://negresseverte.blogspot.com/2007_08_16_archive.html (accessed April 20, 2018).
2. Kutay Onaylı, "Nazım Hikmet: A Loving Revolutionary," *Vagabond Magazine*, February 19, 2014, http://vagabondmagazine.org/nazim-hikmet-romantic-communism/.
3. Nazım Hikmet, *Beyond the Walls: Selected Poems*, trans. Ruth Christie, Richard McKane, and Talât Sait Halman (London: Anvil Press Poetry, 2003), 9.
4. See also, for example, Nazım Hikmet, "The Walnut Tree," in *Nazım Hikmet: Bütün şiirleri* [*Nazım Hikmet: All Poems*] (Istanbul: Yapı Kredi Sanat Yayıncılık Ticaret ve Sanayi, 1957/2008), 1618.
5. Jenny B. White, "Turks in the New Germany," *American Anthropologist* 99, no. 4 (1997): 755.
6. Wim Wenders, "Everything I Loved I Had to Defend," *The Talks*, January 29, 2014, http://the-talks.com/interview/wim-wenders/.
7. Jochen Kuerten, "US Experience Brought Out the European in Me, Wenders Says," *Deutsche Welle*, May 19, 2009, http://dw.com/en/us-experience-brought-out-the-european-in-me-wenders-says/a-4264372.
8. Daniela Berghahn, "Leben . . . ein Blick genügt doch: Der utopische Augenblick in Wim Wenders' 'Road Movies,'" *Monatshefte* 91, no. 1 (Spring 1999): 70.
9. Ibid.
10. Wim Wenders, "An Attempted Description of an Indescribable Film," *Current* (blog), *The Criterion Collection*, November 2, 2009, http://www.criterion.com/current/posts/1289-an-attempted-description-of-an-indescribable-film.
11. Thomas Mohnike, "The History-Accumulator: Berlin as a Foreign Metropolis," in *Nordic Literature: A Comparative History Volume 1: Spatial Nodes*, ed. Thomas A. DuBois, Dan A. Ringgaard, and Steven P. Sondrup (Amsterdam: Benjamins, 2017), 272.
12. For analysis of these representations, see Barbara Mennel, "The Politics of Space in the Cinema of Migration," *German as a Foreign Language* 3 (2010): 40–55; Mine Eren, "Breaking the Stigma? The Anti-heroine in Fatih Akın's *Head-On*," in *Muslim Women, Transnational Feminism and the Ethics of Pedagogy: Contested Imaginaries*

in *Post-9/11 Cultural Practice*, ed. Lisa K. Taylor and Jasmin Zine (New York: Routledge, 2014): 82–109.

13 Benedict Anderson, *Imagined Communities: Reflections on the Origin and Spread of Nationalism* (London: Verso, 1983); Mohnike, "The History-Accumulator," 272.

14 Sara Wallace Goodman, "The Politics and Policies of Immigration in Germany," *German Politics and Society* 85 (2007): 99; Sara Miller Llana, "A New, Unlikely 'Nation of Immigrants': Germany," *The Christian Science Monitor*, December 12, 2014, https://www.csmonitor.com/World/Europe/2014/1212/A-new-unlikely-nation-of-immigrants-Germany.

15 Kwame Anthony Appiah, *Cosmopolitanism: Ethics in a World of Strangers* (New York: W. W. Norton & Company, 2006).

16 Appiah, *Cosmopolitanism*, xv.

17 Paul Richard, "Putting the World in a Box: Joseph Cornell's Inside Stories," *Special to The Washington Post,* November 19, 2006, http://www.washingtonpost.com/wp-dyn/content/article/2006/11/17/AR2006111700301.html; Joseph Cornell, *Navigating the Imagination* (New Haven, CT: Yale University Press, 2008); Anke te Heesen, *The World in a Box: The Story of an Eighteenth-Century Picture Encyclopedia* (Chicago: University of Chicago Press, 2002).

18 Here I refer to the title of Cornell's study *Navigating the Imagination.*

19 Muriel Cormican, "Goodbye Wenders: *Lola Rennt* as German Film Manifesto," *German Studies Review* 30, no. 1 (February 2007): 130.

20 Robert Philip Kolker and Peter Beicken, *The Films of Wim Wenders: Cinema as Vision and Desire* (Cambridge: Cambridge University Press, 1993), 11, 17.

21 Berghahn, "Leben . . .," 70.

22 Ibid., 66.

23 Nicole Huber and Ralph Stern, "From the American West to West Berlin: Wim Wenders, Border Crossings, and the Transnational Imaginary," *Places Journal*, April 2014, placesjournal.org/article/from-the-american-west-to-west-berlin/.

24 Christian Hayes, "Phantom Rides," *BFI Screen Online*, July 7, 2014, www.screenonline.org.uk/film/id/1193042/.

25 Wim Wenders and Beat Wismer, *4 Real & True 2: Landscapes, Photographs* (Munich: Schirmer/Mosel, 2015).

26 Josef Braun, "Outsider's Eye: The Peculiar Case of Wim Wenders," *Vue Weekly*, May 20, 2015, http://vueweekly.com/outsider-eye-the-peculiar-case-of-wim-wenders/.

27 Huber and Stern, *From the American West*.

28 David Horrocks and Eva Kolinsky, *Turkish Culture in German Society Today* (Providence, Oxford: Berghahn Books, 1996), xviii.

29 Rita Chin, "Imagining a German Multiculturalism: Aras Ören and the Contested Meanings of the 'Guest Worker,' 1955–1980," *Radical History Review* 83 (Spring

2002): 45; Aras Ören, *Was will Niyazi in der Naunynstrasse: Ein Poem* (Berlin: Rotbuch Verlag, 1977).
30. Chin, "Imagining a German Multiculturalism," 46.
31. Les Caltvedt, "Berlin Poetry: Archaic Cultural Patterns in Wenders's *Wings of Desire*," *Literature Film Quarterly* 20, no. 2 (1992): 122.
32. Caltvedt, "Berlin Poetry," 122.
33. bell hooks, "The Oppositional Gaze: Black Female Spectators," in *Reel to Real: Race, Sex, and Class at the Movies* (New York and London: Routledge Taylor & Francis Group, 2009), 204.
34. White, "Turks in the New Germany," 757.
35. Morrison's phrase is quoted in hooks, "The Oppositional Gaze," 203.
36. Nadia Fadil, "Not-/Unveiling as an Ethical Practice," Islam in Europe, *Feminist Review* 98 (2011): 86.
37. Sabine Hake and Barbara Caroline Mennel, eds., *Turkish German Cinema in the New Millennium: Sites, Sounds, and Screens* (New York: Berghahn Books, 2014).
38. hooks, "The Oppositional Gaze," 202.
39. Laura Mulvey, "Visual Pleasure and Narrative Cinema," in *Film Theory and Criticism: Introductory Readings*, ed. Leo Braudy and Marshall Cohen (New York: Oxford University Press, 1999).
40. hooks, "The Oppositional Gaze," 205.
41. hooks, "The Oppositional Gaze," 199; Manthia Diawara, "Black British Cinema: Spectatorship and Identity Formation in *Territories*," *Public Culture* 3, no. 1 (1990): 33–48.
42. hooks, "The Oppositional Gaze," 213.
43. Ibid., 212.
44. Anne Cieko, "Voyeurism as an Epistemological and Narrative Device: Wim Wenders's *Wings of Desire*," presented at the Salisbury Literature/Film Conference, 1990, http://cinema.usc.edu/assets/101/16176.pdf; Braun, "Outsider's Eye."
45. Annette Kuhn, *Power of the Image: Essays on Representation and Sexuality* (London: Routledge, 2016).
46. hooks, "The Oppositional Gaze," 209.
47. Kolker and Beicken, *The Films of Wim Wenders*, 18.
48. See hooks, "The Oppositional Gaze," 202.
49. hooks, "The Oppositional Gaze," 205.
50. Ibid., 213.
51. Walter Murch, Foreword to *Audio-Vision: Sound on Screen* by Michel Chion, trans. Claudia Gorbman (New York: Columbia University Press, 1994), xix, xx.
52. Adam Bingham, "DVD Reviews: Wings of Desire," *Cineaste* (Spring 2010): 68.
53. David Desser, "Tokyo Story (1953), Ozu Yasujiro," in *Film Analysis: A Norton Reader*, ed. Jeffrey Geiger and R. L. Rutsky (New York: W.W. Norton & Company, 2005), 465.

54 Coco Fusco, "Angels, History and Poetic Fantasy," *Cineaste* 16, no. 4 (1988): 14–17.
55 Cormican, "Goodbye Wenders," 135; Christian Rogowski, "To be Continued: History in Wim Wenders's *Wings of Desire* and Thomas Brasch's *Domino*," *German Studies Review* 15, no. 3 (1992): 549; Caltvedt, "Berlin Poetry," 253; Wim Wenders, cited in Eric Rentschler, *West German Filmmakers on Film: Visions and Voices* (New York: Holmes & Meier, 1988), 153; Mark Luprecht, "Opaque Skies: *Wings of Desire*—Angelic Text, Context, and Subtext," *Post Script* 17, no. 3 (Summer 1998): 47–54.
56 Rogowski, "To be Continued," 550.
57 Karen J. Campbell, "Rilke's *Duino Angels* and the Angels of Islam," *Alif: Journal of Comparative Poetics* no. 23 (2003): 194.
58 Omid Nikfarjam, "Dreaming a Continent," *New Statesman*, July 12, 2007, www.newstatesman.com/arts-and-culture/2007/07/european-film-cinema-pictures.
59 Jonathan Rosenbaum, "City of Angels (on *Wings of Desire*)," *Chicago Reader*, July 15, 1988, https://www.jonathanrosenbaum.net/2017/08/city-of-angels/.
60 Murch, Foreword to *Audio-Vision*, x.
61 Bingham, "DVD Reviews," 68.
62 Ibid.
63 Raymond Barglow, "The Angel of History: Walter Benjamin's Vision of Hope and Despair," *Tikkun Magazine*, 1998, http://barglow.com/angel_of_history.htm.
64 Herfried Münkler, "The Fall of the Wall and German Reunification," *Young Germany*, April 9, 2013, http://www.young-germany.de/topic/live/settle-in-adjust/the-fall-of-the-wall-and-german-reunification.
65 Nikfarjam, "Dreaming a Continent," 38.
66 Ibid., 41

10

Blandness and "Just Seeing" in the Films of Wim Wenders

William Baker

Wenders's producer for *Wings of Desire* (1987), Anatole Dauman, commented that "at the center of the Wendersian creation always remains a fascination for the 'act of seeing.' To see objectively and subjectively. To see from the sky, to see in dreams, to see inside oneself."[1] Dauman was not alone in acknowledging the visually phenomenological themes in Wenders's works. Scholars, too, have taken a phenomenological approach when interpreting his films, but such discussions are greatly enriched by acknowledging the influence of the Japanese director Yasujiro Ozu. In an early interview with Jan Dawson, Wenders claimed that Ozu was "the only influence. Or at least the only master."[2] Although Wenders's own statements on Ozu's influence seem hyperbolic, their importance is not to be downplayed. Rather than charting this influence through a reading of *Tokyo-Ga* (1985), which explicitly addresses Ozu's influence, I investigate a common aesthetic shared by these two directors that is most clearly located in Wenders's early road films, in particular *Alice in the Cities* (1974) and *Kings of the Road* (1976). François Jullien's concept of "blandness" represents the point of convergence in my view of these two directors and helps negotiate the grounding of this aesthetic in the phenomenological traditions of Europe and Japan. Blandness is a state of nondifferentiation in the field of perception that nonetheless manifests the potential of differentiation.[3] Both Wenders and Ozu create bland scenes and present blandness as a sight that privileges seeing in their films.

In a 1989 interview with Peter W. Jansen, Wenders provided an answer to the question "What is so great about seeing?":

> Beim Sehen ist für mich toll, daß es anders als das Denken nicht eine Meinung von den Dingen beinhalten muß. Im Denken ist eigentlich in jedem Gedanken

auch gleich die Meinung zu einem Ding, einem Menschen, einer Stadt, einer Landschaft immer mit enthalten. Das Sehen ist meinungsfrei, im Sehen kann man eine Einstellung finden zu einer anderen Person, zu einem Gegenstand, zur Welt, die meinungsfrei ist, wo man einer Sache oder einer Person gegenübersteht, ein Verhältnis dazu hat, wahrnimmt. Das ist ein schönes Wort für Sehen; *das schönere Wort für Sehen ist Wahrnehmen*, weil da das Wort wahr drin ist. Das heißt, im Sehen ist für mich Wahrheit latent möglich. Viel mehr als im Denken, wo man sich viel mehr verirren kann, wo man sich entfernen kann von der Welt. Für mich ist das Sehen ein In-die-Welt-Eintauchen und das Denken immer ein Abstand-Nehmen. Und ich glaube, ich bin ein ganz intuitiver Mensch, und für mich ist das Sehen die Ausdrucks- und Eindrucksform überhaupt.[4]

(The great thing about seeing for me is what distinguishes it from thinking, namely that it doesn't entail having an opinion. In thinking, every thought also contains an opinion of a thing or a person or a city or a landscape. There are no opinions in seeing: in seeing, you can come to view another person, an object, the world, that doesn't imply an opinion, where you just confront the thing or person, take it on board, perceive it. I like the word *insight*. It suggests you can have truth and understanding just from seeing. Much more than from thinking, where you can lose yourself, or lose touch with the world. For me, seeing is immersing myself in the world, while thinking is distancing myself from it.[5])

Although he tends to display his "theory" through his films, here Wenders discusses the act of "just seeing" that is fundamental to his approach. As is particularly clear in the translation of the original German "das schönere Wort für Sehen ist Wahrnehmen, weil da das Wort wahr drin ist," where *wahrnehmen* is translated once as "to perceive" and once as "insight," the idea of "just seeing" goes beyond visually sensing. Rather, *wahrnehmen* has a wider meaning that encompasses all the senses, and this wider sense of *wahrnehmen*—incorporating perception and insight—is included in "just seeing."

Some of Wenders's characters—often children—exhibit this wider meaning of "just seeing." One such character appears in *Kings of the Road*; near the end of the film, Robert approaches a boy writing in a notebook. Robert asks what he is doing, to which the boy responds that he is writing down everything he sees. The boy views his surroundings without categorizing them and seems to be viewing with no other goal in mind than taking note of what he sees. When asked about the role of children in his films, Wenders commented:

> In my films, children are present as the film's own fantasy, the eyes the film would like to see with. A view of the world that isn't opinionated, a purely ontological

gaze. And only children really have that gaze. Sometimes in a film you can manage a gaze like a child's. Like the little boy at the end of *Kings of the Road*, sitting at the station, doing his homework. He's actually my dream of a film director.[6]

Concerning the scene, Alexander Graf states that "what Robert glimpses here is the possibility of seeing without requiring an understanding beyond the fact of the existence of the things seen: *simply remaining open to visual stimulation, to ordinary phenomena.*"[7] This kind of scene is not exclusive to *Kings of the Road*, nor is it limited to the sense of sight. In *Lisbon Story* (1994), Phillip Winter sits outside, accompanied by a girl; while he records the ambient sounds of Lisbon, she names the source of each sound that she hears. In both scenes, the children list what they experience without further evaluation. The presence of each sight and sound is acknowledged, and nothing more.

It is likely that Wenders's idea of "just seeing" was initially influenced by the theories of Béla Balázs and Siegfried Kracauer: "I'm no great theorist. I tend not to remember things I've read in books. So I can't give you Béla Balázs' exact words, but they affected me profoundly all the same. He talks about the ability (and the responsibility) of cinema 'to show things as they are.' And he says cinema can 'rescue the existence of things.'"[8] Wenders mentions only Balázs in the above excerpt, but the reference to cinema "rescu[ing] the existence of things" seems to evoke Kracauer as well. Concerning the true nature of an object or scene, here referred to as "physiognomy," Balázs states that

> children have no difficulty understanding these physiognomies. This is because they do not yet judge things purely as tools, means to an end, useful objects not to be dwelt on. They regard each thing as an autonomous living being with a soul and face of its own. Indeed, children are like artists, who likewise want to depict objects, not make use of them.[9]

The children that Robert and Phillip encounter exemplify this tendency to perceive and depict the world around them rather than making use of it. The importance of this ability is not lost on the grown men: Robert trades his sunglasses and his suitcase for the notebook in which the boy has been writing, and Phillip seems impressed with everything that the girl has noticed. Although not exclusive to children, similar importance is given to the act of seeing by Kracauer as he quotes Alfred North Whitehead in *Theory of Film*:

> Whitehead was the first to see our situation in this light and to comment on it accordingly. He blames contemporary society for favoring the tendency toward abstract thinking and insists that we want concretion . . .: "When you

understand all about the sun and all about the atmosphere and all about the rotation of the earth, you may still miss the radiance of the sunset. *There is no substitute for the direct perception of the concrete achievement of a thing in its actuality.* We want concrete fact with a high light thrown on what is relevant to its preciousness." And how can this demand be met? "What I mean," Whitehead continues, "is art and aesthetic education. It is, however, art in such a general sense that I hardly like to call it by that name. Art is a special example. *What we want is to draw out habits of aesthetic apprehension.*" No doubt Whitehead is right in thus emphasizing the aesthetic character of experience. *The perception of "concrete fact" presupposes both detached and intense participation in it; in order to manifest its concreteness, the fact must be perceived in ways similar to those which play a role in the enjoyment and production of art.*[10]

The "habits of aesthetic apprehension" that Whitehead describes parallel the importance that Wenders places on seeing, as can be seen by the "detached and intense participation" necessary for this kind of perception. While the intellect remains detached, one still engages intensely in the act of seeing. The complexities of abstract thinking detract from the immediacy of perception.

An instance of "just seeing" in *Alice in the Cities* exemplifies Balázs's and Kracauer's statements well. Philip Winter and Alice spend time viewing the city from the binoculars on top of the Empire State Building. Both characters begin by looking at the surrounding skyscrapers, but Philip is quickly distracted from the sites to keep track of Alice's mother. Alice spends more time examining the World Trade Center and the Flatiron Building before being distracted by a bird. Concerning this scene, Norbert Grob states that

> the camera thereafter *forgets* the story it is trying to tell for a few moments and assumes [Alice's] perspective. Thereby is it clear that Wenders's unexpected perspectives that disclose reality are more important than the continuous formulation of the story. Through the flight of the seagull, the subject and space of the film are experienced as duration and location.[11]

Alice does not differentiate between the sights of the city and the bird; they are equal under her gaze. As described by Balázs, Philip is focused on using his sight as "a means to an end," while Alice wordlessly accepts the landscape before her. Although Alice "just sees," Philip has yet to do so. Through interactions with Alice and by examining his Polaroids, Philip develops a new sense of aesthetic apprehension, as described by Whitehead.

When taking pictures at the beginning of *Alice in the Cities*, Philip seeks to capture something noteworthy about the landscape with his camera, but no matter how many pictures he takes, his attempts fail. They do not adequately capture that which Philip found noteworthy about the landscape and are added to a lineup of other pictures that fail to meet Philip's expectations. But when he and Alice make their way to Europe, Philip takes a picture from the window of the plane. This wing extending into the visual void above the clouds, one of Wenders's signature shots, is not an innovation of *Alice in the Cities*, but appears multiple times in Wenders's first feature, *Summer in the City* (1970), among the film's constant scenes of travel, whether it be by car, train, or airplane. It is only in *Alice in the Cities* that the shot is admired for its beauty and its emptiness. The picture shows little except for the wing of the plane and clouds, but it is dwelt on more than any other picture Philip has taken in the film thus far (Figure 10.1). In *On Film*, Wenders comments on the empty and open nature of such images:

> If there is too much to see, that is, if an image is too full, or if there are too many images, the effect is: you don't see anything any more. Too much turns quickly into "nothing." You all know that. You also know the other effect: if an image is empty, or almost empty, and sparse, it can reveal so much that it completely fills you, and the emptiness becomes "everything." . . . Just as much as you want to frame something in order to show it, you have to be aware of keeping things out of your frame. What you want to show, what you want *in*, is defined by what you keep *out*.[12]

In Wenders's effort to frame a shot that "becomes everything," he creates a plain shot of simple construction, a bland shot. It is this same blandness that Ozu

Figure 10.1

captures in his films, and the same blandness that François Jullien theorizes on in *In Praise of Blandness*.

Jullien begins by defining the term, which he claims undergirds not only the arts but also one's sensory perception of all things:

> Blandness: that phase when different flavors no longer stand in opposition to each other but, rather, abide within plentitude. It provides access to the undifferentiated foundation of all things and so is valuable to us; its neutrality manifests the potential inherent at the Center. At this stage, the real is no longer blocked in partial and too obvious manifestations; the concrete becomes discrete, open to transformation.[13]

Jullien defines blandness through negation: it is the absence of a strong, bold, clearly defined stimulus. Within the absence of these strong stimuli exists their potential; one would not be able to identify a strong stimulus without having experienced its absence. Blandness represents one side in a dichotomy of presence and absence. But blandness is the antithesis not only of one stimulus but also of *any* stimulus. Therefore, blandness can be imagined as a central point from which radiate numerous stimuli of increasing strength. The center represents the average, the neutral, and the real. The way in which this nondifferentiation facilitates plentitude is well displayed when Jullien discusses music. When any single note is chosen and played, a distinction is made between that sound and all other potential sounds; one sound *is* while the others *are not*. When no note is played, all notes are present to the same extent: not at all. This state of nondifferentiation with respect to sound is, of course, silence, but within this silence exists the potential that any note could be played—a potential that is the plentitude mentioned in the definition of blandness.[14] Silence is the undifferentiated foundation of all potential sounds; music cannot exist without the corresponding idea of music's absence. Rather than playing emotional crescendos and diminuendos in music, or painting vibrant colors in a work of art, bland music, poetry, or painting is created by minimizing the difference between the two sides of this dichotomy between presence and absence. By preventing the work from straying too far from this nothingness, blandness in art can gesture toward that from which the art has been created: silence, emptiness, or a blank field: "The arts can facilitate our perceptual apprehension of this basic blandness. Indeed, it is their mandate to reveal it; through music, poetry, and painting, the bland is transformed into experience."[15]

160 Wim Wenders

The bland work of art eschewing ornamentation resembles phenomenological reduction, in which all but the most fundamental qualities of a phenomenon are stripped away. This removal of all but the most essential qualities—in both art and phenomenology—allows the resulting essence to speak to any given viewer. These reductions can apply to the experiences of many points of view. For example, concerning painting,

> the artist, Ni Zan (fourteenth century), painted virtually the same landscape throughout his life. He did this not, it seems, because of a particular attachment to these motifs but, on the contrary, to better express his inner detachment regarding all particular motifs and all possible motivations. His is the monotonous, monochromatic landscape that encompasses all landscapes— where all landscapes blend together and assimilate each other.[16] (Figure 10.2)

Figure 10.2 The Artist Ni Zan (fourteenth century), The Collection of National Palace Museum, Taiwan.

The way in which the paintings of Ni Zan encompass the qualities of all landscapes resembles statements Wenders makes about Ozu:

> Ozu's films always tell the same simple stories, of the same people in the same city of Tokyo. They are told with extreme economy, reduced to their barest essentials.... His films may be thoroughly Japanese, but they are also absolutely universal. I have seen all the families of the world in them, including my parents, my brother and myself. Never before or since has the cinema been so close to its true purpose: to give an image of a man in the twentieth century, a true, valid and useful image, in which he can not only recognize himself, but from which he can learn as well.[17]

Just as Ni Zan iterated the same style of landscape painting, Ozu iterated the family drama. Perhaps Ozu, like Ni Zan, chose to create works of similar composition in order to show detachment from all genres. His families, as Wenders notes, encompass all families. This universal quality mirrors the "undifferentiated foundation" that Jullien describes in the definition of blandness. But Wenders is not the first to identify the bland qualities of Ozu's films; as noted by Paul Schrader, Ozu integrates emptiness into the form of his art in the same way as Chinese landscape painter Ma Yuan, founder of the "one-corner style." As seen in *Angler on a Wintry Lake*, a small painted portion of the canvas stands in contrast to an unpainted void (Figure 10.3).[18] A number of scenes from *Alice in the Cities* make even better comparison. Just as the boat in Ma Yuan's painting is surrounded by a void, so too are the planes in *Alice in the Cities*. The film opens with an extreme long shot of a plane centered in a clear sky. As Philip and Alice take off for Europe, their plane is filmed in the same way (Figure 10.4). The boat and plane that inhabit these voids define their surroundings as water and air respectively. The composition of these shots is as simple as possible, a form surrounded by emptiness.

A similarly exemplary shot appears at the beginning of Ozu's 1959 remake of his 1934 film *Floating Weeds*: the foreground is inhabited by the ground and a dark glass bottle; the middle portion of the frame presents a white lighthouse on a piece of concrete jutting out into the calm water, which fills the space between the two visual weights (Figure 10.5). These components are situated under an empty sky that fills the upper two-thirds of the frame. The visual composition of this opening shot resembles the traditional Chinese landscape painting described by Jullien. Although the viewer knows the lighthouse to be a larger, heavier form than the bottle in the foreground, both objects take up the same space within the frame. Additionally, the white color of the lighthouse lessens its visual weight, and this—in combination with the dark color of the bottle—

Figure 10.3 Ma Yuan, Angler on a Wintry Lake, Tokyo, National Museum

Figure 10.4

Figure 10.5

balances the scales between the two objects, as exemplified in a 1797 description of the rule of thirds: "And to give the utmost force and solidity to your work, some part of the picture should be as light, and some as dark as possible: These two extremes are then to be harmonized and reconciled to each other."[19] This harmonization is, in part, achieved through Ozu's well-known use of the 50-mm lens, which flattens the perspective of the image; though neither the lighthouse nor the bottle appears to be entirely in focus, they are both in focus to the same degree. The way the opposite poles of these dichotomies are brought together by minimizing the difference between them is one element that makes this shot bland.

Jullien makes similar statements concerning Ni Zan's landscapes: "Near and far are fundamentally homogeneous, 'reflecting each other,' . . . and becoming equals under the viewer's gaze":

> No decorative, or merely pleasing, touch relieves the platitude of the whole. Yet, drained of all opacity—unburdened of all weightiness—as such a landscape is, it does not lack its own substance. . . . Nothing here strives to incite or seduce; nothing aims to fix the gaze or compel the attention. Yet this landscape exists fully as a landscape. The Chinese critics traditionally characterize this in one word: *dan*, the "bland."[20]

It is this blandness from which *Floating Weeds* begins. Following the opening credits, the introductory music quickly fades away, leaving the viewer in silence when presented with the first shot. From this stillness, the visual and aural blandness of Ozu's first shot, the following four shots begin to gradually grow in complexity and tempo, each shot one second shorter than the last. Many of Ozu's films, especially his color films, begin in a similar manner: *Tokyo Story* (1953), *Ohayo* (1959), and *An Autumn Afternoon* (1962) all begin with motionless, unpopulated shots which gradually grow closer to the characters with each take. This allows what follows to stand in contrast to the introductory blandness. The same blandness of composition and harmonization of near and far can be found in Wenders's signature "wing shot," seen, as discussed earlier, in *Summer in the City* and twice in *Alice in the Cities* (once through Wenders's film camera and once through Philip's Polaroid camera), as well as in *Tokyo-Ga* as Wenders begins his journey to Japan.

In addressing the act of seeing through the visual aesthetic of blandness, Wenders's works explore the future of the bland image in an increasingly vibrant, visual world. It is therefore noteworthy that *Tokyo-Ga*, a film that directly acknowledges the importance of Ozu, displays far fewer bland images than other Wenders films. At the beginning of *Tokyo-Ga*, Wenders states:

> My trip to Tokyo was in no way a pilgrimage. I was curious as to whether I still could track down something from this time, whether there was still anything left of this work, images perhaps, or even people, or whether so much would have changed in Tokyo in the twenty years since Ozu's death that nothing would be left to find.[21]

This search for Ozu's images is a search for traces of the blandness that Ozu captured in his films. The city of Tokyo and the medium of film have undergone constant development since Ozu's time. Although *Tokyo-Ga* occasionally displays calm, everyday scenes (people picnicking in the cemetery, the visit to Ozu's grave, and interviews with Chishu Ryu and Yuharu Aysuta), these bland scenes are contrasted with the vibrant colors and fast movements of the city. Blandness would, at first, seem to be elusive and outdated within the context of the city and the torrent of images therein, but blandness stands as a counterpoint to the most vibrant of scenes. For instance, while filming the creation of wax food replicas, Wenders raises questions of authenticity with regard to the new, mass-produced images of the city. As the workers shape the wax, it takes the form of various enticing and realistic dishes. Near the end of the scene, Wenders's voiceover says: "I spent the whole day there. Only I was not allowed to film at lunchtime, which was a pity. The employees sat surrounded by the wax artifacts and ate packed lunches which looked just like the imitations. You were afraid someone might take a bite out of a wax sandwich by mistake."[22] These words are accompanied by stationary close-ups of the completed replicas. This bland camera treatment invites the viewer to play out the otherwise absent comedic climax of the scene on their own. In turn, allowing the viewer to contribute part of their own experience to the film-viewing experience narrows the gap between the experience of reality and the experience of the film. According to Wenders, the distance between cinematic and everyday experience has grown too wide. His films both narrow and problematize this distance:

> People are by now so used to the wide gulf between cinema and life that it makes you sit up and catch your breath when you see something true or real happening on the screen, even if it's just a child's gesture in the background, or a bird flying across the screen, or a cloud casting its shadow over the picture momentarily. It has become a rarity in today's cinema for such moments of truth to take place, for people and things to show themselves as they are.[23]

By facilitating these moments through his films, Wenders's idea of "just seeing" falls in line with Kracauer's and Whitehead's idea of "aesthetic education," Jullien's mandate that the arts reveal blandness, and Wenders's own evaluation of Ozu's films, which present "a true, valid and useful image, in which [man] can not only recognize himself, but from which he can learn as well." The issue of presenting truth in the cinema continues to drive Wenders following *Tokyo-Ga*, as can be seen in his initial mistrust and eventual acceptance of video as an authentic means of filming in *Notebook on Cities and Clothes*: "The video images even felt more accurate sometimes, as if they had a better understanding of the phenomena before the lens."[24] This acceptance of technology is a moment of divergence from Ozu. Where Ozu waited until 1958 to shoot in color and never entertained the idea of a wide-screen film, Wenders has accepted not only video but also, more recently, 3-D in *Pina*, *Every Thing Will Be Fine*, and *The Beautiful Days of Aranjuez*. By incorporating these innovations in the medium, Wenders acknowledges the potential of new visual technology to enable "just seeing" and to show things as they really are.

Notes

1 Anatole Dauman, *Pictures of a Producer* (London: British Film Institute, 1992), 154.
2 Jan Dawson, *Wim Wenders* (New York: Zoetrope, 1982), 8.

3 François Jullien, *In Praise of Blandness* (New York, Zone Books, 2008).
4 Wim Wenders, *The Act of Seeing: Texte und Gespräche* (Frankfurt/Main: Verlag der Autoren, 1992), 59; italics are mine.
5 Wim Wenders, *On Film* (New York, Faber and Faber, 2001), 326.
6 Ibid., 323.
7 Alexander Graf, *The Cinema of Wim Wenders: The Celluloid Highway* (London, Wallflower Press, 2002), 67; italics are mine.
8 Wenders, *On Film*, 159.
9 Béla Balázs, *Béla Balázs: Early Film Theory*, ed. Erica Carter (New York, Berghahn Books, 2010), 46.
10 Siegfried Kracauer, *Theory of Film: The Redemption of Physical Reality* (New York, Oxford University Press, 1960), 296; italics are mine.
11 Norbert Grob, *Wenders* (Berlin: Wissenschaftsverlag Volker Spiess, 1991), 104. "Die Kamera *vergißt* danach für einige Augenblicke die Geschichte, die sie zu erzählen sucht, und übernimmt [Alices] Blick. Wodurch deutlich wird, daß Wenders unerwartete Perspektiven, die sich auf die Realität eröffnen, wichtiger sind als die kontinuierliche Formulierung der Story. Im Flug der Möwe wird plötzlich jenseits des Sujets die filmische Zeit erfahrbar: als Dauer. Und der filmische Raum: als Ort" (translation is mine).
12 Wenders, *On Film*, 381.
13 Jullien, *In Praise of Blandness*, 24.
14 Ibid., 69–78.
15 Ibid., 27.
16 Ibid., 37.
17 Wenders, *On Film*, 219.
18 Paul Schrader, *Transcendental Style in Film: Ozu, Bresson, Dreyer* (Los Angeles: University of California Press, 1972), 27.
19 John Thomas Smith, *Remarks on Rural Scenery* (London: S. and R. Bentley, 1797), 16. The opening shot of *Floating Weeds* also adheres to other aspects of the rule of thirds:
Analogous to this 'Rule of thirds,' (if I may be allowed so to call it) I have presumed to think that, in connecting or in breaking the various lines of a picture, it would likewise be a good rule to do it, in general, by a similar scheme of proportion; for example, in a design of landscape, to determine the sky at about two-thirds; or else at about one-third, so that the material objects might occupy the other two: Again, two thirds of one element (as of water), to one third of another element (as of land); and then both together to make but one third of the picture, of which the two other thirds should go for the sky and aerial perspectives. (16)

20 Jullien, *In Praise of Blandness*, 35 and 37.
21 Wenders, *Tokyo-Ga*, 0:04.35.
22 Wenders, *Tokyo-Ga*, 0:48.55.
23 Wenders, *On Film*, 222.
24 Ibid., 368.

11

The Heart of Things: Wim Wenders and the Evocations of Peace

Mary Zournazi

In Wim Wenders's 1994 film *Lisbon Story*, the main protagonist, Phillip Winter—a character who appears across several Wenders films—arrives in Lisbon to document sound for the director Friedrich Monroe. But Friedrich has disappeared from his Lisbon house. All that is left appears to be his journal, his favorite philosophical text, and a strange and elusive child who seems to know where the missing director has gone. As the film progresses, it seems the film director is having some kind of breakdown; he wanders around the city like a haunted figure, talking to himself, and shooting the city of Lisbon with a camera on his back. He's doing an experiment: What happens if you capture images without any purpose? Without any respect for the process and the experience?

The film is part love story, part documentary, and part commentary on the state of images. For the disillusioned Friedrich, images have lost all their meaning and have been consumed by the global forces of marketing and advertising. Friedrich's disenchantment seems to come from loss of a cinematic purpose and its role in documenting reality. I watched *Lisbon Story* again recently, and I laughed out loud at Friedrich and his crazy experiment, but the laugh echoed that strange realization when something dawns on you. What Wenders was addressing in 1994 is even more urgent and more poignant now: How do we understand the rapid circulation and explosion of images around the globe? What does it mean for identities and our sense of place? How do we create images and stories that matter?

It is Phillip Winter who brings Friedrich back to reality, with a soliloquy about the necessity of images that he sends to Friedrich via a tape recorder (emblematic of his work practice). It is worth quoting in full here:

> Now you are at a dead-end street,
> face to the wall.

Turn around and trust your eyes again.
They are not on your back.
Trust your old camera.
It is still able to capture life.
Why would you want to produce trash
if you can shoot indispensable pictures?
With your heart.
On celluloid.

Wim Wenders's love and care for images and the creation of indispensable pictures is, in my mind, a common theme across his work, and it is this love for images and their role in the art and craft of filmmaking that brought us together. Our book *Inventing Peace* (2013) is a philosophical treatise and dialogue on the nature of perception and images. Our emphasis on dialogue was twofold: it involved a dialogue on the nature of perception itself, and a dialogue between ourselves as we explored different possibilities for a moral and visual vocabulary for peace. We considered how to approach peace through sacred, ethical, and spiritual means to help make peace more visible and tangible in our daily lives and experience. In the spirit of our collaboration, this chapter is a dialogue *with* Wim Wenders's work rather than about it. I put forward some films and written texts that resonate with issues around peace that brought us together in the first place, and signal for me his ongoing commitment to "indispensable pictures."

listening

The character of Philip Winter first appears in Wenders's film *Alice in the Cities* (1973). This movie is part of his road movie trilogy, together with *Wrong Move* (1975) and *Kings of the Road* (1976). In *Alice in the Cities*, Winter is a German journalist traveling by car through the United States to write a story about his experience, but he gets writer's block and instead of writing he takes photographs with his Polaroid camera as a way of remembering and capturing the desolation and strangeness of the American landscape. Viewing his mission as failed, he decides to return home, but through a chance encounter he is thrown together with the young Alice, who has been abandoned by her mother. Together, they embark on a journey to find her grandmother in the Ruhr region of Germany.

There is a wonderfully strange moment in *Alice in the Cities* that I want to focus on: Philip Winter is selling his car, and toward the end of the transaction, he hears music in the distance and asks the dealer where it is coming from. The dealer responds that it's the organ playing at Shea Stadium. The film cuts to a pan of the stadium, and in a small booth above the stadium a woman is playing the organ in a very matter-of-fact way. The music lingers into the next scene where Winter is catching a train at Shea Station to meet his publisher in downtown New York.

For me, this moment highlights a type of listening, a moment that gives atmosphere and a sense of place to the film. I can feel the crowd at Shea Stadium, and in the small booth where the woman is playing, I can almost feel her boredom. There is something reverential in this quality of listening that connects us not only with the film but also something that is beyond the sphere of human countenance; it brings us into the realm of the unseen, the "invisible" elements of film and its enduring power.

To listen, then, is an important element across many of Wenders's works, and this listening extends to nonhuman objects as well, such as buildings, cultural remains, rocks, rivers, trees, and other objects (c.f. *Cathedrals of Culture*, 2014).[1] This listening animates the potential for cinema and for peace. As he writes in *Inventing Peace*:

> I've photographed remote locations on this planet,
> from the deepest Australian desert to the American West,
> from the heart of Africa to Armenia.
> But I'm not only attracted to faraway places.
> I've taken pictures in my own city of Berlin, in
> New York or on skyscrapers in Sao Paolo.
>
> What I did in all these places
> was to look for their company. I
> tried to just be there,
> lose myself in those spaces
> and listen to them, as much as possible.
> Yes, just listen.
> One can do that.
> We have that ability.
> We call it "a sense of place".
>
> Just sit by a river and let it flow by for a while.
> The river starts talking to you.
> Its presence gets strong and convincing.
> Its time superimposes itself on your own sense of time. It

tells you to calm down
and become part of its flow.
"Listen!" the river says.
Before you know it,
the waves splashing onto the stones or the sand in front of you
will have stories to tell.
After all, that river saw history.
We always think that we are the only ones witnessing the past.

But that is just what I'm convinced of.
Places speak to us.
All of them!
They have messages,
they tell stories.
Some are sad, some
are hopeful, some
are joyful.
And, yes, some have stopped talking.
They're all talked out.[2]

Wenders's approach to listening resonates with the work of the French philosopher Michel Serres, who asks us to consider nonhuman and human forms of perception. So rather than the world being merely the object of our perception, the world itself *perceives* and, in many ways, humans are a *small* part of this process of engagement. Both are concerned with how to extend our vision of the world and how to enable the different perceptions of it to take hold and move us in some ways, and change how we think, see, and feel.

In this regard, how the world speaks is pivotal to Wenders's films and their sensibility. In the opening sequence of *Paris, Texas* (1984) we see the figure of Travis (Harry Dean Stanton) walking across the desert accompanied by the haunting musical composition of Ry Cooder. It is the desert imagery itself, so present and vivid, that conveys Travis's experience and speaks to us in unexpected ways: the landscape shares its memories and experience with us. And it is often this kind of listening to the world that brings forth a spontaneity and presence that is *unexpected*; it can teach us things. It is a gift that is given to us, if we choose to hear it.

In a different way, the final scene in Wenders's film *Land of Plenty* (2004), which is a response to the effects of 9/11, has this reverential listening through the two main characters: Paul, a former soldier, and his niece, Lana, who has been a missionary and returns to the United States after being abroad. Throughout the film, Paul experiences paranoia after the September 11 bombings, and he is fighting his own "war on terror." It is Lana who is able to help him see through this paranoia, and her character provides an alternative response to the war on terror. In the very last scene Lana and Paul are at the site of the World Trade Center looking out across the wounded territory. Lana says:

> Let's just be quiet.
> Let's just listen.

seeing

In the final stages of writing our book, we spent some time near Joshua Tree National Park in the Mojave Desert. Unbeknownst to us, in the distance was a military base, and occasionally we would hear detonations, and at other times, grey mushroom clouds would hover over the desert. Some evenings we would go outside our cabin, and through the uncannily eerie desert silence we could hear different birds and the wanderings of animals. We decided to include in our book a "postcard from Joshua Tree" that captured the paradox of the peace we were living and the "war" that was surrounding us. On several occasions, Wim took out his camera and waited for the right moment in which to take shots of the military base, which looked like a phantom city in the distance.

As both a filmmaker and a photographer, it is this perceptive quality, this way of seeing, that moves across Wenders's works, and locates a relationship of presence and "witnessing" that is evocative of his encounters with place. It is in this way that the act of seeing and peace coalesce. This quality of vision involves a certain radiance and awareness of things. As Wenders comments on the nature of Andrew Wyeth's painting in *Inventing Peace*, this is about learning how to "see," which involves a responsibility toward the image, whether it is through painting, photography, or filmmaking. Indeed, it is about responding to the presence of a person, or a landscape or thing that we encounter.

We explored this idea of presence and responsibility through some of Martin Buber's work.[3] In Buber's terms, what we see and encounter in this world exists only when there is real responding to it—what he calls *I-Thou* relations. Genuine responsibility arises "between man and man," but this relationship is not limited to the traffic between humans; it is about *becoming aware* of all things, the world as we encounter it and its sacredness. There is nothing necessarily dramatic about becoming aware of things: it allows us to connect with the world to see others and ourselves and to encounter reality *as it is*; in some ways, this *reality* may be why peace is considered as "boring."

Buber documents this kind of reality through a wonderfully careful examination of a "tree." He offers a full sense of this kind of reverential listening and seeing that encompasses the respect that we can bring to life, images, and the world in which we live—something that resonates deeply and strongly in Wenders's work. I quote Buber here for the beauty and the intelligence of perceiving reality and our responses to it:

> I consider a tree
> I can look on it as a picture: stiff column in a shock of light, or splash of green shot with the delicate blue and silver of the background.
> I can perceive it as a movement: flowing veins on clinging, pressing pith, suck of the roots, breathing of the leaves, ceaseless commerce with earth and air—and the obscure growth itself.
> I can classify it in a species and study it as type in its structure and mode of life.
> I can subdue its actual presence and form so sternly that I recognise it only as an expression of law—of the laws in accordance with which a constant opposition of forces is continually adjusted, or of those in accordance with which the component substances mingle and separate.
> I dissipate it and perpetuate it in number, in pure numerical relation.
> In all this the tree remains my object, occupies space and time, and has its nature and constitution.
> It can, however, also come about, if I have both will and grace, that in considering the tree I become bound up in relation to it. The tree is now no longer *It*. I have been seized by the power of exclusiveness.
> To effect this it is not necessary for me to give up any of the ways in which I consider the tree. There is nothing from which I would have to turn my eyes away in order to see, and no knowledge that I would have to forget. Rather is everything, picture and movement, species and type, law and number, indivisibly united in this event.
> Everything belonging to the tree is in this: its form and structure, its colours and chemical composition, its intercourse with the elements and with the stars, are all present in a single whole.
> The tree is no impression, no play of my imagination, no value depending on my mood; but it is bodied over against me and has to do with me, as I with it—only in a different way.

> Let no attempt be made to sap the strength from the meaning of the relation: relation is mutual.
>
> The tree will have a consciousness, then, similar to our own? Of that I have no experience. But do you wish, through seeming to succeed in it with yourself, once again to disintegrate that which cannot be disintegrated? I encounter no soul or dryad of the tree, but the tree itself.[4]

As Buber once noted, that reality is "inseparable, incomparable, irreducible, now, happening once only, it gazes upon me with an awesome look."[5] It is this awesome quality that is about the sacredness of the world, and how we might understand it. In his collection *On Film* (2001) Wenders reflects on Béla Balázs's notion of the sanctity of images, and "the ability (and responsibility) of cinema to 'show things as they are.'" And he says, "Cinema can rescue the existence of things." It can also "teach us how to live."[6]

We see this kind of "awesome quality" in *Alice in the Cities*. Toward the end of the film, Alice and Philip Winter are seated in a café after a long and failed search for her grandmother in Wuppertal. A young boy is eating ice cream, seated by a jukebox that belts out Canned Heat's "On the Road Again." Philip orders a coffee and Alice orders a large ice cream. After some time, Alice says that her grandmother never lived in Wuppertal. There's a long silence, and then Winter gets up and goes to the bathroom. In the documentary *One who Set Forth: Wim Wenders' Early Years* (2007; dir. Marcel Wehn), Rüdiger Vogler, who plays Winter, reflects on this scene as one of most beautiful moments in cinema:

> I could have shouted at her, or told her to go to hell,
> I could have smacked her, or I could have done loads of things.
> But I don't really do anything.
> It's a very long scene without dialogue.
> I go to the toilet
> and look in the mirror and say:
> "Oh, boy!"

In many ways, it is Alice and her childlike vision of the world that enables Philip to open up to a way of relating and experiencing the world which he had not been privy to before. Throughout the film, both Alice and Philip Winter are finding themselves and each other. At the end of the film, Alice and Philip travel by train to Munich after the search for Alice's grandmother ends. Together they seem to have found some solace. Alice asks Philip what he will do in Munich, and Winter replies that he will finish his story.

dreaming

Reflecting on his most adventurous film, *Until the End of the World* (1991), Wenders writes how a film must be preceded by a dream, "either a real dream of the sort that you wake up and remember, or a daydream."[7] In this film, we see a world where dreaming has gone mad. The story follows Claire, who is undertaking a kind of odyssey: She is intrigued by Sam Farber, a man with a double identity, and follows him around the world. She in turn is followed by Eugene, her ex-partner, who still loves her and who records her story. Philip Winter makes another appearance in this film, this time as a kind of detective to help track for Claire the mysterious Farber and his machine.

Farber is capturing images for his blind mother by using a device invented by his father that allows blind people to see. The machine is revolutionary in that it can extend visual parameters and eventually develops the ability to extract images of people's dreams and memories. As the film progresses, the device becomes addictive: the main characters, Claire and Sam, can see inside their own dreams, becoming enclosed within the space of their own existence. In the film, indigenous people will not let their dreams be "stolen" and their images violated.

In the Director's Cut, we see the full extent of the logic of images, the beauty of the world that is beholden to us, just as we witness the loss of the sacredness of images when technology is misappropriated. Addicted to their dreams and memories, Claire and Sam can no longer see each other, or anyone or anything else. They are driven by their narcissism, echoing the myth of Narcissus who is captivated by his own self-image. One of Eugene's statements in the film resonates with many of Wenders's concerns: "In the beginning was the word. What would happen if only the image remained in the end?" Toward the end of the film, the *healing* comes through the power of stories and being able to "see" the world again. The film could be imagining the future of today: our current obsession with image-making—our selfies, our Facebook worlds, our Instagram personalities.

In the light of today's world, the question "Which future of seeing?" preoccupied us and was central to our discussions around peace. We considered some of Heidegger's work on technology and the ways that technology can be used to enhance the world and human capacity, or to destroy it. In his writings on technology, Heidegger often cites the German poet Friedrich Hölderlin's line, "poetically man dwells." Heidegger saw the implications of technology as both creative and artful in orientation, just like the human capacity for thought. Whereas Hölderlin's work searched for the sacredness of god and men, for Heidegger he looked at the mystery that could unfold in the skillful use of technology. Both poet and philosopher believed that the holy could appear in new and still unanticipated forms.

In different ways, Wenders's work pushes the boundaries of cinema and technology, whether it is the innovative neon lighting in *The American Friend* (1977), the exploration of video in *A Notebook on Cities and Clothes* (1989) and most recently through 3-D and its potential. In *Pina* (2011), Wenders uses 3-D as way to open out the potential of cinematic experience and as a way of documenting life. What 3-D enables is a form of presence: a new connection between the human body and technology that enhances and extends visual and cinematic language. Crossing the boundaries of dance and the cinematic image, the camera that *dances* with us demonstrates the grace and beauty of the human body and its unique language. Wenders reflects on the curious act of seeing that 3-D enables, as well as its precarity:

> Still, my deepest desire, or biggest hope
> is that this future 3D cinema will in fact ignite a new interest in *the act of seeing*,
> in the *physiology* and *psychology*
> of what our eyes and our brains do together, in unison in
> the most amazing perfection,
> to *create* space, depth, volume and presence.
> Every day, right now, "in life,"
> when you put down this book and go outside,
> when you see the world, your friends, or kids, or neighbours,
> your eyes and your spatial perception are miracles!
>
> That is what 3D tries to imitate and could *become*:
> a miraculously new/old way to perceive life,
> in which we are more immersed and concerned again.
> There is still a long way to go;
> this is an adventurous road
> into a territory that is still largely unexplored, cinematically,
> yet so well known, humanly and physiologically.
> I look at it as a chance,
> but it might very well be
> that the new language is wasted before it can fulfil its promises.[8]

In his 3-D film *Everything Will Be Fine* (2015), Wenders uses the sense of "volume" and presence to bring us closer to the fictional characters and their realities. The main protagonist, Tomas, causes the death of a child through a car accident and the film traces his journey toward redemption and forgiveness. In the film, it is the immersion in and proximity to his experience that allows us to see the world which Tomas inhabits and to feel ourselves into it. There is a remarkable moment in *Everything Will Be Fine* that materializes Buber's tree: a tree standing in its entirety—there is a sense of its "roundness"; we can feel its presence, its uniqueness and its beauty. The presence of the tree is a reminder of the potential for healing in the film—the forgiveness and redemption that is possible not only for Tomas but also for us: how we can respond to tragedy through love and tenderness rather than regret, and this is a love that endures.

The unforgettable

In April 2018, Wenders delivered a lecture for Harvard University's Norton Lecture Series entitled "The Visible and the Invisible." Wenders spoke of the contradistinctions that often frame the way we "define the world of movies as well as their (and our) relation to the world." In particular, Wenders discussed the relationship between the *visible* and *invisible* in cinema; he argued that we tend to concentrate on the visible elements of cinema which are the "dominant" realm of motion pictures, but the other important realm of cinema is invisible, the unforgettable elements that linger long after we see a film: the feelings, the memories, the spaces in-between, and how we can see and imagine or dream ourselves into a film (or a book, for that matter).

So what makes films unforgettable? It is the difference between films that are "products" and films that are a form of expression. (This echoes Friedrich's disillusionment in *Lisbon Story*.) This notion of "making visible" involves a moral and ethical language for cinema in general, and Wenders's notion of film involves a sense of the sacred and the invisible elements that can teach us something about the world, where we can feel and experience things. In my mind, they enable us to *think* and *feel*: the affective qualities that change our perceptual habits.

During the question-and-answer period at the Harvard lecture, an audience member asked about the films that may not have any sense of "action" or instant gratification, those films that might be considered "boring." In his astute response, Wenders described how this inspired a new logic: the relationship between the *boring* and the *unforgettable* in cinema. Wenders has had a long and deep admiration for Japanese film director Yasujiro Ozu. And in many ways the logic of the boring and the unforgettable in cinema might seem to correspond with Ozu's work. Today's audiences may find Ozu "boring," and yet his films speak to the heart of the human condition. For example, *Tokyo Story* (1953) is a moving story of a family and their inherent selfishness, and it is perhaps a masterpiece of the "boring" because of its real-time affectation and plot. The power of this film is that we feel and we are moved by the story, and we learn something about ourselves.

It is the common or shared collective memory that evokes the unforgettable elements of film. What Wenders argues belongs to common territory between the filmmaker and the audience—in other words, the space that enables you to encounter the story and to feel and be moved by it. This is what endures and what enables a kind of sense or sentience of time where we can remember, care, and love aspects of a film. And, in what Wenders refers to as the "architecture of time," the moments that create the totality of a film is where we might find glimpses of other stories and experiences that may change our lives. And it is these moments in cinema and in life that may enable us to see, dream, and be re-enchanted with the world once again.

Notes

1   See Michel Serres, *Eyes*, trans. Anne-Marie Feenberg-Dibon (London: Bloomsbury Press, 2015).
2   Wim Wenders and Mary Zournazi, *Inventing Peace: A Dialogue on Perception* (London: I.B. Tauris, 2013), 137–39.
3   Martin Buber, *I and Thou* (London: Routledge Classics, 2004).
4   Ibid., 14.
5   Martin Buber, *The Way of Response*, ed. N. N. Glatzer (New York: Schocken Books, 1966), 22.
6   Wim Wenders, *On Film* (London: Faber and Faber, 2001), 159.
7   Ibid., 297.
8   Wenders and Zournazi, *Inventing Peace*, 175.

Bibliography

Adorno, Theodor and Max Horkheimer. *Dialectic of Enlightenment*. 1944. Translated by John Cumming. New York: Herder and Herder, 1972.

Alter, Nora M. "Documentary as Simulacrum: Tokyo-Ga." In *The Cinema of Wim Wenders: Image, Narrative, and the Postmodern Condition*, edited by Roger F. Cook and Gerd Gemünden, 136–62. Detroit: Wayne State University Press, 1997.

Alter, Nora. "Global Politics, Cinematographic Space: Wenders's *Tokyo-Ga* and *Notebooks on Cities and Clothes*." In *Projecting History: German Nonfiction Cinema, 1967-2000*, 103–49. Ann Arbor: University of Michigan Press, 2002.

Anderson, Benedict. *Imagined Communities: Reflections on the Origin and Spread of Nationalism*. London: Verso, 1983.

Appiah, Kwame Anthony. *Cosmopolitanism: Ethics in a World of Strangers*. New York: W. W. Norton & Company, 2006.

Bachelard, Gaston. *The Poetics of Reverie*. Translated by Daniel Russell. Boston: Beacon Press, 1971.

Balázs, Béla. *Béla Balázs: Early Film Theory: Visible Man and the Spirit of Film*. Edited by Erica Carter. New York: Berghahn Books, 2010.

Barglow, Raymond. "The Angel of History: Walter Benjamin's Vision of Hope and Despair." *Tikkun Magazine*, 1998. http://barglow.com/angel_of_history.htm.

Bausch, Pina. "Etwas finden, was keiner Frage bedarf. Rede beim '2007 Kyoto Prize Workshop in Arts and Philosophy' am 12. November 2007 in Kyoto." In *O-Ton Pina Bausch: Interviews und Reden*, edited by Stefan Koldehoff and Pina Bausch Foundation, 317–32. Wädenswil, Switzerland: Nimbus, 2016.

Bausch, Pina. "Was mich bewegt. Rede aus Anlass der Verleihung des 'Kyoto Preises' am 11. November 2007 in Kyoto." In *O-Ton Pina Bausch: Interviews und Reden*, edited by Stefan Koldehoff and Pina Bausch Foundation, 295–315. Wädenswil, Switzerland: Nimbus, 2016.

Benjamin, Walter. "The Formula in Which the Dialectical Structure of Film Finds Expression." In *Selected Writings, vol. 3, 1935-1938*, edited by Howard Eiland and Michael W. Jennings, translated by Edmund Jephcott, Howard Eiland, et al., 94–95. Cambridge, MA: Belknap Press of Harvard University Press, 2002.

Benjamin, Walter. "The Image of Proust." In *Illuminations: Essays and Reflections*, edited by Hannah Arendt, translated by Harry Zohn, 201–16. Suffolk: Fontana, 1982.

Benjamin, Walter. "The Work of Art in the Age of Its Technological Reproducibility: Third Version." In *Selected Writings, vol. 4, 1938-1940*, edited by Howard Eiland and

Michael W. Jennings, translated by Edmund Jephcott et al., 251–83. Cambridge, MA: Belknap Press of Harvard University Press, 2006.

Benjamin, Walter. "Theses on the Philosophy of History." In *Illuminations*, edited by Hannah Arendt, translated by Harry Zohn, 253–64. New York: Schocken Books, 1968.

Berghahn, Daniela. "Leben ... ein Blick genügt doch: Der utopische Augenblick in Wim Wenders' 'Road Movies.'" *Monatshefte* 91, no. 1 (Spring 1999): 64–83.

Bingham, Adam. "DVD Reviews: *Wings of Desire*." *Cineaste* Spring 2010: 68–69.

Bloomaert, Jan. *Discourse: A Critical Introduction*. Cambridge: Cambridge University Press, 2005.

Bourdieu, Pierre. "Social Space and Symbolic Power." *Sociological Theory* 7, no. 11 (1989): 14–25. Doi: 10.2307/202060.

Brady, Martin and Joanne Leal. *Wim Wenders and Peter Handke: Collaboration, Adaptation, Recomposition*. Amsterdam: Editions Rodopi, 2011.

Brandes, Peter. "Wim Wenders und die romantische Ästhetik des Sehens." *komparatistik online*, no. 1 (2007): 1–4.

Bratu Hansen, Miriam. Introduction to *Theory of Film: The Redemption of Physical Reality*, by Siegfried Kracauer, vii–xlv. Princeton, NJ: Princeton University Press, 1997.

Braun, Josef. "Outsider's Eye: The Peculiar Case of Wim Wenders." *VueWeekly*, May 20, 2015. http://vueweekly.com/outsider-eye-the-peculiar-case-of-wim-wenders/.

Buber, Martin. *I and Thou*. London: Routledge Classics, 2004.

Buber, Martin. *The Way of Response*. Edited by N. N. Glatzer. New York: Schocken Books, 1966.

Buchka, Peter. *Augen kann man nicht kaufen: Wim Wenders und seine Filme*. Munich: Carl Hanser Verlag, 1983.

Busnel, François, in conversation with Wim Wenders and Peter Handke. "Wim Wenders adapte au cinéma la pièce de Peter Handke 'Les beaux jours d'Aranjuez.'" *La Grande Librairie*, October 28, 2016. www.youtube.com/watch?v=A4sLktgdJ0U.

Caltvedt, Les. "Berlin Poetry: Archaic Cultural Patterns in Wenders's *Wings of Desire*." *Literature Film Quarterly* 20, no. 2 (1992): 121–26.

Campbell, Joseph. *The Hero with a Thousand Faces*. New York: Pantheon, 1949.

Campbell, Karen J. "Rilke's *Duino Angels* and the Angels of Islam." *Alif: Journal of Comparative Poetics*, no. 23 (2003): 191–211.

Chin, Rita. "Imagining a German Multiculturalism: Aras Ören and the Contested Meanings of the 'Guest Worker,' 1955–1980." *Radical History Review* 83 (Spring 2002): 44–72.

Cieko, Anne. "Voyeurism as an Epistemological and Narrative Device: Wim Wenders's *Wings of Desire*." In *Presented at the Salisbury Literature/Film Conference*, 1990. http://cinema.usc.edu/assets/101/16176.pdf.

Cook, Roger F. "Postmodern Culture and Film Narrative." In *The Cinema of Wim Wenders: Image, Narrative, and the Postmodern Condition*, edited by Roger F. Cook and Gerd Gemünden, 121–35. Detroit: Wayne State University Press, 1997.

Cook, Roger and Gerd Gemünden. *The Cinema of Wim Wenders: Image, Narrative, and the Postmodern Condition*. Detroit: Wayne State University, 1997.

Cormican, Muriel. "Goodbye Wenders: *Lola Rennt* as German Film Manifesto." *German Studies Review* 30, no. 1 (February 2007): 121–40.

Cornell, Joseph. *Navigating the Imagination*. New Haven, CT: Yale University Press, 2008.

Corrigan, Timothy. "Wenders's *Kings of the Road*." In *New German Film: The Displaced Image*, 19–32. Bloomington: Indiana University Press, 1983.

Coury, David N. *The Return of Storytelling in Contemporary German Literature and Film: Peter Handke and Wim Wenders*. Lewiston, NY: Edwin Mellen Press, 2004.

Dauman, Anatole. *Pictures of a Producer*. London: British Film Institute, 1992.

Dawes, Bridget. "Celluloid Recoveries: Cinematic Transformations of Ground Zero." In *Media and Cultural Memory / Medien und kulturelle Erinnerung: Transnational American Memories*, edited by Udo Hebel, 285–309. Berlin: de Gruyter, 2009.

Dawson, Jan. *Wim Wenders*. Translated by C. Wartenberg. New York: Zoetrope, 1982.

De Campos Martins, Pablo Gonçalo Pires. "As Espirais Dos Arquivos: Lento Retorno e as Paisagens de Um Filme Sem Telas." *Galáxia (São Paulo)*, no. 33 (2016): 94–106. Doi: 10.1590/1982-25542016225353.

Deleuze, Gilles. *Cinema I: The Movement Image*. London: Continuum International Pub., 2005.

Deleuze, Gilles and Félix Guattari. *A Thousand Plateaus: Capitalism and Schizophrenia*. Minneapolis: University of Minnesota Press, 1987.

Deleuze, Gilles and Félix Guattari. *What Is Philosophy?* New York: Columbia University Press, 1994.

Desser, David. "*Tokyo Story* (1953), Ozu Yasujiro." In *Film Analysis: A Norton Reader*, edited by Jeffrey Geiger and R. L. Rutsky, 456–72. New York: W.W. Norton & Company, 2005.

Diawara, Manthia. "Black British Cinema: Spectatorship and Identity Formation in *Territories*." *Public Culture* 3, no. 1 (1990): 33–48.

Eichendorff, Joseph von. "Sehnsucht." 1834. In *Deutsche Gedichte. Von den Anfängen bis zur Gegenwart*, edited by Benno von Wiese, 376. Berlin: Cornelsen, 1993.

Eisenschitz, Bernard. *Nicholas Ray: An American Journey*. Translated by Tom Milne. London: Faber and Faber, 1993.

Eißel, Katharina. *Er-Fahrung neuer Horizonte: Reise und Wahrnehmung in Filmen von Wim Wenders*. Saarbrücken: VDM, 2007.

Eisert-Rost, Elisabeth et al. "Heimat." In *Der deutsche Heimatfilm. Bildwelten und Weltbilder. Bilder, Texte, Analysen zu 70 Jahren deutscher Filmgeschichte*, edited by Wolfgang Kaschuba, 15–32. Tübingen: Tübinger Vereinigung für Volkskunde, 1989.

Eitner, Lorenz. "The Open Window and the Storm-Tossed Boat: An Essay in the Iconography of Romanticism." *The Art Bulletin* 37, no. 4 (1955): 281–90.

Eleftheriotis, Dimitris. "Global Visions and European Perspectives." In *Aliens R Us: The Other in Science Fiction Cinema*, edited by Ziauddin Sardar and Sean Cubitt, 164–80. London: Pluto Press, 2002.

Elsaesser, Thomas. *New German Cinema: A History*. New Brunswick, NJ: Rutgers University Press, 1989.

Elsaesser, Thomas. "Spectators of Life: Time Place and Self in the Films of Wim Wenders." In *The Cinema of Wim Wenders: Image, Narrative, and the Postmodern Condition*, edited by Roger F. Cook and Gerd Gemünden, 240–56. Detroit: Wayne State University Press, 1997.

Eren, Mine. "Breaking the Stigma? The Anti-heroine in Fatih Akın's *Head-On*." In *Muslim Women, Transnational Feminism and the Ethics of Pedagogy: Contested Imaginaries in Post-9/11 Cultural Practice*, edited by Lisa K. Taylor and Jasmin Zine, 82–109. New York: Routledge, 2014.

Evans, Walker and Jerry L. Thompson. *Walker Evans at Work: 745 Photographs Together with Documents Selected from Letters, Memoranda, Interviews, Notes*. New York: Harper & Row, 1982.

Fadil, Nadia. "Not-/Unveiling as an Ethical Practice." Islam in Europe. *Feminist Review* 98 (2011): 83–109.

Franke, Yvonne. "Wim Wenders' *Im Lauf der Zeit*—No Place to Go." In *Heimat Goes Mobile: Hybrid Forms of Home in Literature and Film*, edited by Gabriele Eichmanns and Yvonne Franke, 190–211. Newcastle upon Tyne: Cambridge Scholars Publishing, 2013.

Fuchs, Anne and Mary Cosgrove. "Introduction: Germany's Memory Contests and the Management of the Past." In *German Memory Contests: The Quest for Identity in Literature, Film, and Discourse since 1990*, edited by Anne Fuchs and Mary Cosgrove, 1–24. Columbia, SC: Camden House, 2010.

Fusco, Coco. "Angels, History and Poetic Fantasy." *Cineaste* 16, no. 4 (1988): 14–17.

Gaffez, Fabien. "Le rouge et le vert: D'Edward Hopper à Robby Müller." *Positif* no. 621 (November 2012): 104–5.

Geist, Kathe. *The Cinema of Wim Wenders: From Paris, France to Paris, Texas*. Ann Arbor: The University of Michigan Press, 1988.

Gemünden, Gerd. *Framed Visions: Popular Culture, Americanization, and the Contemporary German and Austrian Imagination*. Ann Arbor: University of Michigan Press, 1998.

Goethe, Johann W. *Werke: Hamburger Ausgabe in 14 Bänden*. Vol. 7: Romane und Novellen II. Edited by Erich Trunz. Munich: dtv, 2000.

Gonçalo, Pablo. "Film in Words/Words in Pictures: Ekphrasis Modulations in Peter Handke and Wim Wenders' Cinematic Collaborations." *Journal of Screenwriting* 8, no. 1 (2017): 83–97.

Goodman, Sara Wallace. "The Politics and Policies of Immigration in Germany: A Rearview Look at the Makings of a 'Country of Immigration.'" *German Politics and Society* 85 (2007): 99–110.

Graf, Alexander. *The Cinema of Wim Wenders: The Celluloid Highway*. London: Wallflower Press, 2002.

Gramling, David. "Seven Types of Multilingualism: Or, Wim Wenders Enfilms Pina Bausch." In *The Multilingual Screen: New Reflection on Cinema and Linguistic Difference*, edited by Tijana Mamula and Lisa Patti, 37–56. New York: Bloomsbury Academic, 2016.

Grimm, Jakob and Wilhelm. *Werke. Abt. III, Bd. 42.1: Deutsches Wörterbuch. Dritter Band: E—Forsche*. 1862. Edited by Wilfried Kürscher. Hildesheim / Zürich / New York: Olms, 2003.

Grob, Norbert. "'Life Sneaks Out of Stories': *Until the End of the World*." In *The Cinema of Wim Wenders: Image, Narrative, and the Postmodern Condition*, edited by Roger F. Cook and Gerd Gemünden, 191–204. Detroit: Wayne State University Press, 1997.

Grob, Norbert. *Wenders*. Berlin: Wissenschaftsverlag Volker Spiess, 1991.

Hagener, Malte and Thomas Elsaesser. *Filmtheorie zur Einführung*. Hamburg: Junius, 2007.

Hake, Sabine and Barbara Caroline Mennel, eds. *Turkish German Cinema in the New Millennium: Sites, Sounds, and Screens*. New York: Berghahn Books, 2014.

Halle, Randall. *The Europeanization of Cinema: Interzones and Imaginative Communities*. Urbana: University of Illinois Press, 2014.

Handke, Peter. *Der kurze Brief zum langen Abschied*. Frankfurt/Main: Suhrkamp, 1972.

Handke, Peter. *Falsche Bewegung*. Frankfurt/Main: Suhrkamp, 1975.

Handke, Peter and Wim Wenders. "Die Helden sind die Andern." In *Wim Wenders, Die Logik der Bilder: Essays und Gespräche*, edited by Michael Töteberg, 18–22. Frankfurt/Main: Verlag der Autoren, 1988.

Haskell, Barbara. "Edward Hopper: Between Realism and Abstraction." In *Modern Life: Edward Hopper and His Time*, edited by Barbara Haskell in collaboration with Ortrud Westheider, 48–55. Munich: Hirmer Verlag, 2009.

Haugen, Einer Ingvald. *The Ecology of Language: Essays by Einar Haugen*, selected and introduced by Anwar S. Dil. Stanford: Stanford University Press, 1972.

Hayes, Christian. "Phantom Rides." *BFI Screen Online*, July 7, 2014. www.screenonline.org.uk/film/id/1193042/.

Heesen, Ankete. *The World in a Box: The Story of an Eighteenth-Century Picture Encyclopedia*. Chicago: University of Chicago Press, 2002.

Helfer, Martha. "Gender Studies and Romanticism." In *The Literature of German Romanticism*, edited by Dennis F. Mahoney, 229–50. Rochester, NY: Camden House, 2004.

Hernandez, Tanya. "The Buena Vista Social Club: The Racial Politics of Nostalgia." In *Latino/a Popular Culture*, edited by Michelle Habell-Pallan and Mary Romero, 61–72. New York: NYU Press, 2002.

Hikmet, Nazım. *Beyond the Walls: Selected Poems*. Translated by Ruth Christie, Richard McKane and Talât Sait Halman. London: Anvil Press Poetry: 2003.

Hikmet, Nazım. "The Walnut Tree." In *Nazım Hikmet: Bütün şiirleri [Nazım Hikmet: All Poems]*, 1618, 1957. Istanbul: Yapı Kredi Sanat Yayıncılık Ticaret ve Sanayi, 2008.

Hoffmann, E. T. A. *Des Vetters Eckfenster*. 1822. Stuttgart: Reclam, 2014.

hooks, bell. "The Oppositional Gaze: Black Female Spectators." In *Reel to Real: Race, Sex, and Class at the Movies*, 197–213. New York and London: Routledge Taylor & Francis Group, 2009.

Horrocks, David and Eva Kolinsky. *Turkish Culture in German Society Today*. Providence, Oxford: Berghahn Books, 1996.

Huber, Nicole and Ralph Stern. "From the American West to West Berlin: Wim Wenders, Border Crossings, and the Transnational Imaginary." *Places Journal*, April 2014. placesjournal.org/article/from-the-american-west-to-west-berlin/.

Hutcheon, Linda. *A Theory of Adaptation*. New York: Routledge, 2006.

Huyssen, Andreas. *After the Great Divide: Modernism, Mass Culture, Postmodernism*. Bloomington: Indiana University Press, 1986.

Jacobs, Jürgen. "Bildungsroman." In *Reallexikon der Deutschen Literaturwissenschaft: Neubearbeitung des Reallexikons der Deutschen Literaturgeschichte*, edited by Klaus Weimar and Harald Fricke, 230–33. Berlin: de Gruyter, 2007.

Jullien, François. *Ein Umweg über China: Ein Ortswechsel des Denkens*. Berlin: Merve, 2001.

Jullien, François. *In Praise of Blandness*. New York: Zone Books, 2008.

Kahana, Jonathan, ed. *The Documentary Film Reader: History, Theory, Criticism*. Oxford: Oxford University Press, 2016.

Koebner, Thomas. *Unbehauste: Zur deutschen Literatur in der Weimarer Republik, im Exil und in der Nachkriegszeit*. Munich: Ed. Text + Kritik, 1992.

Kolker, Robert Philip and Peter Beicken. *The Films of Wim Wenders: Cinema as Vision and Desire*. Cambridge: Cambridge University Press, 1993.

Köster, Werner. *Wim Wenders und Peter Handke: "Kongenialität"—intermediale Ästhetik—Kommentarbedürftigkeit*. Marburg: Tectum-Verl., 2015.

Kracauer, Siegfried. *Theory of Film: The Redemption of Physical Reality*. New York: Oxford University Press, 1960.

Kramsch, Claire. "Ecological Perspectives on Foreign Language Education." *Language Teaching* 41, no. 3 (2008): 389–408.

Krätzsch, Dana. "Was ist 'falsch' an *Falsche Bewegung*? Zu Peter Handkes Wilhelm Meister-Adaption." In *Poetische Welt(en): Ludwig Stockinger zum 65. Geburtstag zugeeignet*, edited by Martin Blawid and Katrin Henzel, 29–40. Leipzig: Leipziger Univ.-Verl., 2011.

Kreimeier, Klaus. "Die Welt ein Filmatelier oder: Herzkammerton Kino." In *Wim Wenders*, edited by Frieda Grafe, 15–42. Munich: Hanser, 1992.

Kuerten, Jochen, "US Experience Brought out the European in Me, Wenders Says," *Deutsche Welle*, May 19, 2009. http://dw.com/en/us-experience-brought-out-the-european-in-me-wenders-says/a-4264372.

Kuhn, Annette. *Power of the Image: Essays on Representation and Sexuality*. London: Routledge, 2016.

Kuzniar, Alice. "Wenders' Windshields." In *The Cinema of Wim Wenders: Image, Narrative, and the Postmodern Condition*, edited by Roger F. Cook and Gerd Gemünden, 222–39. Detroit: Wayne State University Press, 1997.

Linsel, Anne. *Pina Bausch: Bilder eines Lebens*. Hamburg: Edel Books, 2013.

Littlejohns, Richard, "German Romantic Painters," In *The Cambridge Companion to German Romanticism*, edited by Nicholas Saul, 227–41. Cambridge: Cambridge University Press, 2009.

Llana, Sara Miller. "A New, Unlikely 'Nation of Immigrants': Germany." *The Christian Science Monitor*, December 12, 2014. https://www.csmonitor.com/World/Europe/2014/1212/A-new-unlikely-nation-of-immigrants-Germany.

Luprecht, Mark. "Opaque Skies: *Wings of Desire*—Angelic Text, Context, and Subtext." *Post Script* 17, no. 3 (Summer 1998): 47–54.

Malaguti, Simone. *Wim Wenders' Filme und ihre intermediale Beziehung zur Literatur Peter Handkes*. Frankfurt/Main: Lang, 2008.

Mann, Charles C. *1491: New Revelations of the Americas before Columbus*. New York: Random House–Vintage, 2005.

Mann, Klaus. *Mephisto: Roman einer Karriere*. Frankfurt/Main: S. Fischer, 2000.

Mariniello, Silvestra. "Experience and Memory in the Films of Wim Wenders." *Substance* 34, no. 1, Issue 106 (2005): 159–79.

Martinec, Thomas. "'Some Kind of Film Poem': The Poetry of Wim Wenders' *Der Himmel über Berlin/Wings of Desire*." *Studies in European Cinema* 6, no. 23 (2009): 165–78.

Marx, Karl. *The Eighteenth Brumaire of Louis Bonaparte*. 1852. Beijing: Foreign Languages Press, 1978.

Mazierska, Ewa and Laura Rascaroli. *Crossing New Europe: Postmodern Travel and the European Road Movie*. London: Wallflower Press, 2006.

McCormick, Richard W. "'Wilhelm Meister' revisited: 'Falsche Bewegung' by Peter Handke and Wim Wenders." In *The Age of Goethe Today: Critical Reexamination and Literary Reflection*, edited by Gertrud B. Pickar and Sabine Cramer, 194–211. Munich: Fink, 1990.

Medeiros, Paulo de. "Representing Lisbon: Wenders, Memory and Desire." *Journal of Romance Studies* 1, no. 2 (Summer 2001): 73–88.

Medina, Alberto. "Jameson, 'Buena Vista Social Club' and Other Exercises in the Restoration of the Real" *Iberoamericana (2001–)* 7, no. 25 (March 2007): 7–21.

Meinecke, Friedrich. *Die deutsche Katastrophe: Betrachtungen und Erinnerungen.* Wiesbaden: Brockhaus, 1946.

Mennel, Barbara. "The Politics of Space in the Cinema of Migration," *German as a Foreign Language* 3 (2010): 40–55.

Modern Languages Association Ad Hoc Committee on Foreign Languages. "Foreign Languages and Higher Education: New Structures for a Changed World." *Profession* 12 (2007): 234–35. www.mla.org/Resources/Research/Surveys-Reports-and-Other-Documents/Teaching-Enrollments-and-Programs/Foreign-Languages-and-Higher-Education-New-Structures-for-a-Changed-World.

Mohnike, Thomas. "The History-Accumulator: Berlin as a Foreign Metropolis." In *Nordic Literature: A Comparative History Volume 1: Spatial Nodes,* edited by Thomas A. DuBois, Dan A. Ringgaard, and Steven P. Sondrup, 262–74. Amsterdam: Benjamins, 2017.

Mora, Gilles and John T. Hill. *Walker Evans: The Hungry Eye.* London: Thames and Hudson, 2004.

Morley, David and Kuan-Hsing Chen, eds. *Stuart Hall: Critical Dialogues in Cultural Studies.* New York: Routledge, 1996.

Mulvey, Laura. "Visual Pleasure and Narrative Cinema." In *Film Theory and Criticism: Introductory Readings,* edited by Leo Braudy and Marshall Cohen, 833–44. New York: Oxford UP, 1999.

Münkler, Herfried. "The Fall of the Wall and German Reunification." *Young Germany,* April 9, 2013. http://www.young-germany.de/topic/live/settle-in-adjust/the-fall-of-the-wall-and-german-reunification.

Murch, Walter. Foreword to *Audio-Vision: Sound on Screen,* by Michel Chion, vii–xxiv. Translated by Claudia Gorbman. New York: Columbia University Press, 1994.

Nagib, Lúcia. *Impure Cinema: Intermedial and Intercultural Approaches to Film.* London: I.B. Tauris, 2014.

Négresse Verte. "Nazım Hikmet Ran—Zülfü Livaneli: 'Karlı Kayın Ormanında' ('In the snowy night woods')." *Négresse Verte* (blog), August 16, 2007. http://negresseverte.blogspot.com/2007_08_16_archive.html (accessed April 20, 2018).

Neumann, Erwin. "Frühromantische Künstlerromane in den Spuren des Goetheschen 'Wilhelm Meister': Ludwig Tiecks 'Sternbald,' Friedrich Schlegels 'Lucinde' und Novalis' 'Heinrich von Ofterdingen.'" In *Wilhelm Meister und seine Nachfahren: Vorträge des 4. Kasseler Goethe-Seminars,* edited by Helmut Fuhrmann, 53–74. Kassel: Wenderoth, 2000.

Nikfarjam, Omid. "Dreaming a Continent." *New Statesman,* July 12, 2007. www.newstatesman.com/arts-and-culture/2007/07/european-film-cinema-pictures.

Novalis. *Heinrich von Ofterdingen: Berlin 1802.* Edited by Joseph-Kiermeier-Debre. Munich: dtv, 2014.

Novalis. *Vorarbeiten zu verschiedenen Fragmentsammlungen*. 1798. In *Novalis: Schriften, Bd. 2: Das philosophische Werk I*, edited by Richard Samuel, 507–651. Stuttgart: Kohlhammer, 1960.

Onaylı, Kutay. "Nazım Hikmet: A Loving Revolutionary." *Vagabond Magazine*, February 19, 2014. http://vagabondmagazine.org/nazim-hikmet-romantic-communism/.

Ören, Aras. *Was will Niyazi in der Naunynstrasse: Ein Poem*. Berlin: Rotbuch Verlag, 1977.

Peucker, Brigitte. "Filming Tableau Vivant: Vermeer, Intermediality, and the Real." In *Rites of Realism: Essays on Corporeal Cinema*, edited by Ivone Margulies, 294–314. Durham: Duke University Press, 2003.

Prager, Brad. "29 February 1972: With *Die Angst des Tormanns beim* Elfmeter New German Cinema Learns to Read." In *A New History of German Cinema*, edited by Jennifer M. Kapczynski and Michael D. Richardson, 436–41. Rochester: Camden House, 2012.

Press, Skip. *The Complete Idiot's Guide to Screenwriting*. Toronto: Alpha-Penguin, 2008.

Reichardt, Ulfried. *Globalisierung: Literaturen und Kulturen des Globalen*. Berlin: Akademie Verlag, 2011.

Rentschler, Eric. *West German Cinema in the Course of Time: Reflections on the Twenty Years since Oberhausen*. Bedford Hills: Redgrave, 1984.

Rentschler, Eric. *West German Filmmakers on Film: Visions and Voices*. New York: Holmes & Meier, 1988.

Richard, Paul. "Putting the World in a Box: Joseph Cornell's Inside Stories." *Special to The Washington Post*, November 19, 2006. http://www.washingtonpost.com/wp-dyn/content/article/2006/11/17/AR2006111700301.html

Richter, Gerhard. *Afterness: Figures of Following in Modern Thought and Aesthetics*. New York: Columbia University Press, 2011.

Rodowick, D. N. "Unthinkable Sex: Conceptual Personae and the Time-Image." In *InVisible Culture: an Electronic Journal for Visual Studies*, 2000. www.rochester.edu/in_visible_culture/issue3/IVC_iss3_Rodowick.pdf (accessed April 14, 2018).

Rogowski, Christian. "To be Continued: History in Wim Wenders's *Wings of Desire* and Thomas Brasch's *Domino*." *German Studies Review* 15, no. 3 (1992): 547–63.

Rosenbaum, Jonathan. "City of Angels (on *Wings of Desire*)." *Chicago Reader*, July 15, 1988. https://www.jonathanrosenbaum.net/2017/08/city-of-angels/.

Russell, Catherine. "The Life and Death of Authorship in Wim Wenders' *The State of Things*." *Canadian Journal of Film Studies / Revue canadienne d'études cinématographiques* 1, no. 1 (1990): 15–28.

Salgado, Sabastião. *Genesis*. Cologne: Taschen, 2013.

Salgado, Sabastião and Eric Nepomuceno. *Workers: An Archeology of the Industrial Age*. London: Phaidon, 1993.

Sander, Gerd. *August Sander: People of the 20th Century*. 1927. Munich: Schirmer/Mosel Verlag, 2013.

Schiewer, Gesine Lenore. "Interkulturelle Philologie am Beispiel der Interpretation von Chamisso-Literatur—Ansätze der Linguistik unter Berücksichtigung der Mehrsprachigkeitsforschung." In *Literatur Interpretieren. Interdisziplinäre Beiträge zur Theorie und Praxis*, edited by Jan Borkowksi, Stefan Descher, Felicitas Ferder, and Philipp David Heine, 361–87. Münster: Mentis, 2015.

Schrader, Paul. *Transcendental Style in Film: Ozu, Bresson, Dreyer*. Los Angeles: University of California Press, 1972.

Serres, Michel. *Eyes*. Translated by Anne-Marie Feenberg-Dibon. London: Bloomsbury Press, 2015.

Smith, John Thomas. *Remarks on Rural Scenery*. London: S. and R. Bentley, 1797.

Smith-Prei, Carrie. "Translating Pina for *Pina*." In *Translation and Translating in German Studies: a Festschrift in Honour of Raleigh Whitinger*, edited by John L. Plews and Diana Spokiene, 175–87. Waterloo: Wilfried Laurier University Press, 2016.

Sontag, Susan. *Regarding the Pain of Others*. London: Picador, 2003.

Speck, Oliver C. *Funny Frames: The Filmic Concepts of Michael Haneke*. New York: Continuum, 2010.

Stam, Robert. "Introduction: The Theory and Practice of Adaptation." In *Literature and Film: A Guide to the Theory and Practice of Film Adaptation*, edited by Robert Stam and Alessandra Raengo, 1–52. Oxford: Blackwell Publishing, 2005.

Strasberg, Lee. "A Dream of Passion: The Development of the Method." In *Star Texts: Image and Performance in Film and Television*, edited by Jeremy Butler, 42–50. Detroit: Wayne State University Press, 1991.

Telgenbüscher, Joachim. *Die Kunst der Romantik: Europas Maler im Zeitalter der Sehnsucht 1790–1860*. Hamburg: Gruner Jahr, 2014.

Troyen, Carol. "Edward Hopper's Stories." *Magazine Antique*, April 2007, 82–91.

Varga, Darrell. "The Bones of Reagan; Or, the Ruins of Art Cinema in Contemporary American Film." *CineAction* 75 (Winter 2008): 4–19.

Virilio, Paul. "Die Dromoskopie." In *Der negative Horizont: Bewegung—Geschwindigkeit—Beschleunigung*, 133–54. Munich/Vienna: Hanser, 1989.

Visarius, Karsten. "Das Versagen der Sprache oder: His Master's Voice." In *Wim Wenders*, with texts by Frieda Grafe et al., 43–64. Munich/Vienna: Hanser, 1992.

Vogler, Christopher. *The Writer's Journey: Mythic Structure for Writers*. Studio City, CA: Michael Wise Productions, 2007.

Weiner, Jonah. "The Dirty Projectors Go Solo." *The New York Times Magazine*, February 2017.

Wenders, Donata and Wim Wenders. *Pina: The Film and the Dancers*. Munich: Schirmer/Mosel, 2012.

Wenders, Wim. "An Attempted Description of an Indescribable Film." *Current* (blog). *The Criterion Collection*, November 2, 2009. http://www.criterion.com/current/posts/1289-an-attempted-description-of-an-indescribable-film.

Wenders, Wim. "Auf der Suche nach Bildern: Orte sind meine stärksten Bildgeber." In *Iconic Turn: die neue Macht der Bilder*, edited by Christa Maar and Hubert Burda, 283–302. Cologne: DuMont Literatur und Kunst Verlag, 2004.

Wenders, Wim. "Commentaries." Disc 2. Pina. DVD. Directed by Wim Wenders. New York: Criterion Collection, 2013.

Wenders, Wim. *Emotion Pictures*. Translated by Shaun Whiteside. London: Faber and Faber, 1989.

Wenders, Wim. "Everything I Loved I Had to Defend." *The Talks*, January 29, 2014. http://the-talks.com/interview/wim-wenders/.

Wenders, Wim. *Falsche Bewegung*. Munich: Solaris Film, 1975.

Wenders, Wim. "Impossible Stories." In *The Cinema of Wim Wenders: Image, Narrative and the Postmodern Condition*, edited by Roger F. Cook and Gerd Gemünden, 33–41. Detroit, Michigan: Wayne State University Press, 1997.

Wenders, Wim. "In Defense of Places." In *Wim Wenders: A Sense of Place*, edited by Daniel Bickermann, 7–38. Frankfurt/Main: Verlag der Autoren, 2005.

Wenders, Wim. *Instant Stories*. London: Thames and Hudson, 2017.

Wenders, Wim. *Instant Stories*. Munich: Schirmer/Mosel, 2017.

Wenders, Wim. *Journey to Onomichi*. Munich: Schirmer/Mosel, 2010.

Wenders, Wim. *On Film*. Translated by Michael Hofmann. London: Faber and Faber, 2001.

Wenders, Wim. *Once: Pictures and Stories*. Munich: Schirmer/Mosel and D. A. P., 2010.

Wenders, Wim. *Pictures from the Surface of the Earth*. Munich: Schirmer Art Books, 2003.

Wenders, Wim. *The Act of Seeing: Texte und Gespräche*. Frankfurt/Main: Verlag der Autoren, 1992.

Wenders, Wim. "The Men in the Rodeo Arena: Lusty." In *Wenders: On Film: Essays and Conversations*, translated by Michael Hofmann, 116–22. London: Faber and Faber, 2001.

Wenders, Wim. *The Pixels of Paul Cézanne and Reflections on Other Artists*. Translated by Jen Calleja. London: Faber and Faber, 2018.

Wenders, Wim. "Was Bilder heute bewirken." In *A Sense of Place: Texte und Interviews*, edited by Daniel Bickermann, 68–96. Frankfurt/Main: Verlag der Autoren, 2005.

Wenders, Wim. "Wim Wenders Explains the Making of His Film *Pina* (2011)." Interview by Zoila Clark, February 12, 2012, *Coral Gables Art Cinema, Florida*. www.youtube.com/watch?v=tAtPS2n3tVc.html.

Wenders, Wim. "Wim Wenders in Conversation with Alain Bergala." In *Written in the West*, 7–17. New York: Neues Publishing Company, 2000.

Wenders, Wim. "Wim Wenders Influencé par Hopper." Interview by Jean-Pierre Devillers, *Grand Palais*, 2012. www.youtube.com/watch?v=SakYrQaOLJQ.

Wenders, Wim. "Wim Wenders Talks with WSWS: 'The Culture of Independent Film Criticism Has Gone Down the Drain.'" By Richard Phillips. *World Socialist Web Site*, January 10, 2000. www.wsws.org/en/articles/2000/01/wwen-j10.html.

Wenders, Wim. "Wim Wenders über seinen Film *Pina*." Interview by Matthias Greuling and Alexandra Zawia, March 30, 2011. *celluloidVideo*. www.youtube.com/watch?v=rvsWg4_b9zI.html.

Wenders, Wim and Beat Wismer, *4 Real & True 2: Landscapes, Photographs*. Munich: Schirmer/Mosel, 2015.

Wenders, Wim and Mary Zournazi. *Inventing Peace: A Dialogue on Perception*. London: I.B. Tauris, 2013.

White, Jenny B. "Turks in the New Germany." *American Anthropologist* 99, no. 4: 754–69.

Williams, Raymond. *Problems in Materialism and Culture: Selected Essays*. London: Verso, 1997.

Wismer, Beat. "Wim Wenders, Photographer: Some Introductory Remarks." In *4 Real & True 2! Wim Wenders: Landscapes, Photographs*, edited by Wim Wenders and Beat Wismer, 10–17. Munich: Schirmer/Mosel, 2015.

Wolfson, Nathan. "PoMo Desire? Authorship and Agency in Wim Wenders' *Wings of Desire*." *Film and Philosophy* 7 (2003): 126–40.

Wood, Jason. *Last Words: Considering Contemporary Cinema*. London: Wallflower Press, 2014.

Žižek, Slavoj. "Rossellini: Woman as Symptom of Man." October 54 (August 1990): 19–44. doi:10.2307/778667.

Žižek, Slavoj. *The Sublime Object of Ideology*. London: Verso, 1989.

Filmography

Baser, Tevfik. *40 Square Meters of Germany* (1986).
Biberman, Herbert. *The Salt of the Earth* (1954).
Bresson, Robert. *Au Hasard Balthazar* (1966).
Cameron, James. *Avatar* (2009).
Fassbinder, Rainer Werner. *Fox and His Friends* (1975).
Fassbinder, Rainer Werner. *Marriage of Maria Braun* (1979).
Flaherty, Robert. *Nanook of the North* (1922).
Ford, John. *Stagecoach* (1939).
Greenaway, Peter. *The Draughtsman's Contract* (1982).
Herzog, Werner. *Aguirre, the Wrath of God* (1972).
Herzog, Werner. *Cave of Forgotten Dreams* (2011).
Herzog, Werner. *Lessons of Darkness* (1992).
Hitchcock, Alfred. *Rear Window* (1954).
Keaton, Buster. *The General* (1926).
Meerapfel, Jeanine. *Melek Leaves* (1985).
Mekas, Jonas. *Cassis* (1966).
Ozu, Yasujiro. *Floating Weeds* (1959).
Ozu, Yasujiro. *Tokyo Story* (1953).
Ray, Nicholas. *The Lusty Men* (1952).
Ruttmann, Walter. *Berlin, Symphony of a Big City* (1927).
Sauper, Hubert. *Darwin's Nightmare* (2005).
Sanders-Brahms, Helma. *Shirin's Wedding* (1975).
Scorsese, Martin. *Alice Doesn't Live Here Anymore* (1974).
Scorsese, Martin. *Hugo* (2011).
Spielberg, Steven. *The Adventures of Tintin* (2011).
Warhol, Andy. *Empire* (1964).
Warhol, Andy. *Sleep* (1963).
Wehn, Marcel. *One Who Sets Forth* (2007).
Wenders, Wim. *Silver City Revisited* (1968).
Wenders, Wim. *Summer in the City* (1970).
Wenders, Wim. *The Goalkeeper's Fear of the Penalty* (UK) or *The Goalie's Anxiety at the Penalty Kick* (USA) (1972).
Wenders, Wim. *The Scarlet Letter* (1973).
Wenders, Wim. *Alice in the Cities* (1973).

Wenders, Wim. *Wrong Move* (1974).
Wenders, Wim. *Kings of the Road* (1976).
Wenders, Wim. *The American Friend* (1977).
Wenders, Wim. *Lightning Over Water* (1980).
Wenders, Wim. *Hammett* (1982).
Wenders, Wim. *Room 666* (1982).
Wenders, Wim. *The State of Things* (1982).
Wenders, Wim. *Paris, Texas* (1984).
Wenders, Wim. *Tokyo-Ga* (1985).
Wenders, Wim. *Wings of Desire* (1987).
Wenders, Wim. *Notebook on Cities and Clothes* (1989).
Wenders, Wim. *Until the End of the World* (1991).
Wenders, Wim. *Faraway, So Close!* (1993).
Wenders, Wim. *Lisbon Story* (1994).
Wenders, Wim. *Beyond the Clouds* (1995).
Wenders, Wim. *The End of Violence* (1997).
Wenders, Wim. *Buena Vista Social Club* (1999).
Wenders, Wim. *The Million Dollar Hotel* (2000).
Wenders, Wim. *The Soul of a Man* (2003).
Wenders, Wim. *Land of Plenty* (2004).
Wenders, Wim. *Don't Come Knocking* (2005).
Wenders, Wim. *Palermo Shooting* (2008).
Wenders, Wim. *Pina* (2011).
Wenders, Wim. *Cathedrals of Culture* (2014).
Wenders, Wim. *The Salt of the Earth* (2014).
Wenders, Wim. *Every Thing Will Be Fine* (2015).
Wenders, Wim. *The Beautiful Days of Aranjuez* (2016).
Wenders, Wim. *Submergence* (2017).
Wenders, Wim. *Pope Francis: A Man of His Word* (2018).

Acknowledgments

Olivier Delers and Martin Sulzer-Reichel would like to thank the following people: Wim Wenders, Marcel Wehn, Laura Holtorf and the staff of the Wenders Foundation; the participants in the 2017 Wenders Conference at the University of Richmond; Yvonne Howell, Kathleen Skerrett, Patrice Rankine, Thomas Bonfiglio, Ray Hilliard, June Wise, Peter Lurie, and Laura Holliday.

Contributors

William Baker is PhD Candidate in German at the Ohio State University.

Peter Beicken is Professor of German, University of Maryland.

Olivier Delers is Associate Professor of French at the University of Richmond.

Kristin Eichhorn is Assistant Professor of German Literature at the University of Paderborn.

Mine Eren is Associate Professor of German at Randolph Macon College.

George Kouvaros is Professor of Film at the University of New South Wales.

Simone Malaguti is Lecturer at the Ludwig-Maximilians-Universität in Munich.

Philipp Scheid is Assistant Professor of Art History at the Philipps-Universität of Marburg.

Oliver C. Speck is Associate Professor of German and Film Studies at Virginia Commonwealth University.

Martin Sulzer-Reichel is Director of the Arabic Language Program at the University of Richmond.

Darrell Varga is Associate Professor of Film Studies at the Nova Scotia College of Art and Design.

Mary Zournazi is Associate Professor in the School of Social Sciences at the University of New South Wales.

Index

4 Real & True 2: Landscapes, Photographs 22, 128–9
40 Square Meters of Germany 141

Adorno, Theodor W. 96
The Adventures of Tintin 110
Agamben, Giorgio 42
Aguirre, the Wrath of God 37
Alberti, Leon Battista 65
Alekan, Henri 139
Alice Doesn't Live Here Anymore 38, 42
Alice in the Cities 1, 4, 11, 17, 20–2, 29–30, 32–3, 35, 37, 40–2, 48, 67–8, 72, 120, 123–7, 154, 157–8, 161, 164, 169–70, 174
Alt, Jakob 66
Alter, Nora 94
Althusser, Louis 94
The American Friend 4, 8, 35, 37, 176
Appiah, Kwame Anthony 137
Armstrong, Louis 115
Au hasard Balthazar 17
Avatar 110
Avventi, Carlo 3

Balász, Béla 18, 156–7, 174
Barglow, Raymond 149
Bastian, Heiner 86
Baudrillard, Jean 70
Bausch, Pina 3, 15–16, 21, 105–15, 127
The Beautiful Days of Aranjuez 3–4, 15, 45, 165
Beicken, Peter 65, 92–3, 96, 138, 144
Benjamin, Walter 5, 21, 42, 84, 88, 96, 101, 104
Bergala, Alain 78–9, 81
Berghahn, Daniela 136, 138
Biberman, Herbert 93
Bingham, Adam 148
Blech, Hans Christian 50
Blommaert, Jan 119
Borzik, Rolf 108
Bourdieu, Pierre 131

Brady, Martin 3, 5, 44
Bratu Hansen, Miriam 83
Bresson, Robert 17
Buber, Martin 19, 172–4
Buena Vista Social Club 11, 14, 113

Caltvedt, Les 140
Cameron, James 110
Campbell, Joseph 95
Campbell, Karen 148
Campos Martin, Pablo de 121
Carey, Peter 4
Cassis 64
Cathedrals of Culture 170
Cave of Forgotten Dreams 110
Chaplin, Charlie 88–9
Chatwin, Bruce 85
Chin, Rita 140
Chion, Michel 145, 148
Close, Chuck 7
Conrad, Joseph 99
Cooder, Rye 12, 171
Cook, Robert 94
Corrigan, Tim 24
Coury, David 3

Darwin's Nightmare 98
Dauman, Anatole 154
Dawson, Jan 154
Deleuze, Gilles 30, 38, 42, 46
De Oliveira, Manoel 14
Derobe, Alain 110, 112, 114
Desny, Ivan 50
Diawara, Manthia 141–2
Diderot, Denis 7
Dommartin, Solveig 106
Don't Come Knocking 1, 4, 8
Dürer, Albrecht 65
Dylan, Bob 85

Eichendorff, Joseph von 54, 61, 67
Eitner, Lorenz 66
Eleftheriotis, Dimitris 12

Elsaesser, Thomas   84, 94
Empire   64
The End of Violence   8
Evans, Walker   21, 81–5, 87
Every Thing Will Be Fine   3, 9–11, 45, 72, 124, 165, 176–7

Faraway, So Close!   44
Fassbinder, Rainer Werner   29, 37–8, 45
Flaherty, Robert   100
Flaubert, Gustave   54, 61, 67
Floating Weeds   161, 163
Ford, John   33, 37–8, 44
Foucault, Michel   71
Fox and His Friends   37
Freud, Sigmund   88, 95
Friedrich, Caspar David   21, 37, 51, 66, 85

Gainsbourg, Charlotte   9
Geist, Kathe   60–1, 93
Gemünden, Gerd   34
The General   37
The Goalkeeper's Fear of the Penalty   3, 34
Goethe, Johann Wolfgang von   4, 9, 20, 31, 36, 48–50
Gonçalo, Pablo   6–7
Graf, Alexander   1, 156
Gramling, David   25, 128, 130
Grimm, Jacob Ludwig Karl   64
Grimm, Wilhelm Carl   64
Grob, Norbert   65, 157
Gründgens, Gustaf   53
Guattari, Felix   38, 42

Hammett   92, 96
Handke, Peter   1, 3–7, 31, 36, 45, 49–50, 54, 57–61, 69, 85, 121, 128, 135
Hegel, Georg Wilhelm Friedrich   55, 98
Heidegger, Martin   175–6
Helfer, Martha   36
Hernandez, Tanya   11
Herzog, Werner   29, 45, 97, 110
Highsmith, Patricia   4
Hikmet, Nazım   136
Hoffman, E.T.A.   20, 63
Hölderlin, Friedrich   175
hooks, bell   140–2, 145
Hoppe, Marianne   53

Hopper, Edward   3, 8, 72, 85
Hugo   110

Instant Stories   26
Inventing Peace: A Dialogue on Perception   1, 9–10, 17–19, 22, 129, 169–70, 172

Jensen, Peter   154
Johannessen, Bjørn Olaf   9
Jooss, Kurt   108
Journey to Onomichi   84–7
Jullien, François   22, 132, 154, 159–61, 163, 165
Jung, Carl   95

Kaynes, Christian   139
Keller, Gottfried   54
Kersting, Georg Friedrich   66
Kings of the Road   11, 20, 29, 32–5, 37, 39–40, 48, 80–1, 88–9, 108, 154–6, 169
Kinski, Nastassja   5, 39, 50, 71
Klee, Paul   5, 147
Kolker, Robert Phillip   65, 92–3, 96, 138, 144
Kracauer, Siegfried   156–7, 165
Kramsch, Claire   123
Kreimeier, Klaus   34, 36
Kreuzer, Lisa   35
Kuzniar, Alice   70

Laban, Rudolf   108
Lacan, Jacques   39
Land of Plenty   1, 11, 72, 171
Lang, Fritz   33
Leal, Joanne   3, 5, 44
Lessons of Darkness   97
Lightning Over Water   92
Lisbon Story   5–6, 11–14, 17, 44, 120–1, 125, 130, 156, 168, 177
Livaneli, Zülfü   136
The Logic of Images   2
Lumière, Auguste   64, 110
Lumière, Louis   64, 110
The Lusty Men   79–81

Malaguti, Simone   3, 131
Mann, Charles   100
Mann, Klaus   53

Index

Mariniello, Silvestra 11
Marriage of Maria Braun 37
Martinec, Thomas 6
Marx, Karl 98
Ma Yuan 161
Medeiros, Paulo de 14
Melek Leaves 141
Meyerowitz, Joel 85
The Million Dollar Hotel 1, 8, 72
Mitchum, Robert 80
Mohnike, Thomas 136
Morrison, Tony 141
Müller, Robby 30
Mulvey, Laura 141
Münkler, Heifried 149
Murch, Walter 148

Nagib, Lúcia 133
Nanook of the North 100
New German Cinema 5, 29–30, 33, 41, 43, 93
Nietzsche, Friedrich 42
Nikfarjam, Omid 148
Ni Zan 160, 163
Notebook on Cities and Clothes 92–4, 99, 165, 176
Novalis 54, 67

Once 22, 124, 126
One Who Sets Forth 174
On Film 2, 158, 174
Ören, Aras 140
Ozu, Yasujiro 2, 6, 13–14, 17, 21–2, 84–6, 93–4, 96, 145, 154, 158, 161, 163–5, 177

Palermo Shooting 124
Paris, Texas 1, 22, 37, 39–40, 71, 78, 92, 126, 128, 139, 171
Percy, Walker 85
Pessoa, Fernando 119, 125, 130
Peucker, Brigitte 7
Pictures of the Surface of the Earth 77
Pina 1, 14–16, 21, 45, 105–7, 114–15, 127–30, 165, 176
Proust, Marcel 85, 96

Rach, Rudolf 109
Ray, Nicholas 33, 79–81, 87, 89, 96

Rear Window 63
Reed, Lou 85
Richter, Gerhard (painter) 7
Richter, Gerhard (scholar) 84
Rilke, Rainer Maria 147–8
Road Trilogy 8, 20, 29–30, 33, 38–40, 49, 169
Room 666 92, 120
Rottländer, Yella 126
Ruttmann, Walter 138

Salgado, Juliano 1, 16, 96
Salgado, Sebastião 16, 21, 85, 94–102
The Salt of the Earth (Biberman) 93
The Salt of the Earth (Wenders and Salgado) 1, 16, 21, 92–102, 127–8, 130
Sander, August 97
Sauper, Hubert 98
Schiewer, Gesine 122
Schrader, Paul 161
Schygulla, Hanna 36, 50
Scorcese, Martin 38, 110
A Sense of Place 2
Serres, Michel 171
Shakespeare, William 57
Shepard, Sam 4
Shirin's Wedding 141
Silver City Revisited 63–4, 66, 72
Sleep 64
Slow Homecoming 121–2
Smith-Prei, Carrie 16
Sontag, Susan 95
Spielberg, Steven 110
Stagecoach 37–8
Stanton, Harry Dean 39, 71, 126, 171
The State of Things 11, 17, 93
Strasberg, Lee 88
Summer in the City 158, 164
Symphony of a Big City 138

Tarkovsky, Andrei 6
Tieck, Ludwig 54, 65
Tokyo-Ga 5–6, 11, 13, 22, 92–4, 154, 164–5
Tokyo Story 84, 178
Truffaut, François 6

U2 109
Until the End of the World 4, 7, 11–13, 22, 33, 44–5, 65, 72, 92, 120, 127, 175

Van Morrison 85
Vermeer, Johannes 7, 85
Virilio, Paul 69
Visarius, Karsten 65
Vogler, Rüdiger 4, 30, 50, 58, 68, 174

Warhol, Andy 7
Wehn, Marcel 174
White, Jenny 136
Whitehead, Alfred North 156–7, 165
Williams, Raymond 94

Wings of Desire 1–2, 5–6, 12, 18, 22, 29, 45, 92, 134–54
Wrong Move 4, 20–1, 29, 31–7, 40, 48–61, 67, 72, 124, 169
Wyeth, Andrew 3, 9–10, 72, 172

Yamamoto, Yohji 93, 97

Zischler, Hanns 81
Žižek, Slavoj 40
Zournazi, Mary 2, 17–19, 22, 129

www.ingramcontent.com/pod-product-compliance
Lightning Source LLC
Chambersburg PA
CBHW052044300426
44117CB00012B/1967